M000165503

RED STAR
AGAINST
THE SWASTIKA

Vasily Emelianenko, 1945

RED STAR AGAINST THE SWASTIKA

The Story of a Soviet Pilot
over the Eastern Front

Vasily B. Emelianenko

FRONTLINE BOOKS

Red Star Against the Swastika

A Greenhill Book
First published in 2005 by Greenhill Books, Lionel Leventhal Limited
www.greenhillbooks.com

This paperback edition published in 2015 by

Frontline Books
an imprint of Pen & Sword Books Ltd,
47 Church Street, Barnsley, S.Yorkshire, S70 2AS
For more information on our books, please visit
www.frontline-books.com, email info@frontline-books.com
or write to us at the above address.

Copyright © Vasily B. Emelianenko, 2005
Introduction © Vladimir Vershinin, 2005

Publication made possible by the 'I Remember' website
(www.iremember.ru) and its director, Mr Artem Drabkin.

The right of Vasily B. Emelianenko to be identified as the author of this work has been
asserted by him in accordance with the Copyright, Designs and Patents Act 1988.

ISBN: 978-1-84832-803-7

CIP data records for this title are available from the British Library

Typeset by Palindrome
Printed and bound by CPI Group (UK) Ltd, Croydon, CR0 4YY

CONTENTS

ILLUSTRATIONS

INTRODUCTION

Vladimir Vershinin

Il-2: The Birth of the Legend

The Soviet Air Force became a separate combat arm in 1932. According to the book *Fundamental Tactics of the Air Force* by Brigade Commander B. Teplinskiy (Voenizdat, 1940), the main task of the aircraft was to provide assistance to the ground forces during the military operations. General Douhet's book, *Il Dominio dell' Aria*, which was very popular in those years, prophetically discussed the potential power of air forces, but it did not find a response among the Soviet militarists. The Soviet aircraft was not considered an independent military unit that could seriously turn the scale in case of war. It had to co-operate with the ground forces and could only be used in their interests.

Although 'Shturmoviks' became the backbone of Soviet airpower during World War II and replaced the Front bomber aircraft to a great extent, there was no ground-attack section in the Soviet Air Force until the late thirties. After the Spanish Civil War the Soviet military theorists considered that there was no need for special ground-attack aircraft because their functions could be performed by multi-purpose planes, such as the short-range bomber, Sukhoi Su-2, and fighters with air-cooled engine systems. These planes had the best chance of survival in an attack from light-calibre machine-guns and ground-based anti-aircraft guns. The Soviet Air Force therefore developed with N. N. Polikarpov the R-5 reconnaissance aircraft and its variants the R5Sh, R-5SSS and R-zet. These planes were equipped with up to four 7.62-mm machine-guns directing forward fire and two 7.6-mm twin machine-guns on the turret for rear defence. Their bomb-load was up to 500 kilograms and their maximum near-ground speed was about 200 kph. The outdated fighters I-15-bis and I-153 were also used as attack aircraft. They were equipped with four 7.62-mm ShKAS machine-guns, and later with four 12-mm BS machine-guns or two 20-mm ShVAK machine-guns, and missiles. They could carry 200 kilogrammes of bombs and developed a speed of up to 360 kph.

Thus, the Soviet Air Force did not have a single-purpose ground-attack aircraft until the beginning of the World War II. Designers S. A. Kochergin, N. N. Polikarpov and A. N. Tupolev made attempts to create such a plane, but the lack of high-powered engines and construction materials with the required weight and strength characteristics did not allow them to accomplish their projects.

Nevertheless, in 1937 military engineers from the Air Force Research Institute demanded the urgent construction of a single-purpose ground-attack aircraft, which 'could operate at a low altitude, had the highest-powered engine, and was equipped with powerful offensive and defensive weapons'.

In January 1938 bomber designer S. V. Ilyushin volunteered to construct an armoured attack aircraft – 'a flying tank'.

Ilyushin promised to design an aircraft that would have all the essential parts (crew, engine, lubrication and fuel systems and bombs) protected by armour. The plane was to travel at up to 385–400 kph and had an operational range of 750–800 kilometres. It was supposed to be equipped with four wing ShKAS machine-guns and one ShKAS machine-gun on the ring-mount for the navigator/gunner. It would carry up to 250 kilogrammes of bombs.

In May 1938 the Government of the USSR approved the plan for the construction for two years. It included the construction of a twin-seater, single-engine, armoured attack aircraft, the BSh-2. Ilyushin was authorised to carry out the project and provide three flight-ready planes by the end of 1938 or the beginning of 1939.

The designing process and the production of a pilot model took more than a year. The main difficulties were connected with the production of aircraft armour with double curvature and a new engine, the AM-35. This engine replaced the previous model AM-34FRN, which was not powerful enough at low altitudes. On 2 October 1939 V. Kokkinaki performed the first test flight on BSh-2. The flight lasted no more than ten minutes, because the engine was overheating and the plane was banking to the left. The development process went on until March 1940. The designers had serious problems with cooling the engine, because the water and oil radiators were situated inside the armoured shell. The chief engine designer, A. A. Mikulin, noted that the design of the new attack aircraft did not at all correspond to the optimal operating conditions for the AM-35, and the recommendations of the engine designers had been flagrantly ignored. 'There is not a single hole in this iron body, through which the engine could cool down! What performance do you expect from it then?' exclaimed Mikulin.

After numerous alterations and improvements the aircraft finally passed all the factory tests on 26 March 1940. It performed fourteen test flights with a total duration of four hours and forty-six minutes. The flight characteristics of the plane were checked only in four flights.

On 31 March the BSh-2 was subjected to status tests, which lasted for three weeks. The report of the Engineering Council of the Air Force Research Institute dated 11 May admitted that the aircraft was easy to operate, but it failed to correspond to the directional stability and control capability requirements, and did not provide enough forward view for the pilot. The report also noted that despite a year and three months' delay in producing the prototype the performance characteristics of the aircraft were still not satisfactory. For example, the plane's range was only 618 kilometres instead of 800 kilometres, and its maximum near-ground speed was only 362 kilometres. To improve the speed characteristics of the aircraft the Council recommended replacing the AM-35 engine with the more powerful AM-38, which had the same weight and dimensions. The Council also recommended replacing two of the ShKAS machine-guns.

The Council made a motion to construct sixty-five BSh-2 aircraft for battle tests, which had to show the advantages of the new aircraft in combat. The tests could also help to bring out the possible defects and eliminate them.

It should be noted that a new engine model AM-38 was constructed specially for Ilyushin's aircraft. That was unprecedented. The AM-38's critical altitude was only 2,800 metres and it did not fit any other aircraft at that time. This fact shows that Ilyushin was influential and had important connections among the higher authorities.

In his letter to the Head of the Defence Committee dated May

1940, People's Commissar Timoshenko expressed his opinion that it would be inexpedient to construct as many as sixty-five planes for identifying defects. He considered ten to fifteen planes enough for that purpose. In the same letter he mentioned a new variant of the attack aircraft, which was being designed at the time by designer Sukhoy and looked better than Ilyushin's model. Nevertheless, on 24 May 1940 the Head of the Air Force, Ya. V. Smushkevich, addressed People's Commissar for the Aircraft Industry A. I. Shahurin. In his letter he wrote: 'It's been 30 days since Ilyushin's aircraft passed the status tests and he gained the permission from the Engineering Council to introduce the model into production. I consider that the Air Force needs this plane urgently. I ask you to speed up the process of making the final decision on putting the armoured attack aircraft designed by comrade Ilyushin into production.' The letter stated that Ilyushin had given guarantees that he would improve the plane's flight characteristics, install two 20-mm or 23-mm guns and provide the means for aimed bombing and shooting during the dive.

This letter presents a solid testimony to the fact that Ilyushin had patrons among the highest command. The designer 'had given a guarantee' to eliminate defects! It seems that he was ready to do anything to put his aircraft into mass production. It should be noted, however, that the designer would fail to fulfill his promises. His attack aircraft was not capable of dropping bombs during the dive. The majority of the defects were left unimproved until the end of the war, when a new attack aircraft, model Il-10, was produced.

The letter of the Head of the Air Force had its effect. On 16 August the plane was exposed to a new series of status tests in the Air Force Research Institute. The tests failed owing to the malfunction of the engine and on 23 August 1940 the aircraft was transferred to factory 39 for the replacement of the AM-35 engine with the AM-38.

This date also marks the point when the twin-seat aircraft was altered into a single-seater. Designer Ilyushin failed to improve his plane's design in the two-seater model. The more powerful engine increased the plane's flight characteristics remarkably, but the fuel consumption was so high that the range decreased even more. Ilyushin solved the problem by sacrificing one of the cockpits.

It should be noted that the original design of the BSh-2 intended that the aircraft would be used as a bomber-attack aircraft. The second member of the crew not only guarded the rear part of the aircraft from fighter attack, but also performed the role of navigator and gunner. With the elimination of the second cockpit the designer of the aircraft simply made aimed bombing from his plane impossible.

In the second half of the war Ilyushin's attack aircraft *was* equipped with a second cockpit for the gunner, but the real value of this was not in defending the aircraft, but rather in providing information to the pilot. Until the very end of the war the only force that could really protect the attack aircraft from enemy fighters was the accompanying group of friendly fighters.

On 12 October 1940 a single-seat attack aircraft, named the TsKB-57, piloted by V. K. Kokkinaki made its first flight. Since the 23-mm guns were still not ready, the TsKB-57 was only equipped with machine-guns. The plane's maximum speed was 423 kph near the ground and 437 kph at an altitude of 2,800 metres. It could climb up to 5,000 metres in ten minutes. But the performance of the AM-38 engine was very unreliable. The fifty hour tests could not be completed in the autumn of 1940, and further improvement of the model went on in the next year. Despite this, the engine went into mass production.

On 9 December People's Commissar Shahurin signed an order to rename the BSh-2 (or TsKB-57) as the Il-2 (Ilyushin-2). Soon the aircraft was put into production at factories 18, 381 and 380.

Neither the engine nor the armament were ready. The aircraft was not tested in combat conditions. The only tests it had passed were the factory ones. Nevertheless, it was put into mass production! Ilyushin's recent time at Stalin's summer residence might have some bearing on this.

The First Il-2s, June 1941

It was a single-seat cantilever monoplane with the main landing gear retracting inside the nacelles in the wing. The nose and middle parts of the fuselage formed a solid armoured shell protecting the pilot, the engine, the radiators, the lubrication and fuel systems. The armoured shell consisted of plates of iron armour AB-1 four millimetres thick at the cowling, five to six millimetres thick at the bottom and sides, and twelve millimetres thick at the rear armoured plate. The fuselage rear and the keel were made as a veneered semi-monocoque reinforced with wooden stringers and veneered frames. The rear part of the fuselage was connected to the armoured body with a metal belt with rivets. The wings and stabiliser had an all-metal structure. The rudders had Duralumin framing and linen casing.

The transparent parts of the cockpit were made of specially constructed T-4 armour.

The aircraft was equipped with a water-cooled engine, the AM-38, of 1,575 horsepower.

The plane was armed with two wing 20mm ShVAK guns, two 7.62mm ShKAS machine-guns, eight RS-82 or four RS-132 rockets and carried 400 kilogrammes of bombs, 420 shells and 1,500 cartridges.

Carrying 400 kilos of bombs the plane could attain up to 419 kph near the ground and up to 451 kph at an altitude of 2,500 metres. Carrying two FAB-250 bombs it could speed up to 380 kph near the ground and up to 419 kph at an altitude of 2,500 metres. For the RS-132 the corresponding numbers were 378 kph and 423 kph. The flight range was 638 kilometres.

The range of the RSI-3 wireless station installed at the aircraft was sixty kilometres at an altitude of 200 metres and sixty-five kilometres at an altitude of 1,000 metres. It was certainly not enough, besides, the audibility was extremely poor. As the author of this book, Vasily Emelianenko, put it, 'the noise in the headphones resembled the sound of lard frizzling on a frying pan'.

The plane was equipped with a PBP-16 sight that could be used both for the shooting and bombing.

Thus, there was nothing peculiar in the performance characteristics of the aircraft except for the extra armour. However, this armour could not protect the plane from shells or even from large-calibre machine-guns. Besides, the rear part of the fuselage was actually made of wood. The war would show that the speed characteristics and the ability to manoeuvre were far more important for the aircraft than the extra armour.

Vasily Emelianenko made a vivid remark about the performance characteristics of the Il-2: 'I always admired the German "Junkers-87". You should have seen them diving! They swooped down one by one and shot exactly to the point. Il-2 could do nothing like that. Its best performance was to fly at an angle of 30 degrees. And it was shaking like mad! The aircraft was heavy and you could not make it fly faster no matter how hard you were trying...'

But an aircraft itself is only a machine. It would have been nothing without a pilot. It was the pilots who made the mediocre Shturmovik a legend. It was they who flew missions without fighters covering, who dived into the very blaze of anti-aircraft fire, who attacked enemy troops. The Germans had a very high opinion of the Soviet pilots. As Schwabedissen wrote: '...the Soviet ground-attack staff was characterised as aggressive, courageous, and stubborn. Their attacks were amazingly cool-headed. An average Soviet Shturmovik pilot was a fearless rival. The weak sides of the Russian character showed up in the Shturmovik pilots to a much lesser degree, than they did in the fighter pilots.' Schwabedissen claimed openly: 'The ground-attack aircraft was the best organised unit among the Soviet Air Force... the role of the Soviet ground-attack aircraft increased constantly until it became the "backbone" of the Soviet Air Force.'

Such were the pilots who fought in the 7th Guards Ground-Attack Regiment, which is described in the book by Vasily Borisovich Emelianenko.

The history of the 7th Guards Regiment began on 27 April 1938. On that day men from the 8th Reconnaissance Squadron, the 9th Long-range Reconnaissance Squadron, the 10th and 11th Army Reconnaissance Squadrons were assigned to form the 4th Bomber Regiment equipped with R-zet planes.

The 4th Bomber Regiment took part in the Finnish War, being a part of the 13th Army Air Force since January 1940. The regiment performed 1,416 operational flights in a month (including 453 night flights), and dropped 101,146 bombs on enemy infantry, artillery and railway junctions. The Decree of the Presidium of the Supreme Soviet dated 7 April 1940 awarded medals and orders to 105 members of the staff. Having done its part of the work at the Finnish War the regiment returned to the airfield in Kharkov.

On 5 May 1941, the Commander of Kharkov military district issued an order to rename the 4th Bomber Regiment as the 4th Ground-Attack Regiment. The regiment was equipped with single-seater Shturmovik Il-2s.

The Great Patriotic War began on 22 June 1941. Three days later the air crew was put into action. By that time the regiment had received all of the sixty-three planes. The pilots had just begun to master the new equipment, when on 26 June the regiment was ordered to fly to the front. At the beginning of the war the operating units actually had no instructions on the use of the Il-2. The pilots had not launched a single missile, and had no idea about aimed bombing. They did not know how to defend against enemy fighters or how to avoid anti-aircraft fire. They had to pass a survival test facing not an instructor of a flying school, but an experienced and strong enemy.

The 4th Ground-Attack Regiment led by Major Getman began operations from the Stary Bykhov airfield. It attacked tanks and mechanised units of the enemy near Bobryusk, Zhlobin, Roslavl and Metislavl destroying the crossings over the Berezina, Dnepr and Sozh. It also attacked the enemy aircraft at the Bobruysk airfield.

The regiment flew to bomb the crossings without the fighters covering and had to operate under the heavy fire from the enemy anti-aircraft guns. For destroying nine crossings over the Berezina on 2 July the regiment got a citation from the Commander of the Western Front Marshal of the Soviet Union S. K. Timoshenko. But it had to pay a high price for the citation: thirteen pilots were lost in three days and nine more pilots were shot down but survived.

The regiment flew to attack the Bobruysk airfield three times and claimed twenty-three Ju-88 and forty-seven Bf-109 destroyed. But this official score seems to be rather exaggerated. The analysis of the military operation of the Il-2 performed by special commissions of the Air Force Front headquarters, Air Armies, and the Air Force Research Institute showed that in three attacks the 4th Ground-Attack Regiment could not destroy more than thirty Luftwaffe planes.

By 10 July there were only ten Shturmoviks and eighteen pilots left in the regiment. On 20 August the regiment handed over the only three Il-2s left to the 215th Ground-Attack Regiment and flew to Voronezh for re-formation.

On October 4 1941, the regiment was awarded the Order of Lenin for the excellent performance of the missions at the Western Front and for the courage and bravery demonstrated in the struggle against the German invaders. The regiment commander, Major Getman, was made Hero of the Soviet Union. On October 7 1941 thirty-two pilots and mechanics were awarded medals and orders of the Soviet Union.

The regiment was re-formed in Voronezh by 4 September, but now it consisted of two squadrons instead of five. It received new Shturmoviks armed with 23-mm wing guns designed by Volkov and Yartsev. The new guns were more reliable and powerful than the previous 20-mm ShVAK models.

During a short break in the military actions the pilots were trained to hold the formation in the air, to arrange in a defensive circle, to launch attacks and to bomb the airfields. The squadron leader, Major Hushper, was entrusted to carry out test bombing at the training ground and study the Il-2's abilities to bomb in the dive. With the help of other experienced pilots Major Hushper managed to achieve very good results in the accuracy of the strikes and devised an instruction on the dive bombing, which became the basic manual for all the pilots in the 230th Ground-Attack Division.

Nobody provided the pilots with ready directions. They had to study the operating characteristics of the Shturmovik in aerial engagements and to set all the rules themselves.

On 18 September 1941 the 4th Order of Lenin Ground-Attack Regiment was transferred to the Southern Front and joined the 5th Reserve Air Grouping.

From 19 September the re-formed regiment began its mission bombing the enemy units in Dnepropetrovsk, Novomoskovsk, Sinelnikovo, Nikopol and Kahovka. Until the end of 1941 the regiment performed more than 500 operational flights and destroyed or damaged up to 100 enemy tanks, 400 cars, forty artillery guns and ten armoured cars. More than 5,000 German soldiers and officers were killed in the attacks.

The regiment records of that period show that the effectiveness of its actions was often reduced owing to the inadequate work of the service battalions that failed to provide the necessary ammunition, fuel and other important materials on time.

The major losses were caused by the enemy anti-aircraft guns. No armour could protect the Shturmoviks from the 20-mm shells. The losses from the enemy fighters were not really high.

It is noteworthy that the regiment command did not ask to equip the Il-2 with a second cockpit for an aerial gunner at that time. What they did ask for was an extra fighter squadron that could guard the Shturmoviks. Perhaps for that reason the aircraft designer Ilyushin wrote to People's Commissar Shahurin: 'I don't consider it necessary to include the second person into the air crew of Il-2... The experience of the aircraft regiments prove that they do not suffer any casualties from the enemy planes...' Meanwhile mechanics in many regiments installed 1,200 self-made machine-gun mounts on Shturmoviks to protect the rear hemisphere from the fighters attacks.

From 18 January 1942 the regiment took part in the Barvenkovsko-Izyumovskaya operation, being the only attack aircraft regiment in the 57th Army. It attacked the front line of the enemy defence along the Severskiy Donets river pursuing the retreating enemy as far as Krasnoarmeysk.

In the spring of 1942 the Germans transferred a considerable part of the aircraft units to the Donets region airfields. The 4th Regiment was ordered to attack the enemy airfields in Stalino, Makeevka, Artemovsk. Squadrons led by the regiment aces, Captain Zub, Senior Lieutenant Mospanov and Captain Yeliseev, managed to fly to the enemy positions at dusk, or in bad weather conditions and destroyed six Ju-88, sixteen Bf-109 and three He-126.

The Order of the Supreme Headquarters dated 7 March 1942 re-formed the 4th Order of Lenin Ground-Attack Regiment into the 7th Guards Ground-Attack Regiment. On 20 May 1942 the 7th Guards Regiment joined the 230th Ground-Attack Division.

In May and June of 1942 the regiment took active part in the Kharkov offensive. Several freshmen arrived at the regiment at that period. Among them was the author of this book, Lieutenant Vasily Borisovich Emelianenko.

It did not take him long to change from a graduate of a flying school into an experienced ground-attack pilot. In winter of the same year the regiment's record of service noted that 'despite the intensive military operations Senior Lieutenant Emelianenko managed to retrain nine pilots in fifteen days and thus allowed to bring them into action without any delay'.

Emelianenko launched ninety attacks and performed all kinds of military missions, including reconnaissance flights, attacks on the enemy airfields, and 'free pursuit'. He managed to set on fire and damage twenty-three enemy aircraft, he destroyed dozens of tanks and cars and killed hundreds of German soldiers and officers. Emelianenko was awarded the Order of the Red Banner, the Order of the Red Star, and the Order of the Patriotic War of the second degree. On 13 April 1944 Emelianenko was made Hero of the Soviet Union for the courage and bravery he had shown.

In 1943 the 7th Guards Regiment fought as a part of the 230th Ground-Attack Division. One of the most impressing episodes of that period was the attack on the Malorossiyskaya railway station on 26 January 1943. The pilots managed to set on fire four trains, two of which contained ammunition, one was carrying fuel and one was carrying tanks. The railway lines were so severely damaged that railway traffic was blocked for four days.

In 1943 the regiment was equipped with twin-seat Shturmoviks. An extra cockpit for the gunner was situated outside the armoured shell behind the armoured baffle of the rear fuel tank. A 6-mm armoured baffle protected the gunner from the rear side. The gunner was armed with a UTB machine-gun and had 150 cartridges at his disposal. The pilot and the gunner could communicate through a SPU-2 interphone system. The new model of the aircraft had an augmented engine AM-38Ph.

As the battle experience showed, the UTB machine-gun could not provide enough angle of firing. The gunner was unable to repel the enemy fighters' attacks from above and from the sides at high angles. His ability to shoot at the fighters attacking from beneath or at the ground targets was also very limited. Besides, the UTB machine-gun was rather unreliable itself.

But the worst thing was that the aircraft became more inert. It became more difficult to manoeuvre and the plane could now carry less load. The speed of the twin-seater Il-2 was 388 kph near the ground, and 400 kph at an altitude of 1,320 metres. The flight range was 685 kilometres.

The gunner could not provide as much protection for his aircraft as the friendly fighters did. By the end of the war the co-ordination between the attack aircraft and fighters squadrons was well developed and there was actually no need for a gunner. Nevertheless the gunners were kept even on the new model of Shturmovik that replaced Il-2 in 1945.

In 1943 the pilots of the 7th Guards Regiment pursued the barges in the Straits of Kerch and attacked the enemy defence 'Blue Line'.

From the beginning of 1944 the German forces were defending their positions on the Kerch peninsula offering stubborn resistance to the Soviet troops. The Red Army managed to break the Blue Line only in April 1944. The regiment took active part in the struggle for Kerch and for the Crimea.

In summer 1944 the 7th Guards Regiment was transferred to Belorussia and took part in the 'Bagration' operation. Later it supported the ground forces in the Eastern Prussia.

At the end of February 1945 the aircraft operating personnel went to Kuybyshev to study and master a new Shturmovik Il-10. The remaining personnel and the staff of the regiment stayed within the 230th division.

By the end of the war designer Ilyushin constructed a much more reliable Shturmovik Il-10 equipped with an AM-42 engine. Taking into account the war experience Ilyushin considerably improved the flight characteristics of the aircraft and made a more efficient use of the armour. He managed to improve the speed characteristics of the new Shturmovuk and its ability to manoeuvre.

From March until Victory Day the personnel of the regiment was attached to the 103rd and 43rd Ground-Attack Regiments and took part in military operations near Graudenz, Stettin and Danzig.

On 28 April 1945 the regiment moved to the Chkalovsk airfield in Moscow and was getting ready for the May parade.

Thus the 7th Guards Order of Lenin Ground-Attack Regiment met the end of the Great Patriotic War.

1

BEFORE THE WAR

At the beginning of June 1941 I had an unexpected piece of luck. I was an Osoaviachim* pilot at the time. The aeroclub chief Aleksey G. Barsky let me into his office, asked me to sit down and clapped me on my knee. 'Here's a ticket and reservation for you. You may go!'

I stared at him in amazement. It was the very height of the flying season, and he was sending me on vacation! It seemed quite contrary to the aircraft saying 'Autumn, cold and puddles are deep – time for pilots to go on leave...'

'It's a special offer,' he explained. 'We can't miss such an opportunity.'

I looked at the reservation. A mysterious romantic name 'Bujur-Nus' was written on it in bold embossed letters. The place was in the Crimea, at the Black Sea. I'd never been there. And the bathing season was right at its height! The packing did not take long: I picked up my trunk and went to the railway station.

The train was carrying me further and further away from the green town of Nikolayev and the Vodopoi airfield. What we called an airfield was in fact just a flat green field with a row of several large wooden boxes, padded with roofing felt on the inside. We usually received the planes in such boxes, and used them later for equipment storage or as airfield dwellings. One of the boxes was a permanent home for uncle Jasha, a watchman, and his sheepdog. He had a rare last name – Jaschik† – and we made a lot of jokes about it. The name 'airfield' was something of an exaggeration. Nevertheless, U-2

* Union of Societies for Assistance to Defence and Air-Chemical Construction of the USSR.
† The word *jaschik* means 'a box' in Russian.

21

training biplanes were buzzing, coming up and down, circling around the green field from dawn to dusk.

That year the flying was really intensive. Instructors never left the cockpit. We even ate our sandwiches in the air. Only during refuelling did we jump out, stand for a while by the tail, our back to the students, and then go a few metres further off to have a smoke. Everyone wanted his log to show the longest flying time, so that his name come first in *Startovka* – a daily paper, published on the airfield. We competed on the quality of training and the number of students who passed their exams successfully.

Our aeroclubs were already established. The work now was really easy compared with the time of the second *pjatiletka*★ when almost all investment went into industry development. At that time students in aeroclubs did not stop working for the period of study, and the aeroclubs were funded only from subscriptions made by the so–called physical and legal members of the voluntary society Osoaviachim. The former were individuals who entered the society and the latter corporate members. It often happened that there was no money on the aeroclub current account, so salaries were paid in parts once in several months. In 1934–7 the situation was the same in the Nalchik aeroclub, where I worked after graduating from a Moscow School of Pilot Instructors. Our first chief, Kutyrev, looked like a village carrier with his field bag always on his shoulder and his boots covered with dust and worn out. He had to walk round the town all day long trying to get 'legal' subscriptions from the heads of enterprises… He had to walk on foot, because there was only one regular transport unit in the airfield – a sorrel horse led by a barefoot coachman, who carted pilots to the flights. Kutyrev was seldom seen in the airfield. When he came he would take a pay-roll out of his bag. 'Here's an advance,' he would say as he gave ten roubles to each pilot and five roubles to each mechanic.

But still none of the instructors could imagine life without flights. After experiencing the thrilling excitement of flying I didn't regret that I had given up studying in the Moscow Conservatoire in the lean winter of 1932. There was a slogan at that time: 'Komsomolets†

★ A five-year plan of work covering all fields of activity in the USSR promulgated by the government.
† A member of the Youth Communist Union, Komsomol.

22

– to the aircraft!' And to be a pilot was at those times an honour no less than to be an astronaut nowadays.

When the first aeroclubs appeared students had a hard time there. Now a shop superintendent would deny a lad or a girl the night shift, so that he or she could go to the flights in the morning; now a foreman would detain a person up at the plant – he had to keep pace with the plan... But it was not only the plants that had a plan: the aeroclubs had their plan as well. 'To train 150,000 pilots for the country!' – that was the slogan. And thus about 200 aeroclubs were training Komsomol members – working youth, collective farmers and students, all of them true devotees of flying.

By 1940 students were no longer required to work while they were studying. They lived in dormitories and were provided with food, shoes and clothes. Instructors got their salaries regularly. I remember one occasion when I did not have to send down a single student for poor studying and also trained an extra student. That time I won in the competition. The extra student, the thirteenth, was our aeroclub coachman Pashka Sazanov. I began to teach him secretly. He often came to my place and stayed until late at night, even spending some nights there. I taught him flying theory, helped him to study the engine and the aircraft. Every morning I seated him in the cockpit instead of my mechanical engineer, Sajenko, who was supposed to sit in the second cockpit during the so-called test flight by the instructor according to the rules. When Sazanov was almost a competent pilot, I took an extra step for him, which became public in the aeroclub. The authorities didn't want to recognise the coachman as a pilot at first, so they brought up his inadequate education. Nevertheless Sazanov passed an exam on theory, and made a successful flight with a representative of a State Entrance Examination Commission. Later he served for many years in the air force, and took part in the war at the Caucasus.

The further our train was from the airfield at Vodopoi, the less I thought about the aeroclub. And when I first saw the sea from a bus window on an awful mountain road, I forgot everything. In the sanatorium I breathed the smell of the sea, which for me was at that time like the smell of a watermelon from Kamyshin near Astrakhan. My neighbour at the table was a bomber pilot, a junior lieutenant Petya (I don't remember his last name). Together we spent evenings at dance parties.

On the fifth day of the vacation we were going up the steep road from the beach to Bujur-Nus, when we saw our *massovik-zatejnik*★ running towards us. He was gesticulating like a madman, shouting, 'Comrades! The war!'

We began to laugh, taking it for a joke, but Kolya swore by God that it was true and we believed him. Hearing Molotov's speech I thought: 'Now I'll become a military pilot at last!'

I had graduated from Saratov Osoaviachim Pilot School in 1933, but I didn't have an opportunity to enter a military school. My instructor Panfilov did write in my graduation report 'Can be sent to an aerial reconnaissance unit', but I was ordered to go to the Central Flying Training School of the Osoaviachim in Moscow. I graduated from it, and got stuck in the aeroclubs: in Nalchik, in Chernigov, in Nikolayev. How long was I going to crawl in the air around the airfield in a U-2 biplane? I wanted to fly on a real war-plane! Of course, I wrote many requests to our military commissar Kandaurov, but he refused. Only in 1937 was I sent to serve in Novocherkassk. There was a School of Junior Aircraft Specialists (SJAS) there and it had a flying subunit. But I did not get a chance to fly there. After our hair was cut close to the skin, there came time for drilling and learning service regulations. It was a Young Soldier Training Course; everyone was equal there, both the conscripts and the pilots who had served as instructors for a long time.

It appeared that during our first year in SJAS we were to study theoretical subjects only. After that we could start our flying lessons on – U-2s! It meant that I would be taught what I had actually been teaching others! I had to wire a telegram of almost a hundred words. I put the form into a window at the telegraph office. A young telegraphist read it for a long time looking at me from time to time: the telegram was addressed to Voroshilov† personally! She finally took the telegram, and soon there came an order to send me back to the aeroclub.

The war found me in Gurzuf, near Yalta. I had to get to Nikolayev as soon as possible. There I intended to press for being taken into a military unit, where I could learn to navigate a war-plane in no time!

★ The person in charge of leisure time in a sanatorium.
† Marshal of the Soviet Union, a prominent military leader during the Civil War.

But it appeared that it was not easy to get even as far as Simferopol. All transport was mobilised on the first day of war. They had just started to move the military officers according to seniority. How long would a reserve junior lieutenant have to wait for his turn?

Petya and I decided to try hitchhiking. After dinner we took our trunks and climbed up to the highway. Overloaded lorries and buses were sweeping past us like hell. Nobody paid any attention to us. We went for more than twenty kilometres along the highway and by night came to Alushta. A driver felt sorry for us, and let us ride in the back of his lorry, which was heaped up with sacks. Several times we had to help the driver to mend broken parts. When we finally reached Simferopol it was already late at night.

The city was blacked out. The railway station was overcrowded. People were sitting on their trunks and packs, children whimpering, men cursing. People were scurrying about in the dark stepping carefully over those sleeping. The entrance to the ticket-office was blocked by a crowd. There was no chance of getting tickets. A voice said: 'Let the General pass!' But people were reluctant to move; everybody wanted to get to their unit as soon as possible...

Petya and I decided to stow away. We were going the same way: he wanted to get into Kirovograd, and I was going a bit further. We wandered along the sleepers near the trains for quite a time. The cars were locked, and there were no conductors. Finally we found an open door. It seemed that the car was empty. I lit a match. From every berth and corner people began hushing: we had broken the blackout. The car was jammed, but there was no noise. Only whispers could be heard.

We departed. Men smoked on the platform, hiding their cigarettes in their fists. Flares flashed above the steppe. Passengers stared at the windows: 'It's the Germans, they are signalling to their aircraft.'

Nikolayev was crowded: it was a holiday. A loudspeaker near the cinema was transmitting a popular song at full volume. The matinee had just finished, and people were coming out of the cinema, dressed up for a holiday. Something flapped high in the sky, as if somebody was beating the dust out of a carpet. Everyone looked up in curiosity. There were puffs of black smoke in the sky, and above them a dark twin-engined plane. A white trail was stretching behind it. It was a German plane. I could not identify the model. The plane vanished. Only two white melting lines drifted eastwards.

25

On that day the Sovyetskaya street was most crowded. Hundreds of people were greeting a cavalry column. Hooves clattered on the pavement which was covered with flowers thrown by the crowd. Ahead of the column a scrawny man was riding a sorrel horse. I knew him. He was Major Zmozhnykh, the chairman of our Osoaviachim regional council. He had taken part in the Civil War, and had been a frequent guest at the Vodopoi airfield. Two bearded men were following him holding a red banner. The inscription was thrilling: 'To Berlin!'

Reaching the Nikolayev military commissar was no easier than getting a ticket in Simferopol. His eyelids were red. He told me in a dull tired voice: 'You know that you are reserved. Mind your own business, they can manage without you at the front. If we need you – we'll send for you...'

But I could not agree to that. My thoughts were: 'Just let me go, and I'll start thrashing the fascists in heaps. I must catch up with Major Zmozhnykh and his cavalrymen!' It took me a week to persuade the military commissar.

With an order in my pocket I was flying to my aeroclub with the speed of a young deer. I ran upstairs jumping over three steps at once. Barsky, the head of the aeroclub, was looking for something inside his safe. He had became rather absent-minded and hot-tempered in recent days. Despite the reserve the aeroclub was slowly falling apart. The head of the flying unit, Mikhail Vorozhbiev, and instructors Bogza, Zalyubovsky and Onishuk had already gone to the front. And now I turned up with a surprise. I hesitated for several seconds, and then put the order on the table.

'What's that?' he asked.

'To the front!'

Barsky turned to face me. He stared at me with his big grey eyes, turning purple with rage, and when he began to speak his voice trembled like a stretched string that was going to snap, 'Does the head of the training flying unit expect me to replace the instructors with the chief accountant, Kursky, and the manager of the household, Goldman?' he stammered.

I felt sorry for my chief, but what could I say to console him? We stood facing each other for a long time, and I was the first to break the silence: 'May I go, sir?'

'Go!' he screamed.

I turned round and went out. When I was closing the door I heard an insulting word, which Barsky threw at my back like a stone. But I was not upset. Running downstairs I kept thinking about Major Zmozhnykh on his horse and a warplane like a distant mirage waiting for me in Kirovograd. That's where I was ordered to go.

The train was slowly passing Znamenka station. Most of windows had no glass in. Burnt freight cars were lying along the railway embankment. When I reached Kirovograd I had to spend a long time trying to find out where my unit was. I finally reached the airfield somehow. I saw about 150 Osoaviachim pilots near the barracks. Someone called me. I saw Misha Vorozhbiev and Anatoliy Bogza running towards me. An unexpected meeting indeed!

'What are you flying?' I asked them.

'A cock-horse!' answered my aeroclub fellows. 'Nobody knows when or on what models we are going to start flying.'

'What are you doing then?'

'Morning check-ups, reports on political issues, evening check-ups... Learning to march to the canteen... Mastering gas-masks, rifles, learning to shoot.'

So there was no plane waiting for me in Kirovograd. We could only watch DB-3 bombers and I-16 Ishak★ fighters as they pursued the reconnaissance aircraft. People were fighting. Meanwhile we were sorted into groups of about fifty men. I was enrolled into a group named the 48th Independent Spotter Squadron (ISS) and was at once appointed the staff head under a cadre commander Captain Gart. I was in this position until evening drill. During drill I didn't notice that the commander, who came up from behind me, had not reported in time: he was downgraded to squad commander.

I would take my squad and go to a shooting-range. We were bad at shooting: rifles recoiled too hard and our right shoulders swelled. Our collarbones ached. On one occasion we were lying opposite the targets, watching nine bombers flying north-west in wedge formation. They were going to bomb tanks near Berdichev and Belaya Tserkov, about 250 kilometres away. We felt jealous: they were flying as if on a parade, it was really beautiful. We kept looking at our

---

★ Ishak was a nickname: in Russian *ishak* means 'donkey'.

27

watches, waiting for them to return. Finally we saw smoke on the horizon, and then dark spots in the sky. There were only five of them. The one that smoked fell behind the others. It looked strange: there was no transparent glass canopy at the fuselage forward section. The bomber glided directly to the airfield, landed, and rolled as an injured bird with one wing hanging. We rushed to the airfield with our rifles and gas masks, but the guards did not let us come closer.

The plane stopped just few metres from the hangar wall. The place where the canopy had been hit by a shell was stained with red drops. The rubber on one wheel was torn to shreds. There were shell-holes everywhere: in the propeller blade, in the mutilated wings and the fuselage. These were the traces of anti-aircraft guns and fighters. An ambulance car arrived. The pilot slowly got out of the cockpit. His face was black from oil. In silence he looked at the nurse and the driver. They put the gunner's body on the stretcher and placed it in the car. The nurse came up to the pilot, took him by the elbow and pointed at the car. He drew her hand aside, and plodded across the airfield without looking at anybody. When he took his helmet off, I recognised him. It was my friend from Bujur-Nus. I dashed to catch him up, but a guard blocked my way with a rifle: 'Halt!'

We were not a real unit yet, we were only recruits. We could not go there.

At night Mikhail Vorozhbiev and I were off-duty. Life is strange: we had served together in the same aeroclub in Nikolayev, we had lived in the same house, and now we were walking together in clumsy greatcoats with our rifles and gas-masks slipping down all the time.

We walked in silence. I was recalling my last talk with Natasha – Vorozhbiev's wife, who remained in Nikolayev with little Edik and Lera. When I was leaving for Kirovograd I dropped in on her for a minute. Bidding me goodbye Natasha had said: 'Misha convinced me that two months wouldn't pass before he came back in victory. You know, I believed him. It's true, isn't it?'

'Of course it's true,' I answered without the slightest hesitation.

Vorozhbiev and I were walking side by side. The searchlight rays were crossing the black sky. An enemy aircraft was howling closer and closer. Soon something whizzed above our heads. We leaped into a trench. A blinding flash came immediately; air beat our faces. The ground beneath us heaved, sand poured from the parapet. Raids went on until the morning. Every now and then we had to jump into a trench. Privately we cursed our rifles and gas-masks, which were a real burden in slit trenches.

Some days later a tractor dragged a twin-engine bomber to the airfield. The plane was labelled with crosses and swastikas. It was a Heinkel-111; we'd heard a lot about it already. They said that our fighters forced it to land – it was brand new, without a scratch. The cockpit still smelled of paint. Each of us longed to sit on the pilot seat, to hold the control stick. We began to study the aircraft spontaneously. One of us found out how to black out the transparent canopy: one just had to pull a cord, *shhh!* – and a light-tight curtain covered the plexiglass. It grew dusky inside. Pulled the cord again and the curtain rolled up – it was a bright day again. That was the anti-searchlight protection. Junior Lieutenant Berezansky, who knew German, was practically forced into the cockpit: 'Read what's written on the instruments, and translate!'

For fighter pilots the Heinkel was a real treasure. They revolved its machine-guns, defined the arcs of fire, searched the 'dead' sectors – those not exposed to fire – and looked for the best attack directions. A stocky lieutenant from a fighter aircraft unit was the one most excited. They said that he had vast experience in pursuing reconnaissance aircraft in the Ishak. 'Why don't these bastards burn?' he kept asking.

Before that we used to think that the aircraft had some special armour. Now the legend was dispelled. There was nothing peculiar in the armoured back with a cap; the armoured bubble of the lower gunner was also familiar. The wing fuel tanks appeared to be covered with ordinary crude rubber protectors. Could it possibly protect the aircraft from fire? Our fighter pilots concluded that if the Ishak were to be equipped with heavy cannons instead of machine-guns, and fly thirty kilometres an hour faster, Heinkels would not escape so easily.

Next day we watched an air fight. Our Ishak was pursuing a German reconnaissance aircraft. The fighter flew higher. It gained extra speed while descending, and was rapidly approaching the German plane. This was already spitting out blue tracer shells, but our pilot was not firing yet. We were wondering if the weapons broke down. The Ishak was already very close, when we saw a black track following the German aircraft and then it caught fire. Soon we saw two white canopies in the air. And our hawk flashed in sunlight, dived steeply and hoicked himself up again triumphantly. Incidentally, the pilot was the guy who had been so interested in the captured Heinkel.

The parachutists drifted to the wheat field. They landed behind the forest near the trackman's sentry-box. A lorry full of soldiers went there and was soon back with the captured German pilots, and a soldier who was hit in the stomach by a stray bullet during the encircling manoeuvre.

We were ordered not to spend the night in the barracks, so we dozed in trenches. In the middle of the night there came an order: 'Battle alarm! Fall in with the luggage!' We fussed about in the dark passages, grabbing the wrong bags. Then we followed our attendant along the field in single file. We stopped by a row of lorries and were ordered to load bombs. We stacked our trunks, and started loading. Later we set off in the same lorries, sitting on the bombs packed in boxes.

'Where are we going?' we asked the driver.

'If they don't turn off anywhere, we'll come to Dnepropetrovsk.'

I was sitting next to Vorozhbiev. In silence we looked at the flashes of distant blazes. It was difficult to concentrate. 'What kinds of troubles are waiting for us? What are we going to fly at: fighters, bombers, reconnaissance or attack aircraft?' I was wondering.

On that disturbed night I was thinking about Nikolayev and our airfield, Vodopoi. The front line was approaching them. For the first time I remembered the insulting word of the airfield chief Barsky. The word he had shouted after me in a fit of temper as I was leaving was 'deserter'!

2

A 'MERCHANT'

The airfield dried out and turned green – summer weather set in. Everything was in perfect order. White and red flags were fluttering in straight rows dividing take-off, landing and neutral strips. Landing panels were set strictly upwind. Five Su-2s were standing wing-to-wing, their wheels along the row of flags. The take-off detail – the flight duty officer, the starter, the finisher and the time-keeper – were wearing red arm-bands and holding red and white signal flags. A duty lorry was standing at its place – flights were forbidden if it was not present. There was supposed to be an ambulance car, but we did not have one. In general everything looked exactly like the scheme in 'Flying Instructions'.

Training flights were to start soon, and the squadron leader, Major Afanasiev, was repeating familiar instructions to a rank of pilots: that was the routine. He was in proper uniform: a dark-blue flying suit, a wide belt, a map-case on a long strap, and of course a helmet with goggles.

The squadron leader was talking in a low, burring voice. He did not hurry – we had enough time. The first plane was to take off right on time, according to the flight schedule. Afanasiev was a perfect pilot, calm and accurate. He had tried to join a military unit, but failed. Now he was in the ideal place: in TC – the Training Centre of the Southern Front. At that time the front required not only planes, but also pilots. Before the war, pilots were trained in Military Flying Schools and aeroclubs. Now additional aircraft brigades and flying centres were organised. They were attached to the front VVS (Air Force). Our TC trained pilots before sending them to the front. Progress was slow: there were too few planes, not enough fuel and not enough spare parts...

I was tired of the TC already. After Kirovograd I was sent to the outskirts of Dnepropetrovsk. Our airfield was granted a silvery twin-engine aircraft, an SB. Though it was a 1933-year model, we still called it a high-speed bomber. It was a fighting machine all the same! But even that single plane was taken away. I had to spend winter in Kotelnikov, near Stalingrad. From time to time I flew SBs or Su-2s. By spring our TC moved to Millerovo. The graduates were assigned to the Southern Front reserve.

But on that bright day, from that very moment on, the course of events in the Millerovo airfield began to change with incredible speed. The squadron leader was still talking when one of the pilots whispered to his neighbour. He nudged the next person in the line, and so it spread all over the rank. Nobody was listening to the squadron leader any longer. Everybody was looking in the same direction, just above the hangar roof. A dark sharp-formed aircraft was rapidly approaching the airfield making no noise. It turned round the building, came closer to the ground, and whizzed so low above the 'T' that the finisher fell down in fright. Then it pulled up sharply, and climbed roaring. The air-blast blew off the landing flaps. The Shturmovik★ banked, circled the airfield, and did a perfect three-point landing in the right place. It was quite a show.

Such an intrusion was an audacious challenge to the airfield rules. First, the aircraft landed unexpectedly, without a prior request. Second, in no time the pilot managed to break a dozen landing rules! Even now he was not taxiing to the dispersal area at a brisk walking pace, but he rushed at the speed of an automobile. The pilot slammed on the brakes beside the row of Su-2s, wheeled around, covered the rank of pilots with dust, and stood in a line with other planes in perfect symmetry.

The unknown pilot impressed everybody by his boldness and accuracy. Afanasiev grew noticeably pale. We were all wondering how the squadron leader was going to tear a strip off the uninvited guest.

The situation developed rapidly. We hardly had time to follow the train of events. As soon as the propeller made its last revolution and stopped, a dirty-faced mechanic in an oily suit jumped out of the

★ Shturmovik comes from the phrase *Bronirovanni Shturmovik* meaning 'armoured attacker', commonly used for ground-attack aircraft. During the war it became synonymous with the Il-2 aircraft.

fuselage hatch behind the cockpit. It was a single-seat plane, but there were two men inside! A new violation! The mechanic immediately began to deal with the engine. The pilot jumped out of the cockpit on to the wing. He was rather short, lean and not particularly young. He threw off the parachute, pulled off his helmet and threw it roughly on the parachute. Then he took out a cap, pulled it on to his grizzled head almost down to his ears, smoothed down the creases under his belt, and tidied his soldier's blouse. There was an Order of Lenin on his breast, a big Parachute Instructor badge with a pendant, and two 'rectangles' in the tabs. So he was of the same rank as our squadron leader. Forces were equal...

Afanasiev was standing at the same place waiting. He was holding red and white flags – the symbol of authority of the flight dispatcher. Everyone must obey him at the airfield. There could be no exceptions.

The pilot jumped down from the wing and walked quickly towards Afanasiev. 'Who is the senior officer?' he asked severely as he moved.

'Flight dispatcher Major Afanasiev,' answered the squadron leader, his hand by his helmet. The major with the Order of Lenin did not return the salute, but simply shook hands with Afanasiev. Our squadron leader pretended not to notice the familiarity. 'May I ask your name and purpose of arriving, sir?' he asked in official manner.

'From the front. Kholoba-a-ev!' drawled the guest. 'And my purpose I will discuss at your headquarters with the head of the TC.' Before Afanasiev could open his mouth the major added insistently: 'I need a car, urgently, to go to the town.'

'We only have a duty car, but the flights are to start soon.'

'I'll take it. Don't worry, it won't take long.' Without waiting for approval he waved his hand confidently to the driver. The driver started the engine, the car rode up, the major jumped inside, slammed the door, and the vehicle was gone, as if a hurricane swept past us.

The flights could not start until the duty car came back. Meanwhile the pilots surrounded the Shturmovik. The mechanic, named Kozhin, was eagerly answering numerous questions.

'Did this plane take part in military operations?'

'Why, of course! There was even an article in *Pravda* devoted to it. Have you read it?'

33

'No – what was the occasion?' everybody was interested.

'This is the only aircraft in our regiment that exhausted its engine life in military operations.'

'And what about the rest?'

'They didn't have time. This one also returned with holes in it many times. We patched it up, and it flew again. They mentioned its number in the article: 0422.'

Kozhin pronounced the number as if it were the name of a celebrity. He spoke of the plane as if it were an intelligent being.

'This one is from an anti-aircraft gun,' he showed us a big Duralumin patch on the wing, 'and the dent in the bonnet is from a splinter... And that one in the tail – pecks from Messerschmitts.'*

'And who piloted it?'

'Different pilots did, but I've been its only mechanic. We are now going to drive it into the repair shop and change the engine – it overheats and shows metal filings in the oil filter.'

A war-plane, military injuries... How many pilots pulled the triggers in this cockpit? How many Fritzes† could it kill, how many tanks and cars could it burn down? A war-plane... And next to it stood clean, paunchy, blunt-nosed Su-2s, without a scratch. How could we possibly call them short-range bombers or attack aircraft? They had no armour, they burnt like matches, there were only four machine-guns inside...

On that day I flew with my navigator on an Su-2 to practise bombardment. We used cement bombs. The navigator did something wrong with the sight, and the bombs burst way beyond the target – a white circle with a cross in the middle. We had missed...

The TC pilots lived in private apartments. Usually after the flights were over everybody went home. But on that day men lounged about the headquarters until late at night. A rumour spread that a 'merchant' had arrived. 'Merchant' was a name for those who came from front-line units to recruit pilots. It was unlikely that that was Major Kholobaev's aim: there were no Shturmoviks in the TC, nobody could pilot them... But soon the bush telegraph reported: the major was sitting by the human resource officer reading personal files.

* The Russians commonly called the German fighter Bf-109 by its designer's name.
† German soldiers.

By the time Kholobaev had finished with the files, it was late at night. He went straight to the pilots, 'Are Boiko and Artemov here by any chance?' The pilots exchanged glances in the dark, and he added, 'What about Zangiev?'

'They've just left,' somebody answered.

'What's your name?' he addressed me.

'Junior Lieutenant Emelianenko.'

'Great! I was looking for you. Where do you live?'

'In a private apartment, comrade Major.'

'Is there enough room for a guardsman to spend the night? Would it be OK with your landlady? I've had a quarrel with your command, so I don't want to ask them...'

'There is, comrade Major...'

I felt uneasy. A honoured commander had come from the front, and was looking for a place to spent the night!

We arrived at my apartment and had a drink. The landlady made a bed on the floor, because there was only one proper bed in the room. Kholobaev looked jealously at the feather bed and snow-white pillow and said, 'The one with the senior rank will sleep in bed, and the subordinate will sleep on the floor. I'm tired of sleeping on the ground in dugouts...' In a second he fell asleep.

I lay awake for a long time thinking of that word, 'subordinate'. What could that mean? Why did he mention several names near the headquarters? Could he have chosen the men already? I wished I could become his subordinate. He seemed to be a simple man, who didn't brag.

At 6 a.m. the pilots selected by Kholobaev were standing by the Shturmovik. The Major said: 'I only know you by your personnel records so far. I was interested in those who have vast flying experience. There are Osoaviachim instructors among you, and experienced pilots. But I cannot know a man's soul through documents. I warn you: there are going to be no feather beds at the front. It's not easy to get a decoration. If any of you does not want to pilot a Shturmovik – tell me honestly, I won't take offence. We have a hell of a job, it's not as smooth what as they write about us suggests.'

He did not need to warn us about feather beds and decorations. The pilots were looking at his order with great respect. We understood that he had not received it for having blue eyes. But I guess each of us was thinking: 'Am I in a dream? Am I really going to pilot a Shturmovik?'

Kholobaev explained what he intended to do. As he was talking, the pilots were exchanging bewildered looks. In one day we were to study the cockpit, learn to start the engine and pass a test. And what did it mean: to pass a test? It meant that we must remember all taps, switches, levers, instruments and their normal readings...

We got into the cockpit by turns. Kozhin explained everything to the one who was inside, and the rest stood on the wing listening. The learning process was going rather fast. When the heat of the day subsided we began to practise starting the engine. Kholobaev was standing on the centre section getting a firm grip on the cockpit side. It was a miracle that he was not blown away by the hurricane air-blast from the propeller. The engine was roaring deafeningly, and Kholobaev was bending into the cockpit and shouting in your ear: 'More throttle!' It was difficult to believe he demanded more throttle! It already seemed that nearly 2,000 horsepower raging inside the engine would smash him into pieces. After each attempt the water in the engine started to boil, and we had to wait until it cooled down.

The day passed in a flash. Pilots were glad to have studied a new plane in such a short time. Kholobaev did not expect us to remember unnecessary numbers like the wingspan or the keel height, fortunately. When Boiko asked out of pure curiosity what was the length of the mean aerodynamic chord of the wing, Kholobaev asked him in return: 'Have you ever seen this mean aerodynamic chord?'

'No...'

'Well, forget this rubbish!'

In the evening he declared: 'Tomorrow we'll try the flights. At dawn everyone must be here, we must use the cool hours.' And what we were going to use those hours for? That he did not tell.

In the morning Kholobaev called me up and ordered: 'Put a parachute on, fasten the belts and taxi out to the take-off. I'll be there.'

'Yes, sir!' I said and thought to myself: 'I'll taxi out, and then he will start explaining the details of the flight on a Shturmovik. He has mentioned the parachute and the belts as a formality.'

So I taxied up to the take-off line and was going to stop the engine, but Kholobaev said: 'You hold down the brakes, step hard on the gas to lance the plugs, and then release the brakes and go. Just before the take-off you reduce speed, slow down until you stop, and taxi in. Don't take off! Did you get that?'

I did everything that he told me, taxied back and was going to leave the cockpit, but Kholobaev jumped up on the wing again: 'Now fly round in a circle. Imagine that you are piloting an Su-2, it will seem even smoother! You'll see... Go!'

I made a flight round in a circle as if in a dream. Only after I had landed accurately on the T did I realise that I was sitting in an Ilyushin. I taxied in. Kholobaev crossed his arms above his head: stop the engine! 'It's boiling – Kozhin explained to the pilots...'

The TC pilots surrounded me: 'How was it?'

'It was fine...' I answered trying to look totally calm. In my mind I was thinking over the two training systems: Kholobaev's and the one in the TC. In a week Kholobaev had managed to train five pilots whom he had selected. And he trained us on a Shturmovik with an exhausted engine, which boiled after each circuit. We also studied battle operation: we blew up real bombs, launched the RSs★, fired cannons and machine-guns. For the first time we were allowed to use as much ammunition as we needed. Perhaps that's why all the targets that had served the TC for so long were smashed to pieces. The white circle that we had missed with my navigator grew noticeably brown.

A day came when Major Kholobaev said: 'Now you will be assigned to the 7th Guards Regiment.'

The 7th Order of Lenin Guards Regiment – that was the name given to the 4th Ground-attack Aircraft Regiment on 7 March 1942. The order to rename the regiment read: 'For the courage shown in fights with the enemy, for the steadfastness, fortitude, discipline and excellent organisation, for the heroism demonstrated by the personnel...' Now the regiment would become my home.

★ RS was an abbreviation for *reaktivny snariad* – a missile.

3

1941

I joined the regiment in 1942. But when I began to write this book, several pilots who had entered the war in 1941 were still alive. I thought it would be right to write down their stories about that period of the war and the tasks they had to carry out. It was a terrible time. The regiment had no experience of modern ways of fighting. The pilots did not have time to master the new aircraft. After the defeat of the first weeks of the war our troops did not have enough fighters and anti-aircraft guns left. Consequently, squadrons flew to attack their targets without any cover. German aircraft had complete superiority in the air. Soviet military pilots had to pay tremendous prices, and very few of those who began the war in summer 1941 lasted until victory came. Most of those who managed to survive occupied command posts. As for the rest – they were lost on missions. During the war years the regiment was reinforced with fresh men many times. It fought until the end of the war, but it paid with several hundred lives of its pilots, mechanics and gunners.

In May 1941 the 4th Ground-Attack Aircraft Regiment based at the Bogoduhov airfield near Kharkov was equipped with new aircraft. Before that the regiment had taken part in the Finnish war flying R-Z planes. Now it was the first regiment among the Air Force to be re-equipped with the brand-new plane called 'N'. The pilots had to master the plane and evaluate its operation and its tactical abilities. The most experienced pilots went to the factory to get the planes, and the rest studied tangled wiring schemes, systems of fuel- and oil-feeding, water-cooling and the hydraulics that released the landing gear. Men learned lots of numbers, including the piston stroke, the diameter of the propeller, the wing span, the length of the mean aerodynamic chord, the width of the landing gear tread, the tail height, the instrument readings and numerous warnings to the pilot starting with the words 'in case of malfunction'...

At the factory the pilots sat in the cockpits for a long time studying the instruments, remembering the take-off position of the engine cowling against the horizon line and learning to release the landing gear. But studying was useless without training flights. They needed a dual- control plane of the same kind with the second cockpit for an instructor. But such a plane had not yet been constructed. The only thing to do was to train pilots on an Su-2 dual-control bomber that had take-off and landing speeds similar to the Shturmovik. Soon the pilots could fly without an instructor, and by the beginning of June seventeen new aircraft were ferried to Bogoduhov.

In the evening the planes were covered with tarpaulin covers. A special unit of soldiers arrived to guard the planes, since they were top secret. But instead of sixty-five planes the regiment had received only seventeen. The rest of the planes arrived in the second half of June.

The vicinity of Bogoduhov now roared with engines from dawn until night. The command was hurriedly re-training pilots. The process advanced very slowly because of the lack of dual-control Shturmoviks.

The first flights were successful, but then one of the engines stalled. The pilot managed to land without damaging the aircraft, fortunately. Soon one more forced landing took place, because the landing gear failed to come out. According to the temporary instruction of that time a pilot was to bale out in such cases. Men were afraid that the Shturmovik could turn over, which would cause a fire, and the pilot would not be able to get out from the cockpit.

When Junior Lieutenant Grigory Chuhno could not release the landing gear, instead of baling out he landed on the fuselage. The Shturmovik crawled along the field creating a cloud of dust. To everybody's surprise the plane neither turned over nor was it seriously damaged. After that incident the instruction to bale out was cancelled. The person to blame for the forced landing was a mechanic, who had left his overalls inside the landing-gear body. He got off with a sharp reprimand. If it had not been for his absent-mindedness, many planes would have been lost!

Some defects found during the test flights had to be eliminated in the following aircraft series. Several pilots and the aircraft's designer,

Ilyushin, were soon to arrive at Bogoduhov from the factory. The flights were well under way, but on one long-awaited Saturday many pilots were going to visit their families in Kharkov and Bolchansk. The regiment was drawn up earlier than usual. 'We'll get home before dark,' many people thought. But unexpectedly Major Kozhuhovsky announced: 'All leave is cancelled! The designer and the pilots and will arrive tomorrow. If the weather allows, we will fly. Fall out!'

The pilots still hoped that they would be dismissed in the morning, since the sky was cloudy and rain was pattering on the tents.

But in the morning they woke up at the 'Get up!' command. In a few minutes there came a thunderous order from Kozhuhovsky: 'Fall in! Quickly!'

'Is it possible that the constructor and the pilots could have arrived so early in such dreadful weather?' People were guessing. Everybody ran out of their tents looking for their place in the formation in the dark, and Kozhuhovsky was already declaring: 'First squadron, remove the tents, gather personal stuff and bedding and put it in the barn. Second, third and fourth squadron, station the planes along the edge of the airfield. Fifth squadron, take shovels and dig trenches for the personnel. Do everything as if there is a real emergency. People from the district headquarters are coming to inspect us. Get started!'

The pilots moved the six-ton Shturmoviks by hand. For some reason Kozhuhovsky forbade starting the engines. Three men lifted the heavy tails on their shoulders, and about ten men pushed the planes by the wing edges. The tents were removed. Wet bedding and heavy trunks were carried to the farmyard. The fifth squadron were digging wide trenches near the wind turbine. Kozhuhovsky came to have a look and rejected the work: 'Are you making a cellar? Make it narrow! Only one person should be able to squeeze through.'

People worked without a break until 11 a.m. Then for some reason everybody was summoned to the wind turbine under a loudspeaker. The regiment commissar Ryabov was walking to and fro with his hands behind his back.

At 12 a.m. sharp the regiment heard him say: 'Without declaring war fascist hordes intruded into our country in the middle of the night...'

Command held a meeting in the drizzling rain. War... For the rest of the day the regiment continued the training flights.

On the fifth day of the war there came an order: 'Fly to the front today!' Most of the men had not expected to be sent to the front so early. They had neither learned to fly in formation nor had they ever fired the guns! Nobody had ever seen the missiles that were supposed to be suspended from the underside of the wings. Nobody had any clue about targeted bombing. The cockpits were equipped with optical sight tubes, and the men guessed that they could help to release bombs over the target. The pilots from the factory were supposed to know how to operate them, but they never arrived from Voronezh...

The 4th Ground-Attack Regiment could not fly to the front on the same day. The delay was caused by unexpected minor problems. For example, when mechanics began to insert small bomb-holders into the bomb bays, they found out that the holders did not fit. The mechanics and armourers led by the regiment engineer, Boris Mitin, slaved over the holders for the rest of the day and the whole night. It took them a long time to understand that the holders were not all the same. Each had its own number and had to be inserted into a certain bay only.

As for the pilots, they had to prepare maps for the flight urgently. The regiment staff did not have the necessary sheets of paper, and the only place where they could get them was Kharkov. To send a car to Kharkov meant losing a day, and to send an aircraft was impossible because Kharkov could not accept planes owing to a storm. Ignoring the advice of the meteorological service not to fly, the regiment commander sent an experienced pilot, Vladimir Vasilenko, together with Lieutenant Yakov Kvaktun, to fly through the storm at his own risk. They got into a heavy rain storm and lost their way trying to escape. Fortunately, they found a railroad and it led them to Kharkov. In the evening the men began to stick together the sheets for a 500-kilometre route. When the huge maps were finally made and folded they would not fit into the map cases! They had to be divided into sections.

The flight was not going to be easy. The first landing was in Karachev near Bryansk. The calculations showed that there would hardly be enough fuel to reach the place. If anything went wrong at the airfield it would be risky to make even one extra circuit. And that was not the only problem. It appeared that the flight duration of seven of the planes was estimated to be several minutes less than that of the rest. The youngest pilots in the regiment, Smurygov and Shahov, were among those who received the 'special' planes.

On that day the division commander, Colonel Putsykin, was rushing about the airfield trying to speed up the process, and telling everybody off. By the evening he lost his voice and could only speak hoarsely and throw furious glances. This went on until late at night. Men fell down to sleep in the hayloft without making beds. Before going to sleep they took the most essential equipment from their trunks: soap, towels, razors, toothbrushes. That was all they were going to take to the front. Smurygov thought of taking a sweater, but changed his mind. 'The war will be over before it gets colder,' he thought.

On 26 June five squadrons lined up along the edge of the airfield evenly spaced. The pilots were sitting in the cockpits waiting for the refuellers to fill the tanks up to the top.

When everything was ready, the squadrons took off one after another and headed to the north-west. The formation broke immediately and the planes flew in a disorderly swarm. Many pilots had not yet got used to the instruments in the cockpit and had to find the switch they needed by reading the labels. It took a lot of time, and as a result planes often came too close to their neighbours. The neighbour would dash aside, interfering with other planes, and so it was a complete mess that lasted for about half the journey. None of the wingmen used the huge maps, because they were too busy watching out for the other planes. Few of the pilots knew where they were flying. All hope rested with the leaders, and fortunately they did their job all right. The squadrons landed at Karachev.

Some planes had to be towed away from the runway, because there was no fuel left in the tanks. Some planes had to land before they reached Karachev. The deputy regiment commander was among the ones whose planes failed to get there. Bad luck for him... The command started to search for the missing aircraft and at the same time people were getting ready for the next part of the flight. The pilots refuelled the planes (the mechanics had not yet arrived) and planned the route to Minsk. The canteen was overcrowded and pilots had to stand in a long queue. Once more they went to sleep late at night, their heads aching...

It seemed that they woke before they could really close their eyes.

There was a real storm outside, but the regiment commander had a strict order to wait by the planes until the weather improved. Each minute was precious. The front was waiting.

The pilots ran to the dispersal areas in heavy rain and in pitch darkness. The planes' numbers could only be seen during the bolts of lightning. Some men hid from the rain inside the cockpits, some squatted under the wings smoking. The clouds were slowly crawling to the west. Finally the rain stopped and the sky cleared up at the east. A green flare shot up giving the sign to start the engines. The squadrons took off.

The command intended to make an intermediate flight stop in Stary Bykhov. Half-way there the unit encountered a heavy rain storm. Trying not to lose the leader the wingmen flew in close formation without any order. That time nobody got lost.

Hundreds of people were swarming over the airfield with shovels and stretchers, building a concrete runway. Piles of road-metal and sand towered in the middle of the field. The airfield was a landing point not only for the attack aircraft but also for fighters and bombers. The planes landed to the right of the runway under construction, and took off to the left of it.

The squadron leaders had to spend much time waiting for Major Getman and the battalion commissar, Ryabov, who were making inquiries about further flights by other units. Those units were the remnants of the regiments that had been attacked in the first hours of the war. Getman and Ryabov talked to a tired-looking lieutenant colonel. The 4th Ground-Attack Aircraft Regiment had an order to join the Western Front air forces, so Getman asked the lieutenant colonel: 'Can I contact the Air Force headquarters through you?'

'No...'

'Where is it now? In Minsk?' Getman asked. He thought that if he could not call up headquarters, he probably had to fly there and report on arrival. Time was precious.

'Minsk is occupied by German tanks,' the lieutenant colonel said.

'Isn't that just provocative rumour?' Ryabov asked, but the lieutenant colonel confirmed that he had seen it with his own eyes. He appeared to be the commander of a unit which had been based in the border area and lost the majority of its planes in the bombardment at dawn on 22 June.

'So where is the front line now?' Getman asked. He took out the map case ready to mark the new data.

'There is no certain information yet... What we have seen with our own eyes looked like a pie with many pieces: to the west of Minsk our forces were fighting, while to the east of Minsk the German motorised columns were continuing to advance.'

Only the pilots arrived at Stary Bykhov by air. The rest of the personnel (and that was about 500 people) were to arrive to the front in sixteen trains. About fifty men were to fly in two transport aircraft. They came later than they were expected, but finally the regiment was ready to go further and take part in operations.

4

RECONNAISSANCE IN FORCE

A U-2 flew low above the Stary Bykhov airfield and landed near the Shturmoviks. 'Could it be Naumenko?' Before the war Nikolai Fedorovich Naumenko had been General Kopets's deputy. Long before the fascist invasion the 'smell of powder' was in the air in the border regions. In June German aircraft were flying across the frontier pretty often. General Kopets addressed the imperious district commander Colonel General Pavlov and asked him to let the frontier forces to 'teach the Germans a lesson'. Pavlov categorically forbade sending fighters to intercept the German planes, referring to the TASS★ report of 14 June, which read that '...the rumours that Germany is going to break the pact and attack the USSR are absolutely groundless...'

'Don't succumb to any provocation!' Pavlov snapped back.

When it became obvious that the enemy had amassed large forces directly on our borders, and the German reconnaissance aircraft were openly flying over the Soviet aircraft bases, Kopets and Naumenko made a second attempt to persuade the commander: 'Let us station the aircraft at the reserve airfields.'

'You are short-sighted,' he answered. 'Don't give any cause for provocation! Follow my directions and get ready for the exercise. Devote your efforts to serious business!' A large-scale exercise was going to take place at the Brest training ground on 22 June.

After the first massive attack by the fascist aircraft General Kopets got into a plane and flew over all his airfields. Wherever he went he saw planes burning. The losses were enormous. The General returned to the headquarters and shot himself in his office. Few people knew about that tragedy.

★ A Soviet news agency.

Now Colonel Naumenko headed the aircraft forces of the Western Front. His difficult job was to assemble the remnants of the aircraft units and organise their operation. The lines of communication had been destroyed by German saboteurs, and it was not easy to command the units. Naumenko had to fly on a U-2 from one place to another giving tasks to the regiments. He also had to maintain communication with the headquarters of the Western Front and the armies and co-ordinate the role of the aircraft with infantry operations. The headquarters changed their locations all the time, and it was not easy to find them. Naumenko had to land near the roads and ask the troops on the move. The usual job in those days was given as 'reconnaissance in force', which meant actually 'find the enemy and destroy him'.

On 28 June Naumenko was seeking the Front headquarters and decided to fly along the road that led from Stary Bykhov along the Dnepr. Approaching Mogilev he noticed a car moving along a country road. It turned and disappeared inside the forest. The colonel circled above the place and saw a few tents and cars in the thicket. He landed on a meadow and went to the car that was standing at the edge of the forest. The driver seemed familiar to him. 'Whom did you bring?' he asked him.

'I brought Sandalov, comrade Colonel.'

'Oh really?' Naumenko was very glad. Quite unexpectedly he found the head of the 4th Army headquarters, Sandalov. Just before the war broke out Naumenko had discussed a plan for a might-have-been exercise with Sandalov.

Naumenko went further into the forest and saw the Commander-in-Chief of the Front, D. G. Pavlov. The Commander-in-Chief looked haggard and did not at all remind the imperious person whom Naumenko had seen in Minsk. He was commanding Sandalov in a quiet voice: 'Recapture Bobruysk... You may go.'

Pavlov was surrounded by staff officers with maps and documents. Everybody was waiting for Marshals of the Soviet Union Voroshilov and Shaposhnikov. They were to arrive from Moscow any moment now. The Commander-in-Chief of the Front noticed Naumenko, who was standing nearby, but immediately turned an indifferent glance in another direction. He began to sign the papers without really looking at them. 'The Air Force does not seem to bother him now,' Naumenko thought and hurried to catch up with Sandalov.

'Where are you located now?' Naumenko asked him.

'Behind the Berezina, three kilometres to the west from Bobruysk. We fly to attack the crossings. Is that right?'

'Perfect! Go on like that!'

'And where is your right-hand neighbour?' Naumenko asked, meaning the 13th Army.

'They are fighting somewhere near Minsk... Come to visit us, we'll talk,' Sandalov said, closing the door of his car.

'Watch the sky as you move. Messerschmitts are patrolling all the roads,' Naumenko advised him at parting.

He tried to get more specific information about the location of the 13th Army headquarters from the staff officers, but nobody knew that for sure. Signal officers were sent there on a U–2 with an order form the Commander-in-Chief of the Front to hold the Minsk fortified area at any price.

Naumenko took off and headed to Stary Bykhov. He flew low, the tops of the trees were just below his wings. He looked up from time to time following his own advice. The sky was cloudless and the sun was shining. As he was approaching Stary Bykhov he noticed four Messerschmitts. For a second Naumenko thought they had not seen him, but at the next moment all four fighters dived, aiming at his aircraft. There was only one thing he could do: land immediately, so he did. He got out of the cockpit, ran away and hid in the bushes. A burst, a new one, and the aircraft caught fire. In an instant the flame spread along the linen wings and the wind scattered the burning fragments.

Naumenko had to hitch-hike to the regiment. He returned to Getman's command post dust-laden and unshaven. Soon there came an order to load the bombs on to the planes and to arm the cannons and sub-machine guns. There were not enough technical personnel in the regiment and one mechanic and one armourer had to deal with five planes at a time. They unpacked big red boxes that had just arrived from Moscow on a transport aircraft. The boxes contained the missiles. It was the first time the mechanics had had a chance to fix them in the planes. A factory engineer was supervising the work. Someone forgot to turn off the electrical current of the aircraft and one of the missiles whizzed like a comet and disappeared in the forest.

The difficult day was already coming to an end, when the commander of the first squadron, Captain Spitsin, and his deputies, Senior Politruk* Filippov and Captain Kholobaev, were summoned urgently to the regiment commander. They introduced themselves to Colonel Naumenko, who looked really stern with his two Orders of the Red Banner and a huge Mauser in a wooden holster. Naumenko instructed the pilots: 'The three of you will fly to scout the Bobruysk region. Don't attack anything to the east of the Berezina river, but destroy whatever you see to the west of it. Got it?'

The task for the first operational flight was formulated in two short sentences. The commander must have known that Spitsin and Filippov had taken part in the Finnish war, and Kholobaev also had enough experience.

As no questions followed, Naumenko said: 'Carry on!'

The pilots saluted and hurried to their aircraft. Too late questions were coming to their minds one by one. What were they supposed to do actually? What targets must they attack and with what weapons? How far to the west should they fly? What route should they choose and at what altitude should they fly?

They had to find the answers by themselves. First of all they set the route. They drew a line on the map which crossed the Berezina to the north of Bobruysk and then turned left, heading to the Slutsk highway. The rest was simple. They decided to fly at an altitude of twenty to thirty metres with Kholobaev to the left and Filippov to the right. Time to go!

Eight missiles were suspended from the underside of Kholobaev's aircraft. The pilot hastily fastened the parachute straps, got inside the cockpit and tried to remember in what position he should set the electrical switch to launch the missiles and drop bombs. He looked round and noticed the regimental armament engineer, Captain Dremlyuk. Kholobaev waved to him and Dremlyuk ran up to the aircraft.

'How should I set the electrical switch on the bombing?'

'Are you going to drop bombs in train, in salvo, or one by one?'

'How on earth should I know? It will depend on the situation...'

---

* *Politruk* is the name of the person responsible for political instruction for the soldiers.

'Then we'll set it at one-by-one position.' Dremlyuk turned the handle at the right point.

'What about the switch for the missiles?'

Dremlyuk turned the handle to the right, then to the left... Then he scratched his head and said: 'Listen, comrade Captain, will you wait for a second? I'll go and bring the factory engineer, he can tell you everything.' And he disappeared.

But there was no time to wait. Spitsin and Filippov were already taxiing. Kholobaev started the engine, throttled up and taxied to the runway. He looked back and saw Dremlyuk running after the plane with the factory engineer. They climbed up the centre-section when the aircraft was already on the starting strip, clutched at the cockpit from both sides, bent over the pilot and began to explain something in his both ears. Kholobaev managed to ask the factory engineer how he should aim when he wanted to launch a missile.

'Set the crosshairs on the target and launch!'

'Right! Jump down quickly, I'm taking off...'

One by one the pilots raised their hands giving the signal 'Ready to take off'. Though the Shturmoviks were equipped with radio transmitters, nobody used them now. Pilots had made an attempt to tune the transmitters already in Bogoduhov, but there was nothing except the permanent loud bang in the headphones. The noise did not allow the pilots to control the engine by ear, so they gave up on wireless communication.

The planes took off, set the course, and noted the time. The pilots were wondering how they would distinguish the enemy. There was no front line on the map, and the situation was not clear. The pilots worried about the possibility of hitting their own forces. Nobody was thinking about anti-aircraft guns. Kholobaev believed in the Shturmovik's armour. Before he flew to the front his son had run up to him at the airfield. When he learned that his father was going to the front he began to cry. 'Won't they kill you, Daddy?'

'Kill me? In such a plane? Look!' Kholobaev had taken out his pistol and shot the side of the cockpit. Then he found a tiny trace from the bullet on the fresh paint and showed it to his son. There was not even a dent!

Of course the real reason for this test was not to calm the boy, but to calm down himself and his friends. Since that time Kholobaev was so sure of the plane's armour that he did not think about the danger that could be waiting for him in Bobruysk.

The engine was working smoothly, and the readings were normal. The Berezina was a rather long way ahead. The roads were deserted. Once they saw a woman with a boy carrying a big bundle. When the woman saw the planes, she grabbed the boy by the hand and rushed in the bushes. The bundle fell on the road raising dust… They flew above a farm with no signs of any living being. The pilots remembered the words of Naumenko: 'Don't attack anything to the east of the Berezina river.' There was nothing to attack here except the depressing and alarming emptiness.

They crossed the Berezina. There were no troops at the eastern side of the river. Where was the force that was supposed to restrain the fascists? The pilots could see Bobruysk and clouds of black smoke above it. The Shturmoviks raced along the river above the very tops of the forest. The estimated time was up. The aircraft began to turn, almost hitting the trees with their left wings. Here was the Slutsk highway and… a column.

Actually what they saw could not be called a column. It was a continuous stream of tanks, lorries, guns and armoured cars. They were moving in several rows heading to Bobruysk. Motorcycles were jolting along the road side. There was no end to the cavalcade. Our pilots noticed the white crosses on the tanks and realised that it was the enemy. But why were the fascists being so impudently careless? Soldiers were sitting on the tank turrets, their sleeves rolled up to the elbows. They were neither hiding nor shooting.

Our aircraft finished the turn right above the column. The pilots pressed the buttons several times. They did not aim, it was impossible to miss flying so low above such a horde. The planes lost their heavy burden and lifted a bit. The pilots did not see the explosions, but they could see panic spreading along the column. Kholobaev saw two lorries clash and fall in the trench. Soldiers were jumping from the cars. Motorcycles raced toward the forest. Luminous lines stretched immediately from the ground aiming at the planes. Whole shafts of sparks were soon piercing the sky. Kholobaev had never seen anything like that before. For a second he froze with astonishment, but then he felt rather than heard a loud click. A white spot appeared on the armoured windshield. He came to his senses. His fingers fumbled for the missile launching button but could not find it at once. He pressed something and a fiery comet rushed forward from under the wing. He pressed again and again, but the missiles disappeared ahead and he could not see where they exploded. Angrily he pressed the button with all his might. The control column moved forward a bit and the plane lowered the nose. This time the missile exploded in the middle of the column. That was an explosion! The pilot could not believe his eyes. Fragments of a lorry, shreds of canvas and something else rose in the air. Wow, that was a shot! But there was no end to the troops ahead and they all were firing at him. Kholobaev knew he had to attack, but with what? Then he remembered: 'The guns!' He pressed the trigger, but nothing happened. 'Am I pressing the right trigger?' Kholobaev thought. Yes, it was the right one. He pushed the reload lever and pressed the trigger again. The guns remained silent. And he was leaving the targets behind…

While Kholobaev was busy with the reload lever, the plane flew up to Bobruysk. The drifting smoke hid the town. The pilot turned left and flew low above the roofs. He got to the northern part of the town and found an enormous gathering of the enemy. He zoomed and then dived, shooting from the sub-machine guns. Suddenly something flashed near him. Kholobaev heard a loud blow and the aircraft jerked so hard that the heavy armoured cover of the fuel tank rose upright. He levelled the plane out but it was hit again. The seat came down under the pilot. The belts cut into his shoulders, and the cover of the fuel tank rose upright again. The anti-aircraft guns were shooting straight at him! 'It seems to be the end of Kostya Kholobaev,' the pilot thought. He yawed from one side to the other shooting in long bursts. There was no sense in sparing the barrels now. He had little chance anyway. At least he could die fighting!

The guns were already empty, but Kholobaev still tossed the plane up and down. At some moment he found himself flying above the Berezina. Burning Bobruysk was left behind. Ahead was the green wood and silence.

Kholobaev turned right and headed to the airfield. The sun was now shining from behind and the pilot saw that the windshield was splashed with oil and water. He looked at the instruments: the oil pressure indicator was approaching zero, while the oil and water temperature indicators were just before the red line. A smell of burning was filling up the cockpit. 'The engine will stall now, and I'll fall in the forest,' Kholobaev thought.

He realised that he was still flying at maximum speed and that he had forgotten to open the armoured screen of the oil radiator. That's why the engine got overheated. He throttled down and pushed the handle of the screen forward. The water temperature slowly came down. 'Perhaps the engine can last until the airfield,' the pilot thought. Only now did he remember about Spitsin and Filippov, but he could not spot them anywhere around.

Kholobaev taxied to the dispersal area and stopped the engine. He leaned against the seat back and closed his eyes. He felt very tired. Then he heard some voices, opened his eyes, and saw pilots and mechanics running to his plane. He pulled off his helmet and the parachute, leaned his hands against the canopy sash, transferred both his legs across the cockpit side as usual, and... fell down with a crash! His suit was torn and his arm was cut with something sharp. A mechanic ran up and helped Kholobaev to get out of a huge hole with ragged edges, which gaped in the centre-section. Kholobaev walked a few steps aside, looked at the aircraft, and could not believe his eyes. The plane was pierced with holes of different sizes. The armoured body was torn to shreds. Oil poured over the fuselage up to the tail. The pilot felt shocked. 'How did I manage to fly in such a sieve?'

People surrounded Kholobaev. Someone asked: 'What was it?..'

He pressed his bleeding hand to his lips and spat angrily on the grass. 'The anti-aircraft guns...' Then he asked: 'Did Spitsin and Filippov return?'

'Yes, they did! They are reporting now.'

'Oh, good. Let them report, and I'll go later...' Kholobaev took a cigarette out of someone's hand and inhaled deeply.

The regimental engineer, Mitin, came up to him, placed his hands on Kholobaev's shoulders and said sympathetically: 'Congratulations on the baptism of fire, Kostya!'

'Are Spitsin's and Filippov's planes damaged much?'

'They have several bullet holes in the wings.'

'But they can fly, can't they?'

'Mechanics are fitting bombs already. They will fly tomorrow.'

'And what about my plane?'

'Its time is over, I'm afraid...'

The regiment commander came up to them, shook hands with Kholobaev and ordered Mitin to drag it into a hangar at once, and not to let anybody see it!

A nine-ship formation of giant low-speed TB-3s flew slowly heading to Bobruysk. No fighters accompanied the bombers. When they flew back, there were only six of them left. A Messerschmitt fussed around behind them. In a few minutes six columns of black smoke rose above the forest.

Kholobaev and Dremlyuk were alone by the plane when they heard a panicky scream: 'Fly! Fly!'

They turned round and saw a twin-engined SB bomber driving directly at them. The Duralumin skin of one of its wings was torn. One of the propellers was not rotating. The bomber came closer and closer, but did not slow down for some reason. A man jumped out of the forward navigator's cockpit and rolled on the ground. The back wheel passed just a few centimetres by him. Kholobaev and Dremlyuk rushed to the side and a second later they heard a crash and a loud crackle behind them. They looked back and froze. The glass canopy of the bomber's forward cockpit had struck the engine of a Shturmovik, collapsing like an eggshell. The Il-2 stood crooked on one wheel. One of its wings leaned against the ground and the other one stuck up just as in a banking manoeuvre. The Shturmovik lay finished off on the ground.

In a few minutes a fighter landed at the airfield and spun round at the end of the runway. Men dragged out the pilot with his young chalk-white face, his left hand hanging on a shred of skin... An SB bomber was coming down with only one engine working. The wind was carrying it across the airfield towards the living quarters of the military camp. The pilot tried to turn, but the bomber banked and turned upside down. It crashed to the ground, and a fiery column rose up to the sky...

That was the first day at the front.

5

THE FIRST ENCOUNTERS WITH MESSERS

Several men were sitting in a tent at the edge of the airfield discussing the combat intelligence that the pilots had brought. Many pilots had spotted large trough-like objects lying in rows at the western bank of the Berezina. They must be the pontoons prepared for bridges. The Berezina river stretched from north to south blocking the enemy's way to Smolensk and Mogilev. But it was clear that without our troops' resistance the river would be no obstacle for the fascists. They would construct bridges and cross the river. And nobody knew where our troops were at the moment. There was no communication with the command. But the Shturmoviks were not going to wait idly!

The men in the tent spent almost the whole night racking their brains over what to do next. At last Colonel Naumenko made the decision: 'When the sun rises fly in small groups as far as the Berezina. Find and destroy the bridges. Don't let the enemy cross the river!'

At dawn the first squad consisting of three aircraft from Captain Spitsin's squadron took off. In ten minutes another three planes headed to Bobruysk. Squad after squad took off at equal intervals. The second day at the front began.

It was not easy to start military operations at one's own discretion, but it was even more difficult to implement that decision. The regiment commander had to set the tasks for all five squadrons. The regiment staff was still on the way from Kharkov, and it was clear that the train would not arrive soon, as the fascist air forces kept bombing the railways. Just a few staff officers managed to get to the front airfield in transport aircraft. The chief communications officer, Captain Buzinovsky, and his assistant Lieutenant Nudgenko were also present, but at first they could neither establish contact between the ground station and the squadrons, nor among the planes in the air.

Before the war pilots used to make jokes about the communication officers: 'There is no combat without communication, but communication services never work.' Now there was no time for jokes. Captain Buzinovsky managed to get telephone sets, but the landing Shturmoviks ripped the wires all the time. The ground station was almost useless, since the planes' receivers only deafened the pilots with crackling and noise. Besides, the communication range was very limited. Many pilots removed the receivers, not being willing to carry extra weight. After the first encounters with Messerschmitts some pilots thought that the enemy fighters were able to locate the aircraft through the working radio stations, so they pulled out the antennas from their planes.

Under those circumstances the regiment had to use the oldest but the most reliable means of communication. Three men from each squadron performed the duties of messengers delivering orders from the command post and bringing back the reports. They also used flares. The green ones gave the signal for take-off, and their number indicated the size of the squadron. The red ones now meant that the pilots had to take off urgently owing to enemy aircraft attack. Mechanics were ordered to set the propellers of the planes according to their readiness. If a Shturmovik was in working order and ready to take off, one of the three blades must stick up. If a plane was not ready, two blades must stick up like horns. Thus the regiment commander could determine how many planes were ready to take off from a distance.

The commander's own gestures were also put to use after the following incident. A messenger ran up to the commander and reported that his squadron had destroyed the bridge near Bobruysk, but the pilots noticed that the enemy was constructing a new bridge near Domanovo. The next squadron was already taking off at that moment. They were going to circle the airfield and fly to Bobruysk. But by now there was no reason for them to fly there. The task had to be changed, but how? Before the squadron approached the airfield Major Getman ran away from his tent. When the planes appeared he began to wave his hands trying to attract the leader's attention. The leader swayed from one wing to the other meaning that he had noticed the commander. Major Getman pointed at the direction of

Bobruysk, raised his arms and crossed them: 'Don't go there!' Then he pulled off his cap and began to wave with it pointing at another direction: 'Fly there!' To everybody's surprise the leader swayed from one wing to the other and set a new course. In an hour the squadron was back and the pilot reported to the regiment commander: 'We attacked a bridge to the south of Bobruysk, near Domanovo.'

'My dear chap, how did you manage to understand my gestures?!'

'But it was obvious! You stopped the flight to Bobruysk and showed a new course with the cap. So I turned to the left.'

On the same day all the squadrons were ordered to fly above Getman's tent after the take off and watch his gestures.

One by one three-ship formations took off from the Stary Bykhov airfield. They hedgehopped to the west to bomb the pontoon bridges across the Berezina. After some time a kind of conveyer-belt was formed in the air. Some groups were taking off, while others were already landing. They were refuelled, loaded with new bombs, and went off again. It was just like a giant conveyer-belt, made up of Shturmovik squads in the air heading to Bobruysk, where it curved along the river, and then stretched back to the airfield. The planes flew to the west in three-ship formations, but often only two or even one of them returned. Their wings were pierced with holes. The pilots reported about the heavy flak near the crossings. They were also frequently pursued by the enemy fighters. The Messerschmitts approached our planes from the tail without any risk and attacked.

The pre-war books on tactics indicated that attack aircraft would be covered by friendly fighters. They were to distract the enemy fighters from your attack aircraft. But there were so few fighters at the Stary Bykhov airfield that they could not even begin to intercept all the German reconnaissance aircraft and bombers that appeared above the airfield. Sometimes they were also loaded up with bombs and sent out as ground-attack planes. The books wrote nothing about the situations when the enemy aircraft had complete superiority in the air.

In the afternoon it was again the turn of the fifth squadron to fly. The squad commander, Lieutenant Zaytsev, set the task for his wingmen Krotov and Smurygov, 'We will attack the restored bridge near Bobruysk and then fly along the Berezina to the north looking for the new crossings... We'll come back along this way,' the commander showed it on the map.

Smurygov was the last to take off. Something delayed him at the start and in the air he fell back considerably. It was difficult to distinguish the dark-green Shturmoviks against the forest, and Smurygov was really afraid he would lose his squad. He throttled up nervously, but the distance was decreasing very slowly.

Smurygov caught up with his group not far from the Berezina. Suddenly he remembered that Zaytsev had given him the instruction to occupy the place to the left of Krotov before the attack. He began to turn and at that time two planes flying in the opposite direction at the same low altitude came into view. 'One of our squads is going back,' Smurygov thought. 'The third plane must have fallen behind just like me, or may be it was shot down...' But in the next moment he felt doubts. The approaching planes had strange-looking wings, as if they were as bit raised and cut at the edges.

They swept past very close and Smurygov noticed that the fuselages of the planes were very thin. The planes looked a bit like wasps. The pilot saw them zoom up, bank and disappear behind his plane's tail. He felt tingles down his spine. 'Were they the Messers?' He looked forward and found out that he had fallen behind again. He sped up, but the distance did not seem to change. 'Zaytsev must be trying to escape from the Messers at full speed,' the wingman thought. At that moment he saw fiery tracks racing past his aircraft aiming at the planes ahead. The planes kept flying straight ahead heading to Bobruysk.

One of the planes came level with his own suddenly, and Smurygov saw the black cross on the fuselage and the spidery swastika on the tail. It was shooting at Krotov's aircraft. The bursts flashed at the Shturmovik's wings. Landing gear fell out of the right nacelle. Both Messerschmitts were already ahead of Smurygov's aircraft. His fingers instinctively found the triggers and pressed them. Tracer bullets raced very close to Krotov's plane, and the Messers climbed up. Smurygov came to his senses and did not shoot any more. He realised that he might hit his friend instead of the enemy.

Bobruysk and the Berezina could already be seen ahead. A line of new pontoons stretched across the river near the first bridge that had been destroyed. The Shturmovik dropped the bombs and aimed at the lorries at the western bank. The Berezina disappeared from view and the air around the planes was now stuffed with black puffs from anti-aircraft guns. Zaytsev banked left, followed by Smurygov, and Krotov's plane fell far behind and was slowly turning to the eastern bank. Two Messers stuck to him like leeches. Krotov headed to the airfield, while Zaytsev and Smurygov flew to the north to look for new crossings.

They flew above the Berezina. The anti-aircraft guns fired at them from time to time from the western side. Then the leader realised that they could fly along the eastern side of the river, and they were outside the firing zone. Nothing special was happening and Zaytsev was already going to head for the airfield when they saw a bridge stretching into the middle of the river near Svisloch. A pontoon was moving from the bank with several men inside it. The pilots opened fire. One person jumped out, but the rest fell down into the bottom of the pontoon. The pilots aimed at a few lorries standing on the western bank. One lorry caught fire, and German soldiers rushed about among the shrubs.

When Zaytsev and Smurygov were landing they saw Krotov's Shturmovik lying flat on the ground. A strip of black soil stretched behind it along the green airfield. Its propeller was bent, part of the landing gear with a wheel and the oil radiator were lying at a distance. The armour of the engine and the cockpit had turned brown. The wings were pierced with holes. All that was left of the rudder and elevator were the rims and shreds of cloth. Krotov was very pale, standing surrounded by the mechanics. He was smoking, pressing his hand against his left shoulder.

'Are you injured?' Zaytsev asked him.

'Guess I hurt something when I was landing.'

'Was it an anti-aircraft gun or the fighters?'

'The Messers followed me as far as the airfield. I tried to escape the bullets, but the rudder would not obey... I flopped on to the ground then, but they still did not leave me alone. I thought they would finish me off on the ground, but their guns were empty. They climbed, circled the airfield and left...'

'Didn't our anti-aircraft gunners drive them away?'

'Have you seen any anti-aircraft gunners at the airfield?'

For some time everybody remained silent. Three Ishaks were taking off from the airfield at that moment. Each of them had two bombs suspended under each wing. Krotov watched them fly and said:

'Messerschmitts fly with no extra weight and hunt the Shturmoviks, and our fighters are loaded with bombs for no real reason...'

'Yes, if they accompanied us, they could drive the Messers away,' said Zaytsev. 'We can do nothing against them. They attack from behind, and our guns can only fire forwards...'

'An aircraft that flew behind could well open fire on the Messers, when they attack a plane ahead of him,' said Krotov casting a glance at Smurygov. The glance was rather reproachful.

'You see, I could hardly manage to catch up with you. And when I did, the Messers were right behind you. I fired a burst, and the tracer bullets passed very close to your aircraft.' Smurygov tried to explain.

The regiment doctor, Tom Fedorovich Shiroky, came up and helped Krotov in a hospital tent. He extracted a splinter out of Krotov's shoulder. He had not had time to notice that he was injured.

The Shturmoviks attacked the bridges for the whole day. Messerschmitts pursued the planes and nobody knew how to repulse them. Still the greatest losses were caused by the anti-aircraft guns, and not by the fighters. Their plane's weapon could not breach the 12-millimetre armoured plate that protected the pilot's back and the rear fuel tank, but they caused much damage to the aircraft.

Our regiment was the only unit equipped with new models of aircraft in those days. It was a real force, and though it was vanishing quickly, it fulfilled the task of delaying the advanced units of the German 'Centre' group of armies on the Berezina. The regiment destroyed nine bridges and contained the forced crossing of the river for three days. But during those three days the regiment lost twenty pilots. Nobody expected such casualties. During the Finnish campaign the regiment had performed more than 2,000 operational flights in planes that had no armour, and it only lost one person. And even that was not a combat loss. A plane hit the top of a tree and caught fire when it was taking off. Now the pilots flew brand-new armoured Shturmoviks, but the tolls were enormous! And on 28 June the second squadron vanished in a second...

The regiment was ordered to transfer to an airfield fifty kilometres to the south-east of Klimovichi. The pilots were already sitting in their cockpits, but the flight was delayed. The command was waiting for the transport aircraft to take away the mechanics and their stuff. There was only one lorry in the regiment. It was loaded with a barrel of petrol, rifles, grenades, a box of canned meat and a bag of crackers. The regimental engineer, Mitin, and a small group of mechanics were to drive to Klimovichi in the lorry after they had handed over six damaged aircraft to the repair shops. But quite unexpectedly the chief of the shops refused to sign the receipt.

'You want to get rid of this rubbish – what am I supposed to do with it? The shops are being transferred as well.'

'You must sign the receipt, and then you can decide what to do with it,' Mitin insisted.

A taciturn field engineer had been treading on Mitin's heels for a long time already. He also wanted to finish his work as soon as possible, and when he heard this conversation, he could not restrain himself: 'Stop this bullshit and get out. I need time to blow these aircraft up.'

After that the chief of the shops signed the receipt immediately, but demanded a reciprocal receipt from the field engineer. The man scribbled it on a scrap of paper. Now Mitin and his five mechanics could finally drive to Klimovichi.

A thick column of smoke rose at the end of the airfield. The quartermasters had set fire to the stores which were full of flying uniforms, so that the enemy did not get it. All the men at the airfield watched the black smoke thinking of the shelves of new coats, boots, flying suits, helmets and other stuff. The quartermasters did not have the right to distribute the uniform among the pilots without the corresponding documents and signatures. They would have had to account for 'the waste of the state property'.

On 1 July the regiment moved to Klimovichi. It barely escaped the Junkers that attacked the airfield. Senior Lieutenant Denisyuk had some problems with his plane's engine and fell behind. When he was taking off German tanks had already forced their way to the airfield and were firing at him. The planes got into a heavy storm and twenty of them made forced landings in different places. The command spent much time looking for them later. A Shturmovik with its fuselage broken in two parts was found near Seshi. Its pilot Alexandr Bulavin bumped his head against the collimator sight and died in the cockpit. This innocent-looking small instrument was situated opposite the pilot's head and was the reason for so many deaths! Pilots nicknamed it 'the instrument that knocks out a pilot once and for all'. It took a long time before they were removed from the cockpit and the sighting grid was marked directly on the windshield. One more plane was found in the forest. The commander of the fourth squadron, Captain Lesnikov, got into a heavy rain, tried to land in the sudden darkness with lights on and took the tops of the trees for a field. The branches cushioned the blow and the pilot got off with bruises, but the aircraft was a total loss.

There were only eighteen Shturmoviks left in the regiment now. Pilots began to use new terms: 'an irretrievable loss', 'horseless'.

The irretrievable loss meant that a Shturmovik had crashed and the pilot was killed. But there were also retrievable losses. For example, captain Kholobaev flew to the airfield after his first sortie on a plane that was not able to be repaired. The plane was written off, but the pilot was safe.

There were other similar cases. Once a pilot failed to return. Men from his group had seen his burning plane fall, and the pilot was considered dead. But the war appeared to be more merciful to pilots than to their 'flying fortresses'. Men were more enduring, that is why there were always more pilots than planes in the regiment.

Then an unshaven man came to the Klimovichi airfield. His cheeks were covered with burn scabs, his swollen lips could not smile, but his eyes were laughing. He unripped his jacket lining and got out a red book and an identity card. Vasya Sorokin was back! Men could not believe it. Sorokin had perished near Bobruysk!

The pilot was showered with questions. He hardly had chance to answer. 'The plane burnt down, and I rolled on a swamp. My clothes were smouldering. I met a woman, and she led me in her house. She gave me new clothes and oiled my face with sour milk... I met a criminal from the Bobruysk prison, who knew those places. Fritzes let all the criminals go. I pretended to be a prisoner myself, and so I came here.

As soon as Vasya Sorokin recovered he demanded a new 'horse'. But there weren't any. Sorokin and his mechanic became 'horseless'. The number of such 'horseless' pilots was increasing and the operational flights were now carried in two shifts. Half of the pilots flew, and the other half rested. The regiment kept losing people. The commander of the fourth squadron, Captain Vladimir Dmitrievich Lesnikov, who had survived in an accident, was killed a few days later.

That was a heavy irretrievable loss for the regiment.

The regiment kept fighting. The main targets for the Shturmoviks were now not the bridges, but the enemy columns heading to Roslavl. Those were very hard days for our troops and our pilots. The enemy had full superiority in the air. Flocks of Heinkels and Junkers raced in the sky. Messers swept in pairs above the roads firing at the troops. It seemed that the Germans had even more aircraft now! It was the twelfth day of the war... Questions were rising in people's minds: 'Yes, we could not withstand the assault on the Berezina because we did not have enough troops present. But why didn't the fresh forces stop the enemy on the Dnepr? When will they deliver the fatal blow, as they promise? Or are they going to lure the Germans far inside the country? Why do we have so few planes? Where is the force that has been demonstrated at the fly-pasts? Where are the planes that fly further, faster and higher than everything?'

3 July: everybody remembered that day for a long time. For the first time since the beginning of the war we heard the familiar voice with its Georgian accent: 'I turn to you, my friends!' Stalin's speech was not reassuring. He told the truth, and that was the end of the cheerful official reports, which did not at all correspond to the real situation. Now the hopes that our defeats would soon be over were lost, but at least we knew that there would be no miracles and the rumours about some fatal blow were groundless. We knew we could only rely on ourselves. In his speech Stalin urged us to realise the gravity of the 'mortal danger' and to be merciless to the deserters and cowards.

On the next day our regiment had to attack the Bobruysk airfield. It was the first time the regiment was given such a task. According to pilots' observations and military information several aircraft squadrons were gathered at the airfield. Some witnesses reported that the airfield looked like an aircraft exhibition. The planes stood without any camouflage in several rows very close to each other. The fascists felt completely at home there. The pilots spent their free time in a casino near the airfield drinking schnapps.

It looked as though with one blow the regiment could cause great damage to the enemy aircraft. Although a few anti-aircraft guns had fired sometimes at the parade wedges of Junkers and Heinkels, our men had rarely seen a burning enemy aircraft. Our fighters also tried to pursue the enemy from time to time, but they was not really effective. The planes sitting on the airfield presented a very attractive target. During one attack many of them could be destroyed, if...

But there were too many 'ifs'. The strike could be effective, if there was enough force. But there was not even one-third of the planes left in the regiment, and some of them were damaged! It might also happen that the Shturmoviks would fly to the airfield and find no planes there. The aircraft were just like birds: at dawn they took off and came back to the nest only in the evening. It meant that the regiment had to take off before daybreak. The problem was that nobody had ever flown a Shturmovik at night. The most experienced pilots had to be chosen for the task.

A few days before the regiment had had a complete staff. Now the squadrons and flights came apart. The pilots were divided into leaders and wingmen. The one flying ahead was the commander for the rest. Take, for example, Junior Lieutenant Nikolai Sinyakov. He was an ordinary pilot, but he appeared to be a good leader. Some men with senior ranks were made to be subordinate to him. The war assigned the men at the proper places and took into consideration neither the list of members of the staff, nor the military ranks.

It had been dark for a long while, but the regiment commander, Major Getman, was still awake. He was sitting in a blindage with a sheet of paper, arranging the aircraft and the pilots for tomorrow's flight. The three-ship formations were drawn in a line on the paper. That would be the battle formation tomorrow. The commander was writing a name of a pilot next to each plane. He would lead the column himself. Now he was carefully arranging the leaders and the wingmen for each group.

There were dispersal areas at the Bobruysk airfield on both sides of the runway. He would lead his wingmen to the first dispersal area, but who would lead the second group? Protocol dictated that it should be his deputy, Major K., but Major Getman had not had time to get to know Major K., because he was appointed his deputy just before the regiment was sent to the front. Nevertheless Major K. had already shown himself as a strict and exacting commander. He noticed each unfastened button and liked to cite a popular pre-war saying: 'There is one step between an unbuttoned collar on the ground and an accident in the air!' People remembered for a long time his vivid speech at the meeting in Bogoduhov on the first day of the war. A tall dark-haired man in a leather jacket and helmet was standing on the platform. He looked so impressive that Captain Kholobaev had whispered to Major Getman: 'Someone should make his sculpture and display it prominently in all the military camps!' Waving his hand energetically Major K. finished his bright speech with the words: 'I will launch my first missile for our Motherland, my second missile for comrade Stalin and my third missile for our people!'

But at the front the major seemed to be out of luck from the very beginning. When the regiment was transferring from Bogoduhov to Karachev he made a forced landing. People searched for his aircraft for several days, and the major did not appear in Stary Bykhov. But he had landed on the fuselage rather masterfully and when the mechanics found him they repaired the plane very quickly. Yet the ill luck did not leave him. From the place of the forced landing he flew to the airfield and landed – without releasing the landing gear! He landed on the fuselage and broke the plane again. Major K. was walking around his aircraft perplexed: 'How could I forget about the landing gear?'

The regiment commander took his deputy aside: 'How could you descend without bothering about how you will be landing?'

'To be honest, comrade Major, it went right out of my mind...'

'But we set up red flares for you, made a warning cross on the runway, showed that you must make one more circuit!'

'That's exactly what I have failed to notice... It can happen to anybody...'

'You are the deputy of the regiment commander! How will your subordinates treat you? It's very easy to lose prestige, and you'll need much time to gain it back...'

'I'll do my best...'

Arranging the groups for tomorrow's mission the regiment commander remembered that conversation and made the final decision: 'Major K. has had enough time to get used to the new place. It's time for him to show what he's worth in a real task... After all I can't make Junior Lieutenant Smurygov or First Sergeant Shahov lead the group!' And so Getman appointed his deputy as leader of the second group.

The engines roared before dawn. The purple flares shot up from the exhaust stubs licking the armoured bodies and even the cockpits of the planes. The flames blinded the pilots and it was difficult to see anything in their reflection.

The regiment commander was the first to take off. The rest followed him, guided by the navigation lights. Getman noted the time and set the course to Bobruysk. His wingmen, Senior Politruk Vladimir Vasilenko and Captain Nikolai Satalkin, were flying behind him. The rest of the group followed the leading flight. In twenty minutes they crossed the Dnepr, which marked the halfway point. Not far from the Berezina Getman turned the navigation light off, and so did the rest of the pilots.

Approaching Bobruysk the Shturmoviks were flying very low. Anti-aircraft guns began to fire. To the left Getman could see the runway and rows of aircraft on both sides. The leader turned and launched the attack. Missiles hit the rows of bombers and exploded, tracer bullets shredded the wings with black crosses. Just above the ground the Shturmoviks dropped their hundred-kilo bombs. Junkers and Messerschmitts ready for operational flights blazed up. Our aircraft came in time and did not allow the enemy planes to take off!

The commander's aircraft came down above the regiment's airfield followed by a smoking trail. The engine was not working properly. Getman landed, taxied to the side, stopped the engine, but did not open the canopy for some reason. Mechanics ran up and immediately began to do something with their hammers near the cockpit. It appeared that the canopy had jammed after the plane was hit by a shell. The mechanics helped Getman out. He was covered with oil from head to foot, and looked exhausted. Men supported him under his arm; he sat on a stump and for several minutes could not utter a word. The major coughed and spat out oil. When he recovered his breath he asked: 'Have all the men from the second group returned?'

He did not ask about his wingmen, Vasilenko and Satalkin. He had seen the two burning planes disappear behind the forest right after the attack.

Getman was told that Major K. and one of his wingmen were the first to return. Major K. had landed on his fuselage near the airfield. 'How could it be?' thought the commander. 'He flew behind me, but returned the first.' He summoned the major, who had already been delivered to the airfield from the place of the forced landing. 'Where did you approach the target from?' Getman asked him.

'From this direction,' the major answered passing his hand over the map.

'Will you be so kind as to take off your gloves and indicate it more precisely!' the commander raised his voice. He hated it when somebody pointed out something on a map with his finger – he expected them to use a pencil. And now this wasn't an ordinary pilot, but his deputy!

'As you wish. I can show it more precisely,' the major answered and began to pull off his gloves from each finger separately.

'Take a pencil, draw the disposition of the planes at the Bobruysk airfield, and show where you approached.'

'Comrade Major,' K. drew himself up to his full height, 'I can't draw pictures.'

'I'm not asking you to draw a picture, make a simple scheme!' the commander had a fit of coughing.

While Major K. was searching in his map-case, Getman wiped his face from oil and saw a young pilot standing nearby. The pilot was one of Major K.'s wingmen. The commander beckoned him with his hand. The man came up and stood with his head down.

'Did you come back with the Major?' the commander asked him.

'Yes.'

'Do you remember the target well?'

'No, comrade commander.'

Getman jumped up from the stump. A terrible guess came into his mind: 'What if my deputy did not fly to the target at all and that's why he can't draw a scheme now?'

'Where did you drop the bombs?'

'In the middle of nowhere...' the pilot answered faintly, casting a glance at Major K.

Getman's heart pounded, and his felt like a bomb exploded beside him. Then he saw tears in the pilot's eyes, and calmed down. He took the pilot by the elbow and drew him to his mutilated plane.

'Tell me how it was step by step.'

'We had not yet reach the Berezina when comrade Major turned left unexpectedly and began to descend. I hardly managed to keep pace with him. Then I saw bombs falling out of his aircraft and automatically pressed the release button. The major began to launch missiles as well, and only then did I realise that there was nothing but

66

a swamp under us. I did not launch my missiles, and decided to fly to Bobruysk by myself. But by that time the rest of the planes were gone, and I did not know where to fly. I had to follow comrade Major.'

At that moment Getman heard Major K.'s voice: 'My engine was not working properly, so I decided not to fly to the target. And I dropped the bombs because otherwise the aircraft would have blown up during the forced landing.'

'And then you landed on your fuselage three kilometres away from the airfield?' the commander barked at him.

'The engine got overheated and couldn't keep going. The windshield was splashed with oil.'

'Get out!' Getman gave a frenzied scream. His hand moved to the holster, but Kozhuhovsky stopped him.

Mechanics set Major K.'s aircraft on its wheels, changed the propeller, and started the engine. During test flights it was working just fine. The committee of investigation drew the conclusion that the pilot had deliberately overheated the engine by closing the oil radiator's screen. In the evening of the same day pilots and mechanics were gathered on a meadow. Three men from the military tribunal were sitting at the table covered with a red cloth. A tall bare-headed man was standing by the table his back to the rest. It was difficult to believe that one and the same man had sworn to launch his first missile for our Motherland and his second missile for comrade Stalin, and then launched them into a swamp.

The chairman pronounced judgement on behalf of the Motherland: 'For the shown cowardice K. is sentenced to be shot. The sentence must be executed immediately.'

Getman asked: 'Not here, please. Take him somewhere as far away as possible.'

Instead of being executed Major K. was sent to the front line 'to redeem his fault with blood'. He was later seen in some rear aircraft unit.

The regiment flew to attack the Bobruysk airfield three times and caused much damage to the enemy. It destroyed and damaged dozens of bombers and Messerschmitts. By 1 September the regiment was transferred to Voronezh for reformation. It required new planes and fresh pilots. Some of the experienced pilots, including Spitsin,

Dvoinyh and Denisyuk, were sent to form new units. Few of those who flew to the front on 27 June were left in the regiment. Among them were Captain Konstantin Kholobaev, Captain Vasily Shemyakin, Lieutenant Pavel Zhuravlev, Junior Lieutenant Nikolai Sinyakov, who had become the commander of the second squadron, First Sergeant Victor Shahov and Junior Lieutenant Nikolai Smurygov. The regiment was reinforced with freshmen and the experienced pilots had to train the newcomers. From dawn until dusk Ils were circling, diving and hedgehopping above the airfield. But as there were not enough aircraft and pilots, the regiment now consisted of only two squadrons. There were twenty-four planes instead of sixty-five.

6

THE REGIMENT

I flew to the front-line airfield in a U-2, which was piloted by Konstantin Nikolaevich Kholobaev. I was sitting in the rear cockpit with my luggage and a *balalaika*.★

Kholobaev was flying just above the tops of the trees and we both were watching the sky for Messers. After some time we crossed a river. Kholobaev stopped the engine and we glided on to a green field with empty caponiers at the edge. 'The regiment must be out carrying on a sortie,' I thought.

We taxied to the dispersal area and got out. A pilot came out from behind a caponier. He had four battle decorations on his breast. To me he seemed a bit flat. The pilot came up to us smiling, shook hands with Kholobaev and said in a high-pitched voice, 'I've been waiting for you. The rest have moved to another airfield...' Still smiling he shook my hand. His handshake was very firm.

'Major Zub,' he introduced himself.

I had come across the unusual name of that outstanding pilot in newspapers many times. In spring 1942 a group led by Major Zub attacked a German airfield and managed to destroy twelve enemy aircraft and damage nine. In my imagination Zub was nothing less than a Hercules.

So now I was a bit surprised by his appearance, but I felt pleased to be treated so simply.

The three of us headed to a nearby house. Major Zub told me, 'Now you'll be fighting with us.' His tone was casual, as if he was speaking about an ordinary kind of work that was not at all dangerous.

★ An instrument used in Russian folk music.

69

A man dressed like a mechanic was approaching us. Zub took my *balalaika*. I thought he was going to ask me about it, but he only wanted to free my hand, so that I could answer to the mechanic's salute. Zub was the regiment commander's deputy, and I expected him to wave off casually, but I was wrong. His salute was accurate and beautiful. He was wearing a proper uniform: a blouse, breeches, and boots. Instead of a helmet with goggles Zub preferred to wear a cap, and instead of a leather jacket or a flying suit he usually wore a dark-blue coat of the pre-war type with stripes on the left sleeve and the pilot insignia.

I had imagined the famous pilot of the Southern Front to be quite a different person, but my imagination let me down as usual.

There were only two planes at the airfield, both waiting to be sent to the repair shops. But the commander consulted with Zub and decided to take the risk and ferry the planes to Morozovskaya. One of the planes had a deformed centre wing section. Zub was going to pilot it. The other one was the famous 'number 0422', on which pilots had trained in Millerovo. I was entrusted to ferry it.

'We'll fly together,' said Zub. 'Do you know the 'scissors' manoeuvre?'

I gave a vague answer. Zub took a pencil, drew a figure-of-eight and began to explain: 'The leader and the wingman are banking from left to right either approaching or moving away from each other. Their courses intersect each time,'– he pointed at the centre of the 'eight' – 'We use this manoeuvre to defend ourselves against fighters. They can't aim properly. And if they pass ahead, we can fire at them.'

I listened to Zub's explanations thinking to myself: 'He tells me everything, as if we were going to make an operational flight. We won't have time to think about these 'eights' in our crippled aircraft!'

At first my leader was flying straight ahead of me at an altitude of about a hundred metres. When he made certain that I was flying confidently to his right, he suddenly gave the command to reform. As soon as I moved to the other side, he ordered me to occupy the previous place. For a long time I was dangling behind the leader, and then his plane also began to bank from right to left. That was the 'scissors' manoeuvre. We kept flying like that for fifty minutes until we reached Morozovskaya.

I got out of the cockpit sweating. Zub wiped his face and took a cigarette: 'Now you have mastered the manoeuvre.' He smiled, pleased. I also remember him saying: 'We have been taught to fly straight, and keep the formation. And the war has proved that a pilot can't last without manoeuvring. It's the same as breathing.'

There were few people at that time who had four decorations, like Major Zub had. Battle awards were not given for long service or for special events. Besides, little time passed since the war began. But Zub already had the Order of Lenin, the Order of the Red Banner, the Order of the Red Star, and a medal 'For Courage'. To be honest, such a medal was a rather modest, not to say insulting, decoration for a pilot. But it depended... Once a correspondent asked Nikolai Antonovich: 'Which decoration is the most precious for you?' and he pointed at Zub's breast.

'This one,' Zub pointed at the medal without any hesitations.

'Why?' The correspondent was very surprised.

'I was recommended for the highest decoration, but I got this one...'

'But you could correct this unfortunate mistake!'

'It is more important what you receive a decoration for rather than which decoration you receive, isn't it?' answered Zub.

When I arrived at the regiment Kholobaev told me: 'You'll be assigned to the third squadron led by Mospanov.'

I was very glad. I had read about the brave Shturmovik pilot in the front newspaper. I wanted to introduce myself to him as soon as possible, but Senior Lieutenant Mospanov was now at another airfield.

There was only one Shturmovik at the airfield. Major Zub and I were waiting for a U-2 to take us to the new airfield in turns. Nikolai Antonovich lay flat on the green grass in the shade of a building and was going to have a nap. As for me, I was studying the Donets Basin region on a map. That was not an easy task, as there were lots of roads in the area and they were intertwined like a web.

A U-2 flew low above our heads and we could see it was carrying a passenger in the rear cockpit. Zub looked up and said: 'It's brought a pilot to ferry the Il!'

The plane taxied in, and a skinny pilot jumped down from the wing. He walked to our side.

'Hello!' Zub shouted, raising himself up on his elbows. The pilot waved back. His tawny unshaven face was covered with dark spots. At first I thought that these were the smallpox marks, but when he came closer I saw that the spots were green. Nurses must have treated him with something bright green...

'Where did you decorate your face?' asked Zub.

'Above the Artemovsk airfield yesterday...' the pilot answered shaking hands with Zub and then with me. He sat down crossing his legs in Tatar manner, got out a pack of Belomore,* and began to smoke. 'An Oerlikon† shell hit the windshield,' he continued his story, 'It swept past my ear, but did not explode. I've brought about a bucket of glass grit in the cockpit...'

'Here is the freshman for your squadron,' Nikolai Antonovich pointed at me.

Now I realised that it was Mospanov. My future squadron leader cast a smiling glance at me and offered me a cigarette.

When Zub was gone on the U-2, Mospanov said: 'Let's do this: you can fly with me inside the fuselage, and the U-2 will come back and take the mechanic. What's the use of waiting here?'

'With pleasure...' My answer was not really sincere. There was little pleasure in flying inside the fuselage of a Shturmovik. You had to squat and it was very windy.

'Do you have a map of this region?' Mospanov asked.

'Yes, I have,' I answered thinking to myself: 'What will I need the map for, if I fly as a passenger facing the tail?'

'Try to navigate. Mark the places that you recognise on the map and write down the time when we fly above them.'

That was not a simple task. When you fly and look in different directions objects do not look as they should. I had little time to recognise anything, because we were to fly low. Besides, I had no navigation instruments, except my wrist watch. The squadron leader did not tell me what route we would take, and I did not dare to ask him. Mospanov went to check the plane, and I suddenly had an idea. 'He will probably chose the shortest way!' I thought. I drew a line between the two airfields and measured off ticks, each marking five minutes of the flight. An impromptu test in navigation, no less!

---

* A Russian brand of cigarette.
† A light anti-aircraft cannon.

We took off. Mospanov flew very low along the course I had marked. In order to see the deserted fields flying past the aircraft tail I had to lift myself up a bit. My legs grew numb very soon. Ten minutes passed but I did not notice anything essential. It was like sitting in a boat facing the stern and seeing nothing but the foamy water. 'It seems like I'm not going to mark anything,' I thought.

But soon I noticed a village and next to it a dry riverbed, which curved in a loop. I looked at the map and saw my line crossing a river that formed a loop. I knew where we were flying! I began to make more marks and cheered up.

We landed and went to have a smoke. Mospanov asked me in a casual tone: 'Did you mark anything on the map?'

'Yes, I did. Here,' I gave him my map-case. Mospanov looked at the map with eager curiosity: 'I have never tried to navigate sitting back to front myself. It must be the same as reading a book from the last line... Did you notice a hay cart turn over when we were flying above it? he asked.

'Yes.'

'Can you show the place on the map?'

'It's here,' I pointed with my pencil.

'I agree!' Mospanov grinned.

I flew as Mospanov's wingman only once. After four sorties I was made a leader myself.

That time we flew in two four-ship formations to attack trains at the Chistyakovo railway station. Mospanov led us masterfully and neither Messers nor anti-aircraft guns noticed us.

We were already approaching Chistyakovo, but the forest to our left did not allow us to see the station. An empty road went along the forest, turning left in one place and disappearing among the trees. Suddenly I saw a motorcycle, which was driving very fast heading to the turn. The Fritzes must have noticed us and hurried to escape.

I had heard rumours that Mospanov never let a moving car pass unharmed and he even insisted that it was necessary to attack them. 'The cars carry the command! You can spare a burst to kill an Oberst, can't you?'

I must say that Mospanov's ideas were absolutely right. A year passed and in 1943 the People's Commissar for Defence issued an order to 'hunt' cars in the enemy rear.

Now it was not a car, but a motorcycle. My leader zoomed, turned a bit to the left and began to descend. At the very last moment, when the motorcycle was already turning inside the forest, a sheaf of fire hit it. Something flashed and the motorcycle rolled to the side, bouncing like a ball. I was very impressed by the accuracy of the shot, which destroyed such a small moving object!

Mospanov climbed and we saw the railway station and a few trains. The anti-aircraft guns began firing at us. The first four planes led by Mospanov dived. I was flying on the right flank of the second squad, but when I saw the bursts so close to my aircraft, I instinctively dashed aside. That was an unconscious reaction. It lasted no longer than a second, but the target was already at my side. I turned left and fortunately managed to drop the bombs at the opposite end of the station.

Back at our airfield Mospanov took me aside and asked: 'How did it happen that you went offside before the attack?'

I was going to explain that I was watching the rolling motorcycle and did not expect the salvo... I stood silent seeking for the right words.

'Was it the fright? Then say so...'

I nodded assent.

'Remember: one time you recoil, and the next time you'll lose your head... I saw your bombs exploding on the station, so I'm not going to proceed with this conversation now...'

To lose one's head was indeed not pleasant. Once I led a group of Shturmoviks to burn German tanks with phosphorus. Before heading to the target I flew to the fighters' airfield to assemble our covering force. I quickly noticed that something was wrong with my engine, but I thought it would improve after a while, and did not go back. I circled above the fighters' airfield three times, but none of the planes were going to take off. I contacted our command post by the radio, and asked if I could fly without the cover. There came no answer. We were already late, and had consumed much fuel, so I made the decision to fly without the fighters. 'One time you recoil, and the next time you'll lose your head...' the words came into my mind.

I set the course, but the engine was getting worse and worse. I had to entrust the group to Fedya Artemov (that was the first and the last time!), and flew back to the airfield. When I looked around I was surprised to see one of the Shturmoviks follow me. Damn! I ordered him to join the group, but the pilot seemed to be deaf.

When I was approaching the airfield the engine was reaching its end. I had to shed the containers with phosphorus before I landed. Fortunately, I managed to land without much problem, but I had to leave the containers full on the ground...

'Why did you come back from the operational flight?'

'Something was wrong with the engine.'

'We'll check it. And why did you fly without the fighters?'

'Because they did not take off. I requested your permission by radio, but you did not hear.'

'I heard!'

'So why did you keep silent?' I was getting angry.

'A leader must make decisions himself. He must not wait for the tips from the ground.'

'So I made the decision.'

'It was a foolish decision. If Messers shoot Artemov down, you'll be responsible. Besides you dropped your containers on our anti–aircraft battery... And why did you drag Neretin with you?'

'I did not drag him...'

Neretin was standing, pale, nearby and did not know what to say. He had no excuses. He had simply followed his leader.

Meanwhile the mechanics surrounded my aircraft looking for the defect. If it was their fault, they would be responsible for upsetting a mission. If they did not find the defect, I would be accused of cowardice. The regiment engineer, Timofey Tuchin, got inside the cockpit and started the engine. To my surprise it worked perfectly. I was standing at some distance, because I did not want the mechanics to see me. Behind my back I heard: 'Perhaps it only seemed to *you* that the engine was not working properly?'

I turned round and looked at someone who always kept apart from the pilots. I could not understand if he was speaking with sympathy or suspicion. Should I tell him about the instrument readings? He would not understand it anyway. He had no technical or even pilot education. I kept silent.

The mechanics removed the cowling and were unscrewing the nuts. Time was hanging heavily. My group was already coming back from the task. I counted everyone except one: the aircraft of Fedya

Artemov was missing... It was too much for one flight: I lost a friend, led Neretin to the airfield, poured phosphorus on the anti-aircraft battery, and the mechanics did not seem able to find any defects in the engine...

Neretin came up to me uncertainly. 'I'm sorry... I thought that everybody would follow you. And I did not obey to your command to return, because I was afraid to get lost.'

What could I say? He was actually right.

Mospanov and Tuchin were coming towards me. The engineer was smiling and the squadron leader was shouting from afar: 'We've found it!'

'Artemov?' I gave a start.

'The defect!' Tuchin proclaimed with his loud voice. 'The head of the block split, and water got into the cylinders. It was a manufacturing defect.'

In the evening we were sitting at the table. I did not receive my hundred grams,* because I had not performed a sortie. In the middle of dinner the door opened and Fedya Artemov entered the room safe and sound. Hurray! Fedya was smiling. The infantrymen had obviously treated him for his good work. His plane had been hit by an anti-aircraft gun, and he had landed by our infantry units.

All's well that ends well, but after that incident all of a sudden I seemed to forget how to take off properly. I almost slid off the runway each time. That was dangerous. The regiment commander warned me: 'You are doing something wrong when you take off... Watch out!' he threatened me with his finger. I wondered whether he thought that I was doing it deliberately.

I also received a reprimand from Mospanov and his words had the right effect. My problems disappeared.

---

* Each pilot received 'A hundred grams for the battle' – about four fluid ounces – of vodka for each operational flight.

7

A FLIGHT WITH MAJOR ZUB

An operational flight that I made with Major Zub remained in my memory for my whole life. That day we did not have any missions in the first half of the day. It was strange after the previous day, when we had to fly from dawn until night. It seemed that the enemy was also having a day off, because not a single plane appeared in the sky. But we knew that the fascist aircraft were gathering in the Donets Basin. Up to a hundred planes were based in Stalino, up to two hundred in Konstantinovo, and more than a hundred in Barvenkovo.

The dinner was delayed for some reason. A lorry was to bring the food from Starobelsk, but it hadn't come. Pilots were sitting under a straw canopy casting sad glances along the road.

Zub and Kholobaev were sitting not far from us smoking. Nothing was worse than to be kept in suspense. We had four hours of daylight time ahead, but there had been no orders from the division command since the morning.

My thoughts were interrupted by somebody shouting, 'The lorry is coming!' At the same moment a messenger came running from the command post.

'General Naumenko is flying to our airfield!' he told the commander.

Kholobaev and Zub jumped in the duty lorry and drove to the runway to welcome the guest. We realised that Naumenko was not coming without purpose.

The landing panels were quickly unrolled. A U-2 came into view soon, flying very low. General Naumenko ignored the landing signs and drove directly to the command post. The lorry went after him. When Naumenko got out of the cockpit the regiment commander and his deputy were already standing at attention waiting for him.

Less than a minute later we saw a messenger running towards us.

'Air crew, to the General!' We forgot about the food and dashed to the command post.

Naumenko was talking slowly in a low voice: 'The enemy has gathered a large amount of aircraft at the Stalino airfield. Our reconnaissance aircraft...' he looked at his watch 'has just gone there to specify the information. As soon as he transmits a confirmation you must take off. Six Shturmoviks will join you in Polovinkino. You will also be accompanied by fighters from the Varvarovka airfield. I have given instructions to other airfields.' The General looked at Kholobaev: 'Who is the leader today?'

'Captain Eliseev, comrade General.'

'The leader is Major Zub!' said Naumenko ignoring the commander's words.

We gave a start at this surprise.

When a pilot was told in the morning that he was included in the air crew, he had time to get ready for the mission. He could consider all the possible dangers and the ways to avoid them. Whatever he was doing, he was always in the state of tension, and that constant strain helped him to suppress the nervousness which spared neither the freshmen nor the aces.

Zub was not included into the air crew on that day, and now the General appointed him a leader!

The pilots stared at Zub. Nothing changed in his face. He addressed the General in a quiet tone: 'May I start getting ready?'

'Yes, we have very little time...'

Zub hurried to the command post. We followed him downstairs, sat round the table, and took out the maps. Our leader was studying the map, planning the route. Finally he named four main points of our journey. Our route looked like a giant rhombus with the opposing corners at Starobelsk and Stalino. We wrote down the flight time and compass courses. The overall flying time was close to the limit, but this would enable us to avoid the enemy anti-aircraft guns and fighters. Zub planned to approach the target from the west, where we were least expected. 'Is everything clear?' he said.

'Everything!'

Nikolai Antonovich drew the battle formation and showed

everyone his place. I was to fly in the first flight to the right of the leader.

We were sitting in our cockpits waiting for the signal. My mechanic, Serezha Temnov, had prepared everything long ago and was now polishing the bulletproof glass of the canopy for no good reason.

The leader's plane was standing to my right. I could see Zub sitting in his cockpit leaning against the back of his seat. I wondered if he felt nervous now. No, he must be as calm as when he was appointed leader unexpectedly. I thought that I probably had no reason to worry. Our reconnaissance aircraft might find the Stalino airfield empty... Or it might fail to get there at all. Naumenko would send another aircraft, and we would be waiting in the cockpits for a long time yet...

My thoughts were interrupted by a sudden flap. A green flare rocketed up above the command post. The signal to take off. In the air I quickly formed up with the leader and felt a bit more confident. We flew straight for several minutes and reached another airfield. From above I could see the Shturmoviks running up raising dust. Following Zub we circled the airfield and the group from the other regiment formed up at the end of our formation. I was really impressed by the accuracy of the manoeuvre.

We set the course, and began to descend smoothly. Soon we could distinguish the bushes scattered along the gully slopes. We flew above a deserted railway line and a signal box. That was the starting point of our route.

We were hedgehopping just above the ground. I looked at the leader. The side window of Zub's aircraft was open and I could see the profile of his skinny face. Zub was performing his usual duty consulting the map, looking around from time to time, and casting glances at the wingmen. He looked confident and calm, and I had a feeling that we were flying to a training ground and not going to carry out a dangerous mission. Only when I saw German lorries driving along the road did I realise that we were in enemy territory.

The leader looked to my side, raised his hand and made a gesture as if he was beckoning me to come closer. We had agreed not to use the wireless communication, so that the enemy could not intercept us. His meaning was clear to me and I reduced the distance. Zub lifted up his thumb – 'well done!'

Above a crossroads the leader's aircraft turned left, smoothly changing the course. The low sun was now shining in our faces. Zub was staring ahead shielding his eyes from the sunlight with his hand. We flew against the sun for quite a long time. Finally the leader's plane began to turn again and the sun was moving to the right. We headed eastwards, and I realised that we were approaching the target already. I had a rather vague idea of our location at that moment. In a minute Zub's plane swayed from one wing to the other (that was the 'attention' command) and sped up considerably. I throttled up trying not to get behind, and so did the rest. Ahead I could see a belt of sheltering forest and a yellow building behind it. The leader's plane began to climb. I looked at the ground and froze: beside the yellow building I saw about fifty twin-engine bombers. Paunchy refuellers were standing between the planes and people were rushing about. Two Messerschmitts were running up the runway from the other end of the airfield.

The leader lowered his nose and fired. The front Messer whirled and one of its wings crashed into the concrete runway. The second plane bumped into the first one shredding its cockpit with its rotating propeller.

It all happened in a flash, before I could come to my senses. The nose of my Shturmovik was already coming down. I set cross-hairs on one of the bombers and pulled the triggers. The missiles darted down and the fire blinded me for a second. The bomber crawled and stopped with one wing sticking up.

I kept descending, firing in long bursts at the rows of bombers and trying to launch as many shells as possible. I dropped the bombs and levelled the plane out so low that I could easily see the huge black crosses and shell-holes at the wings and fuselages of the enemy aircraft.

I looked around trying to spot the leader. His Shturmovik was side-slipping between the bursts from the anti-aircraft guns ahead of me. I could recognise Zub by his flying style. Then I heard his high-pitched confident voice: 'One more attack, one more attack...'

We climbed following the leader. The anti-aircraft guns were firing, the bombs were exploding, the planes were burning on the ground, and we circled the airfield and dived firing. Again I had only one thought in my head: 'To hit, to hit...'

I heard Zub's voice: 'Assemble, assemble.' The wingmen quickly formed up with the leader and the group began to descend.

The engine was working smoothly. Again I could see Zub's tawny profile through the side window. Again he was consulting the map and looking at the wingmen from time to time...

All the men came back from the sortie. General Naumenko listened to Zub's report and waited for the information from the controller aircraft.

Soon it arrived: more than twenty burnt bombers and two destroyed Messerschmitts, which Zub had attacked on the runway.

After dinner Zub summoned his wingmen.

We settled comfortably on the grass and smoked. 'Let's discuss what you have seen on the route. Do you remember,' he addressed Artemov, 'how we flew above a maize field?'

'Of course I remember.'

'Did you notice anything special there?'

'Well, it was an ordinary, big, green maize field...'

'Did you notice any people there?'

'Some women were waving their kerchiefs,' said Vorozhbiev.

'That's right,' Zub said approvingly. 'And how many women were there?'

'About ten, I guess...' Vorozhbiev answered. I had also seen those women but I did not have time to count them.

'There were seven of them,' said the leader. 'And did you see the lorries on the road?'

'Yes, we did,' we answered eagerly.

'How many lorries did you see, and where were they going?'

Again we had different opinions. The wingmen gave more or less the same number of lorries, but not one of us managed to identify the right road on the map. There were many roads in the Donets Basin and it was easy to mix them up. Some said that the lorries were heading to Debaltsevo, some to Gorlovka...

'You must learn to 'take photographs' with your eyes,' the leader concluded.

To help us learn the details Nikolai Antonovich devised a 'game of objects'. 'Those willing to play are welcome,' he would often declare in our leisure time. We would gather at one side of the table and Zub would put different small objects from his pockets on the table. He let us look at them for several seconds and then ordered us to turn aside. We then had to list what was on the table.

At the beginning we mixed things up, but then we became more attentive and showered Zub with answers: 'The knife was not at the same place, it was lying near the pencil!'

'The comb has disappeared!'

It was a cheerful and useful game. It helped us to relax and trained our visual memory.

Zub did not approve of reckless flying. He did not allow any tricks that were made just for show and had no tactical use. His only goal was to achieve maximum results with minimum efforts. He did not like complicated battle formations and re-forming in the air, and always thought and cared about his wingmen. Zub chose the most favourable routes and could quickly assemble the group after the attack. Nobody fell behind in his formations and the enemy fighters could not count on an easy prey.

8

THE SOUVENIR FLINT

On a hot June day I was leading my group to attack an airfield. Airfields are very dangerous targets: they are situated far beyond the front line. Besides, we had to fly above a densely populated area, with all the settlements stuffed with enemy troops. We had to avoid them so that they could not spot us beforehand, and we had to fly at the lowest possible altitude. It's very difficult to navigate in such conditions. A compass is the only help.

We were hedgehopping at a height of twenty-five metres. Every few minutes I consulted the compass, watch and map, and looked at the ground and the wingmen. Everything was going well. We were flying according to the time-schedule, and I recognised the landmarks marked on the map before the flight. What a smart thing a compass is! Don't trust your feelings, if you think you are deviating from your way. Trust your compass, and it will lead you to your destination. You just have to check the flying time, and you won't lose your bearings. It's terrible when you lose your bearings... Long before the war I had experienced what it means, getting lost during a flight. That time I had trusted my feelings, not the compass.

It happened when I was flying U-2 back to Nalchik from Patigorsk. The weather was awful. I forced my way to the steppe through the layers of fog between the mountain peaks, but everywhere there was the same continuous shroud of clouds.

The flight above the railway was monotonous. I got bored and decided to practise blind-flying. I dived into the clouds and decided to have a ten-minute blind flight. Time seemed endless to me... I yielded to the temptation to adjust the compass reading: it seemed to me that the aircraft was constantly swerving to the right. When the time was up I dived beneath the clouds, but... there was neither the

83

railway, nor the settlement that I expected to see. I began to rush aside trying to find my bearings. There was only deserted steppe below the plane, and not a single soul... I calmed down a bit, set course, and flew straight ahead. It took me rather a long time before I saw a railway station and oil derricks in the hills. Which station was it? I descended and tried to read its name but in vain. I was running short of fuel, and it was already dusky. I decided to land and find out where I was in the most reliable way: to ask somebody. On a flat field behind the station I saw a herd of cows. I landed on that field. The shepherd was an old man. I felt ashamed and couldn't just say that I got lost. I began the conversation in a roundabout way: 'Do you have a cigarette, granddad?' I asked as if I landed just because I wanted to smoke. I could think of no better way to start the talk.

We smoked. I talked on different topics and hoped that the man would name some place in the region. He talked with pleasure on any topic, but not about geography. Meanwhile time was pressing. I began to lose patience, and finally asked him, pointing at the railway station, as if out of pure curiosity: 'Are you not from this village?'

'This is not a village, this is a town, Mozdock!' the man looked offended. My hair stood on end under my helmet: it was so far from Nalchik that I didn't have enough fuel to get there. I had to wire a telegram. Next day they brought me some fuel by air. Since then I always remembered: trust the compass!

This time we were heading for the Artemovsk airfield, flying above a deep ravine. A hill towered on the horizon ahead. Judging by the time, our target must be behind it... if only we had not swerved from the course. I felt a wave of heat. 'Trust the compass!' I sped up keeping an eye on the wingmen. They were flying next to me. The aircraft carried containers with granular phosphorus. To set the enemy aircraft on fire we had to open the containers at a very low altitude. Otherwise the fiery rain would die out before it hit the ground, since the phosphorus granules burn out very quickly in the air.

I banked slightly right before the hill, and the overloaded Shturmovik ascended smoothly. The panorama opened up gradually. Suddenly I saw two lines of bombers almost straight on the heading. So I did guide the group to the target!

Now the attack... I started to lower the nose of the Shturmovik when something banged deafeningly. The aircraft jolted and banked abruptly. I saw a hole gaping in the right wing. My hands and feet were working automatically. I straightened the plane out, and it went on descending. The engine was working all right. I kept my eyes fixed on the bomber with crosses on its sides. Missiles darted towards it from under the wings of my aircraft. Machine-guns started firing. A burst, another one, and the bomber caught fire. Meanwhile the ground was approaching. I levelled the plane out its dive, pressed the button, and for a second looked back. The wingmen were flying with fiery trails of burning phosphorus following them, as if the aircraft were burning themselves. White smoke covered the airfield.

I saw a wall of tall pine trees behind the airfield. The cowl of my Shturmovik was below their tops. I made a steep climb, and the plane was immediately hit in the engine. Water showered on me in a very hard spray. I reduced speed sharply in order not to overload the damaged engine. The wingmen raced past me one by one, and soon I lost sight of them.

The oil pressure indicator was slowly approaching zero, while the water temperature was constantly rising: the lubrication and cooling systems were damaged. The engine would stall soon, and the front line was more than five minutes of flying ahead... While the engine was still working I climbed a little. That way I could glide to a suitable spot when the engine stopped working. The windshield grew dim, I could see nothing ahead. My goggles were splashed with oil, I pushed them up on my forehead. I had to look through the open side window. My eyes were watering from the airflow.

I was flying really low; the engine was almost finished. But with every revolution of the propeller I was approaching the front line. I felt a glimmer of hope: perhaps the engine would hold out until our lines? The altitude was two or three metres; speed was critical; the aircraft was responding poorly. The engine stalled. Should I land on the fuselage or on the landing gear? My hand had already grasped the stick releasing the landing gear. I felt the two usual jerks – the wheels came out – and the plane drove down on to the rocky soil at a speed of more than 100 kph. And then a crack – the plane crashed down on the fuselage and crawled...

Silence. The dust hid the sun for some time. I pushed the canopy back. Light wind was slowly dispersing the dust. 'So where have I landed? Is it our territory or the enemy's?' Ahead I could see the metal tower of a high-voltage line with fragments of wiring hanging down. The ground was bare around the plane; but at a distance there was an islet of tall grass with little clumps of yellow flowers. What should I do next? At that moment a burst of machine-gun fire broke the silence. Bullets were hitting the armour-plating behind me. I brought my head down to my knees. After a short pause a new burst hit the Duralumin skin of a wing near the cockpit. The machine-gun was firing somewhere from behind, at a short distance. It was firing one burst after another at regular intervals. It was dangerous to stay inside the cockpit: they would finish me off. I thought it better to hide behind the engine, on the ground.

Without raising my head I got ready to jump. I was waiting for the next burst. It came. In a second I jumped out of the cockpit and lay flat on the ground. Now the sub-machine guns began firing. They had noticed me.

I snuggled up to the hot engine shell near the warped propeller blade. The shooting was coming just from behind. I could crawl forward and hide in the grass. But the whining bullets chained me to the ground; I couldn't lift a finger. I felt doomed. I put my head on my palms and stared blankly in front of me. The sun was shining; the steppe around me was in full bloom. A blade of grass was rocking before my eyes, and a ladybird was crawling up it awkwardly. It got to the very top, spread its wings, and lifted into the air. I turned my head following its flight and flinched: something flashed. No, it was not a shot, it was some gentle glint. What could it be? I turned my head slowly – it flashed again. Finally I saw a small light-brown stone lying very close to me. It had a shaggy surface, but one of its faces was unruffled. In childhood I used to collect such flints and strike fire off them with a file. It had been split open by a bullet or a splinter and glittered in the sun. I took the stone, felt its warmth in my hand, and put it into my pocket. I thought: 'When the war is over, I'll put it on show. I'll have an inscription engraved on it: '21 June, 1942'. This will be the date of my second birth. I'll tell the story of this stone to my children.' I did not have any children at that time, but I was certainly going to have many.

With this thought I came to my senses. The machine-gun kept firing, and I cocked my pistol. At that moment something rustled strangely above me... I pressed my face to the ground and closed my eyes. A sharp blow came from behind the Shturmovik. The machine-gun stopped firing. I guessed that it was our mortar near the pylon of the high-voltage line, and it was shooting. I must crawl in that direction, and do it quickly before the machine-gun started shooting again. I looked from behind the engine. The machine-gun was surely firing from the hill, from the 'dominant eminence'. I crawled like a cat, pressing my whole body to the ground, and moving with the help of elbows, knees and the toes of my boots. Finally I reached the islet of grass, which I had noticed from the cockpit. But the grass obstructed the view, and I couldn't see what was going on around me. What if the Fritzes were somewhere close crawling artfully in order to lay hold of me? I raised my head – something clinked. I pressed myself back to the ground and passed my hand over the helmet – a splinter of glass stuck into my finger. I pulled the helmet off my head; the goggles were completely smashed. A stray bullet? Or was it a sniper, who located me by the glint of the goggles? I threw the helmet aside.

For a long time I was crawling from one grass islet to another, before finally I reached the pylon. Now my way was blocked by a huge skein of barbed wire. You can't jump over these even if you take a run, and I couldn't even raise my head... So I had to crawl along the spiral until I found a big hole, breached by a shell. I squeezed through it and was totally exhausted. I looked at my watch and felt astonished: we had been attacking the target at eleven o'clock, and now it was one o'clock. Had it taken me two hours to get over the two hundred metres from the plane to the pylon? An uneasy thought came to my mind: 'Whose territory is this? The trenches at the front edge are meandering. What if the place has been sacked?' I lay their for a long time listening to the occasional sounds of skirmishing, peering into every knoll, every shrub of grass. The mortar had long since ceased firing; single shots were breaking the silence. Sometimes a bullet would hit a knoll and rebound... And then I realised that the oblong mound, which was being hit by stray bullets, was the camouflaged parapet of a trench. The top of a helmet would appear regularly from the trench, and that was when a shot came. I was wondering, who was in the trench: our soldiers or Fritzes.

A sudden rustle interrupted my thoughts. The grass ahead of me waved, and I saw a faded field cap. I could see no star on it. I cocked my pistol and aimed it at the cap. A long swarthy face appeared for a moment. The man was crawling cautiously, looking around. His sub-machine gun was dragging after him on a belt. I aimed at his head, and at that moment our gazes met. The man became petrified. I had only to pull the trigger, his sub-machine gun was at his side...

We kept silent, gazing at each other. Then a grimace that resembled a smile appeared on the swarthy man's face. I saw a gold tooth. He asked in a low voice, speaking with a strange accent: 'Are you from our lot?' and without waiting for my reply he waved 'Come on!'

'A Fritz!' thought I.

'Don't move...' I hissed and added a round oath. My words had an effect: the man started gabbling:

'Why are you going to shoot?! I'm a friend!'

'You're lying! Where is your star?'

'What star?' he asked a daft question, as if playing for time.

'On your cap.'

The man grasped his cap, felt it all over and turned it inside out. Now I could see a khaki front-star on it. I felt relieved, but my suspicion was not totally dispelled. Having the star in my sights I began the interrogation.

'Name?'

'Do you want my name?'

'Yes, I want *your* name!'

'Then – Birbier...' The name sounded like a German one.

'Where are you from?'

'From Odessa...'

I didn't like the answer. Odessa had long been occupied by the Romanians. I asked: 'Where did you live there?'

'Well, Bebel, 37...' answered Birbier with confidence. He grew bolder obviously, and suggested that I crawl to the parapet and he follow.

'No,' I said roughly, 'You crawl first, and I will have you in my sights... If anything seems wrong I will shoot!'

The soldier was crawling, looking back from time to time, and I was crawling after him as an escort. We crawled up to the parapet and I could already see soldiers with helmets on their heads. The nearest soldier – round-faced and snub-nosed – was grinning broadly. He waved at me and said quietly: 'Come on, pilot, come on, just keep your head and bottom down!'

I dived into the trench, like a walrus into an ice-hole, and first of all took a sip of warm water from a water-bottle, which somebody gave me. Then I lit up some *makhorka*.★

A flaxen-haired soldier squatted in a niche under the parapet with a receiver tied to his head. He was wearing boots with very wide tops and looking at me as he turned the handle of a portable telephone set, calling up someone called 'Akula'.† I was showered with questions by the round-faced man: 'Where is it scarier to fly, comrade lieutenant, high or low?'

'It is safer at a low altitude,' I answered from the point of view of our tactics, and trying to avoid discussing the topic of fear. I'd had enough of fear when I was crawling on the ground.

'So why did you fly so low that you even got into the German trench, comrade lieutenant?'

'Is there a trench there?'

'The first one...'

Now I understood that I had landed close to the enemy, and the wheels of the aircraft had got stuck in the first German trench.

'Why do you raise your heads to face German bullets? Isn't it scary?' I asked him.

'It's bait, we put it on a stick,' explained the soldier, showing me a helmet which already had many holes in it. 'We are teasing their sniper, so that our man could spot him from another place...'

The flaxen-haired soldier hastily unfastened the receiver and passed it to me: 'Battalion commander!' Everyone in the trench went silent immediately, as if the operator had connected to no less than the Commander-in-Chief of the Front. I heard a low voice: 'Well, hello, Stalin's *sokol*!‡ How are you?'

'I'm fine!' I answered, trying to sound cheerful.

'Well, we are waiting for you...'

I thought, what a nice *sokol* would the battalion commander see: my clothes were torn to shreds, my elbows and knees were bleeding...

Bending down I followed the attendant down the trench.

★ Russian (typically Ukrainian) tobacco.
† *Akula* means 'shark' in Russian.
‡ *Sokol* means 'falcon' in Russian. 'Stalin's *sokol*' was a nickname for pilots during World War II. It is also a metaphor for anyone bold and courageous.

In a deep gully I saw a real cave-dwelling. Earth-houses were dug in the slope; their entrances were curtained with waterproof capes. I could see soldiers taking their mess kits and hurrying to the steaming field-kitchen - a cauldron on the wheels with a high chimney. It looked like Stephenson's first steam engine.

The attendant brought me to a blindage. Two men were standing at the entrance smiling at me, as if I was an old friend of theirs. A tall man with big, broad shoulders introduced himself: 'Battalion Commander Misarov.' The other one shook hands with me and introduced himself as Senior Politruk Murakhovsky. They invited me in to the blindage.

There were two trestle-beds and a table of rough wood. On the wall hung a portrait of Stalin – 'The Leader' – in military coat and a slogan: 'Our cause is just, the enemy will be defeated'.

'The infantrymen have made themselves at home,' I thought.

The commander called: 'Tell Lyuda to come!'

Soon there came a blonde with a child's face and full lips. She had a first-aid kit in her hands. She had cocked her field-cap at a jaunty angle, her boots sat well on her slender legs, and her wasp waist was laced with a wide belt. A medal 'For courage' did not hang, but rather lay flat above her left blouse pocket. Casting her blue eyes over the place she saluted awkwardly with her palm up and reported on her arrival. 'You can meet real beauties even on the front line,' I thought.

'Now, deal with the pilot, quickly,' Misarov told her with a smile.

The nurse dealt with my knees and elbows, and was gone. Murakhovsky took out a flask covered in greatcoat cloth, and opened a tin of canned meat with a Finnish knife. Everybody called such canned meat 'the second front', though there was not one then. He also put a mug and a pot of water on the table.

'Come on, pilot, get yourself revived after the long journey. Dilute to your taste. It is pure alcohol, we keep it for the guests,' he told me proudly.

'I will have it neat, then wash it down,' I said, trying to look brave.

I drank up the fiery liquid, and before passing on to water breathed my rank and name. This show had its effect.

'Wow, pilots can do that!' Murakhovsky gave a wink to the battalion commander, who remained calm. The commander nodded assent: 'They can...'

The battalion commander and commissar told me the details of my landing. The front-line observers noticed my Shturmovik flying just above the ground. They saw me landing. I was right to suspect that I had lost the landing gear in the German first trench. After that the aircraft crawled forward on the fuselage for about fifty metres. If I had not let the landing gear out, I would have remained on the German side of the front line. My Shturmovik landed near a place called Nyrkovo, very close to from where I had been machine-gunned.

The observers reported to the battalion commander that the pilot had jumped out of the cockpit. The commander gave an order to the mortar battery to neutralise the attacking machine-gun. Then he summoned intelligence officers and barked a command: 'Find the pilot before he gets blown up on the minefield!' Five men volunteered. They crawled for a long time in the neutral zone, but failed to find me. Only soldier Birbier, who was in the outposts, ran into me.

'Now we have to recommend Birbier for a decoration,' the battalion commander told the commissar. 'We promised an order for the man who would find the pilot.'

'But he was taken prisoner himself!' laughed Murakhovsky. He was obviously fond of jokes.

'Did any Shturmoviks fly over here before I landed?' I asked the question that I'd been keeping in my head.

'Oh yes, they did,' answered the battalion commander. 'They made hell of a noise. Even stung the first company a bit.'

I guessed that 'hell of a noise' and 'stung' meant that they fired at the unit. But I did not want to believe that.

'Were they firing?' I asked the battalion commander.

'Well, just a bit...'

I noticed that 'a bit' was one of his favourite expressions, but it had various meanings.

'Have they made a mess here?'

'Oh, nothing serious... They knocked off our water-carrier horse, and splinters hit two slowcoaches a bit. Lyuda treated them, they remained in the ranks.'

It was hard to believe that my wingmen could do that. I tried to find excuses for the guys: 'They are only inexperienced sergeants. For some of them it was their first operational flight, for the rest – the third. But you should have seen how they dealt with the airfield!'

'It's OK, pilot,' the battalion commander waved off. 'Even the regimental artillerymen make mistakes. They hit our unit from time to time. And when you are flying a plane it's quite natural. Try and distinguish our trench from a German one at such speed... A horse does not wear a uniform. You did everything just fine.' The battalion commander praised us while helping himself with another portion of the 'second front'. 'If only you attacked them more often. You seldom show up...'

'Help yourself, pilot,' Murakhovsky treated me. 'You must have been born under a lucky star. Even the scouts get blown up sometimes, though they know every bush and knob in the neutral zone...'

'Perhaps I have. But I've lost my aircraft. I will have to go to the regiment on my own...' I felt very sorry for the plane.

'Is this thing very expensive?' asked the battalion commander about the plane.

'It costs no less than half a million.' A military representative at an aircraft factory told me this astronomical sum once. I was shocked. Since then I always kept in mind how expensive an aircraft is. I thought about people who had a hard time at the home front, but still gave their personal savings for plane building. Everything for victory. And often an aircraft is shot down during its first operational flight. Now my Shturmovik was lying in the neutral zone. It was in quite good condition still. If only we could drag it out! We could change the engine, patch it up, and it could fly again... I expressed this idea.

'And how much does it weigh?' my interlocutors seemed interested.

'A bit more than five tons...'

'We could try and tow it off with a tank...'

We decided to conduct a rescue mission at night. The battalion commander 'phoned somewhere and asked them to send a machine. They promised. We found a towline of the required length – a strong cable from a high-tension line. Several men volunteered to crawl to the aircraft and fasten the cable.

'What should we tie it to?' they asked me.

I explained that they could wind the cable round the propeller. The blades had been bent, the cable would be fixed.

The tank arrived late at night. ('It wandered about a bit,' said the battalion commander). The tank drove up carefully to the very edge of the gully and stopped its engine. The scouts disappeared in the dark. The battalion commander and I went to the first trench. It was a warm, starry night. The smell of thyme filled the air. There were cicadas chirping, and somebody in Nyrkovo was playing mouth-organ. A German was playing our song 'Katyusha'.★

'They are having good time in Nyrkovo,' the battalion commander explained. If it had not been for the sporadic bursts of sub-machine gun fire, it would have been hard to believe that the war was going on here.

A voice came from the German side: 'Russ Ivan, surrender!'

'F… off, dirty Fritz!' came the answer from our side.

Two bursts of fire came one after another: one red and one green tracer shell raced in opposite directions. I bent down. The battalion commander explained: 'They are distracting attention from the scouts. Perhaps their men are also searching now…'

'So this is what war on the front line is like,' I thought as I stood in the first trench with the battalion commander.

The scouts got back by 1 a.m. very displeased. They had failed to fasten the cable. It appeared that the Germans had already visited the Shturmovik. They had rummaged in the cockpit and gone back. Immediately after that the Germans set up the flares and began to shell – our men had a narrow escape.

The gun fired systematically for a long time. Then something flared up in the dark. In the blaze of the flame we could see the wings of the aircraft spread on the ground. After some time we heard the dry cracking of exploding cartridges. And when the flame began to lick the cockpit, a red flare went up in the dark sky. It was one of the flares stored in the pocket by the left side, near the signal pistol. Squeezing a splinter of flint in my hand I watched my aircraft being incinerated.

Two days later I got off a lorry, tired and exhausted. I made my way through the grass towards my airfield. From afar I could see the caponiers and Shturmoviks covered with camouflage netting. Near the hill people were standing – pilots waiting for a mission. The hill

---

★ Katyusha is a diminutive from Katya (a female name). The Soviet song 'Katyusha' about a girl waiting for her boyfriend, a frontier guard, was especially popular in the war years. The Soviet rocket launchers were called Katyushas after this song.

was actually a mound above a dugout, our regiment's command post.

The pilots were looking at my side. I recognised Kolya Dorogavtsev, Zhenya Ezhov, Fedya Artemov, Vanya Boiko. I smiled at them, but they were looking at me as if I was a stranger. Nobody came to meet me. Only when I was a few steps away did Kholobaev dart towards me. He ran up to me, looked intently in my eyes, and hugged me. Uninvited tears came into my eyes.

In the regiment I learned that none of my wingmen returned from the military operation. I reported that they had crossed the front line. We sent enquiries in every direction and found them all. Some were in Svatovo, some in Starobelsk, some in Polovinkino... They had landed separately in different places. Later they hitchhiked back to the regiment, and their planes were ferried by more experienced pilots.

One of my wingmen, the freckled Lebedev, told me what had happened: 'You had been shot down, and we flew further on. None of us had a transmitter, so we flew in silence. Nobody had the heart to occupy the leading place. Then we began to creep away: some turned right, some left, some kept the same course. I flew alone for a long time before I saw an airfield. I was very glad and was ready to land. I'd already let down the landing gear and extended the flaps, when I saw crosses on the wings of a plane below. I revved up; the engine sneezed, and almost stopped, but the plane sped up. They fired a few volleys after me from anti-aircraft guns. I decided to fly straight eastward, and put the compass on 'E'. I planned to fly that course until I ran out of fuel. After some time I saw an airfield. This time I examined it carefully and saw planes with red stars. It was our airfield! When I landed I found out that it was Svatovo.'

That flight comes back to my memory each time I look at the stone lying before me. There is no inscription on it: no cutting tool can engrave on its surface. Sometimes it disappears after a spring-clean in our apartment, and I have to search for it. My daughter once took it outside for a game... And my son, who is finishing school now, knows its story in detail, but it does not interest him any longer.

9

'NOT A STEP BACK!'

In the spring and summer of 1942 our troops were undergoing new ordeals in the south. The Crimea Front sustained a severe defeat in the beginning of May. Our counter-offensive near Kharkov failed. Our Southern Front troops defending Donbass were under the threat of encirclement. The enemy was fighting his way to the Caucasus.

Our regiment was based on the other side of the Don, near Kagalnitskaya. We flew to attack temporary bridges made by the enemy near Nikolaevskaya and Konstantinovskaya. The situation resembled that of June 1941 when the regiment attacked temporary bridges on the Berezina. We were suffering no fewer casualties now.

Kozhuhovsky read to us order number 227 of 28 July from the People's Commissar of Defence. The words weighed like stones: '...The enemy is sending fresh forces to the front... The German occupiers are forcing their way to Stalingrad, to the Volga. They want to conquer Kuban and the Northern Caucasus at any price... A part of the Southern Front troops left Rostov and Novocherkassk following the panic-mongers... they heaped ignominy upon their banners... People of our country are losing faith in the Red Army... It's time to stop the retreat... We must defend each metre of the Soviet land to the last... Panic-mongers and cowards must be extirpated on the spot... Not a step back!'

We were also a part of the Southern Front troops.

We hedgehopped to attack temporary bridges over the Don in small groups without cover. We blew up the bridges, but large enemy columns were already on the southern side. Major Kholobaev impressed on the young pilots: 'We had it worse on the Berezina... We had to learn shooting and bombing at the front. But you have

95

trained at training grounds, shot at the targets, learned to aim... You have a proper flying experience on Ils. Besides you are guardsmen now – so you get appropriate orders. You must destroy this bridge! Make the dive steeper and release bombs at a lower altitude – they will hit it right.'

The newcomers kept their eyes fixed on Kholobaev. For them he was a living history of the regiment. His hair was now completely grey, though a year ago he had only one grey strand above the right eyebrow. He tossed it back all the time. One hand was holding on to a hot-water bottle under his blouse – he had a disturbing pain in the stomach.

Konstantin Nikolaevich sat in a circle of young pilots and explained energetically:'Never let the enemy understand that a young inexperienced sergeant is flying. A Fritz does not know your rank, does not ask for your ID card. Attack impudently, impertinently... Then he will think:"An o-o-old wolf is flying!"'

Only a few men from those who had made their first combat sortie in Stary Bykhov were left in the regiment. Lieutenant Colonel Getman had become a division commander; Major Kholobaev was appointed regiment commander. Nikolai Smurygov was still in hospital with heavy wounds, the same with Victor Shahov, who lost both legs. Now the heavy burden was passed to Petr Rudenko, Eugene Ezhov, Fedor Artemov, Ivan Boiko, Mikhail Vorozhbiev and Vladimir Zangiev, who were already experienced pilots. Mikhail Talykov and Leonid Bukreev were promoted leaders. Bukreev managed to blow up a bridge during his first operational flight following Kholobaev's instructions.

On those hard days we were often visited by war correspondents from an army newspaper, *Wings of the Soviet States*. They published many good reports about pilots and mechanics in the 'Tribune of Combat Experience' column. Those reports really helped to strengthen people's confidence in the future victory. Once they called Bukreev 'an expert at destroying German bridges'. After that article Lenya believed that he was capable of carrying out any military mission.

Near Rostov Major Kholobaev offered a mission to me and my two wingmen, sergeants Nikolayev and Kladko. The task was to destroy a pontoon bridge across the Don near Nikolaevskaya: but how should we achieve it? For the sergeants it was going to be the first combat sortie. Three planes were not enough for such a mission, and there were no fighters to cover us. Besides, I knew that Messerschmitts were patrolling the air above Nikolaevskaya from dawn until dusk, and there were lots of anti-aircraft guns in the area.

Listening to Kholobaev I thought that we were doomed. I had butterflies in my stomach. I tried to think of something else. An absurd idea came into my head: 'Sergeant Nikolayev will bomb the Nikolaevskaya bridge. What if this coincidence means that we'll be lucky, and Nikolayev will show himself as an expert in his first combat sortie, as Leonid Bukreev did?' I never really believed in omens. That's why I did not grow a beard at the front. I shaved daily, ignoring Mondays,* and the thirteenth day of the month. I often carried out military operations successfully on a thirteenth, which really surprised some pilots. After I was conferred the Hero of the Soviet Union by the Order of 13 April 1944, and my name was the thirteenth in the list, many people lost their distrust in the fateful number. But that would happen much later on...

The three of us were standing before the regiment commander. I doubted that he fancied our chances. He'd got an order from the division – to raise the forces that were available. Certainly he tried to object. I think he even raised his voice, but the order was strict: 'Carry out! Not a step back!' That's why he was so mad now. With his left hand he was holding the water bottle on his stomach, and his right hand was gesticulating as he spoke. I smiled. Kholobaev saw that and barked at me angrily: 'Emelian! What's that?'

Kholobaev often shortened my name when he was in good spirits. Now he was mad, but it slipped out – 'Emelian'.

I didn't say anything. He probably understood that I guessed his thoughts. He knew that we had little chance of return, but he had to be strict: doubts would have paralysed our resolve. That's why he spoke bluntly: 'You will attack from this side, and return here!' Kholobaev scratched the celluloid on the map-case. He enunciated the word 'return' with such deep conviction that it was hard to believe in any other outcome for the flight.

The sergeants stared at the battalion commander in amazement.

---

* The Russians have a saying, 'Monday is a hard day!'

Yesterday evening he was explaining so patiently how important it was to conceal your lack of experience from the enemy. Why was he so mad now? I felt sorry for Konstantin Nikolaevich, not for myself. That was good. When you feel sorry for yourself you can easily give way to despair. The rough words of the commander helped me to concentrate.

'Take your seats in the cockpits!'

We hedgehopped towards Nikolaevskaya. My wingmen kept in the line. 'Well done, guys!' We flew above the quiet steppe. Occasionally we could see tiny villages consisting of just one street. We crossed the wide backwaters of the Manychsky canal above an isthmus. To the right I saw a dam, to the left – the Soleny farm. Our course was right. Then we crossed the serpentine Sal river. A third of our way was still ahead. We were going to cross the Don to the right of the bridge, then turn back, and attack from the opposite side. That was what Kholobaev told us.

I kept looking out for German fighters. The sky was clear as yet. 'Maybe we'll manage to fly up to the bridge unnoticed?' I only hoped they did not intercept us before we reached the target.

I saw something green ahead –the marshy banks of the Don. An enemy column had crossed to the southern bank! It was on our way. I warned: 'The enemy!' We sped up and raced above the fascists' heads. In a minute we must reach the Don. I looked up and saw three pairs of Messerschmitts. It was time to climb. If only we had an opportunity to release the bombs before they attacked.

I pulled the control column back, and banked left. The ground seemed to fall in. I could see the Don, a bell tower on the opposite bank, streets jammed with troops. I looked back to check if Nikolayev had turned to the right and saw his Shturmovik dropping steeply. It hit the southern bank of the Don and caught fire. Two Messerschmitts soared up above the fire. Sergeant Nikolayev was blown up by the bombs that he was going to release above the bridge.

But where was the bridge? I could not see it. There were enemy columns on both banks of the river, but there were no pontoons. I glanced at the water surface again and for a second could not believe my eyes. Two lorries were driving in the middle of the river. I realised that the bridge was sunk below the water surface so that it could not be seen! I had to aim at the lorries. I was still climbing. Just a few seconds more and I could begin to dive. The anti-aircraft guns were silent – they were obviously afraid to hit their own fighters. And where was Kladko? I glanced to the right – my wingman was already followed by two pairs of fighters. The plane was smoking, but it kept flying after me... I dived and aimed at a lorry. A long salvo – the water near the lorry boiled up. I pressed the button releasing the bombs and felt four jolts under the seat. I levelled the plane out and looked back. A huge water column was rising in the middle of the river. I could see no sign of Kladko.

Two Messerschmitts were right behind me! I made a sharp side-slip to the ground... My Shturmovik was flying just above the grass. A pair of fighters with white crosses on their fuselages and yellow cantilever wings was following me a bit higher on the right. On the left – symmetrically - the second pair. The Messerschmitts were flying so close that I could easily see the fascist pilots in helmets and goggles. They glanced at my side. I had never seen them so close... A pair to the left, a pair to the right – like an honorary escort. These were not dangerous at the moment. And where was the third pair? I saw the planes through a small rear-view window. They were at the same height with me. The first one was yawing – it was aiming. I side-slipped sharply. The smoking tracks from the Oerlikons ran past me, the shells hit the ground in front of the plane. The pair that attacked me climbed up, and occupied the place at my side, while one of the escorting pairs slew down and was going to attack me from behind – they were reforming. Again I managed to escape the shells, and again they were changing their places. The German fighters rearranged quickly and accurately. They were going to finish me off easily, as if it was a game... But I had already adapted to their manoeuvres: I concentrated my attention entirely on the pair behind me. Each time they aimed, I side-slipped to the right or to the left alternately, and lifted out just a few metres above the ground. Time was working in my favour. I managed to draw the fighters about thirty kilometres to the south of the Don. The most terrible outcome for me would have been to fall into enemy territory. Now I was not afraid of that at least.

A new attack. The aircraft banked left again, but this time the Oerlikons banged on the upper wing. I tried to lift out, but could not move the control stick: the shells tore up the aileron and the instrument panel jammed. According to the laws of flying my plane was now going to hit the ground on its left wing, and I would be buried under the debris... Instinctively I pressed the rudder foot-pedal to the floor – the plane turned off sharply, and the lower wing rose reluctantly. Without the slightest hesitation I released the landing gear, stopped the engine and taxied along the field. Still moving I looked up: four fighters were heading to the Don, and the pair that attacked me zoomed and banked. Oh no, it was not just banking, they were going to dive at me from the side. I jumped out of the cockpit, and lay on my side, my head near a wheel and my back to the planes. The fighters fired a volley, a second one... Something was flowing under the engine – either water or a stream of petrol. The fighters were turning back again. 'They will finish me off here...'

While the Messerschmitts were turning I rushed to the only bush on the field, which cast a long shadow. It was inconvenient to run: the parachute was banging against my knees. My legs gave way. I fell in the shadow and watched the fighters diving again. 'Damn!' It seemed that they noticed my rush, and were aiming at me, not the plane. The leading Messerschmitt fired a burst. It ploughed the ground near my legs. The fighters flashed above my head. During the last dive the Messerschmitts did not fire a shot. They were out of ammo. They failed to set my aircraft on fire.

My mutilated Il stood as if weeping. A stream of petrol flew from under the cowling on the dry, hot ground. I took off the parachute. The haversack looked as if it was moth-eaten. White silk was peeping out of numerous holes. The sack had been shredded by splinters. It had saved me from injuries.

I realised that German forces would arrive soon. I removed the plane's clock, broke the instruments with the butt of my gun, shot at the lower petrol tank and went southwards. I was thinking about Nikolayev and Kladko, and kept recalling the words from the order: 'Not a step back!' A village came in sight ahead of me. Two rows of houses snuggled up to the road from both sides. I consulted the map – it must be a stud-farm number 36. Near the last house I saw a well. My mouth was dry, but I did not dare enter the village at once. There was no continuous front line near the Don. It often happened that the enemy front-line units outflanked our defence and gained territory. I had seen such situations many times from the air. Just in case, I took off my military blouse and wrapped my map-case, cap, and belt with its holster into it. I put the pistol into my pocket, hid the documents in my bootleg and walked through the steppe in my orange shirt.

On the road to the farm I saw an old woman with a teenager. I hurried up towards them. 'Where are you heading for?'

'Where my old legs will carry me.' The woman adjusted the kerchief on her head. She turned her face towards the Don, raised her arms to the sky, and cried: 'Nothing is sacred for those devils! They drop bombs on the children and the old men who try to cross the river, trample them with tanks, fire at them from machine-guns. Herods! Herods!' Her hands drooped down. She looked at me. 'Are you a soldier?'

'Yes...' I answered in one word. She must have identified me by my trousers and boots.

'And why are you here?' she looked at my bundle.

'I have to struggle forward. It's a long way ahead. I saw a well and wanted to drink, but I'm afraid to go there.'

'I'll send Grisha, he'll check...'

We did not have to wait long.

'There are no Germans there!' reported the boy, when he returned.

I put on my soldier's blouse and the cap, tied on the belt, and hurried towards the village. In a ravine I noticed two soldiers. Neither had boots, belt or cap. I did not see any weapon either. One of the soldiers, a very young boy. was flaxen-haired and short; the second had a thick beard. The first one stared at me either in fright, or in surprise. I thought, 'They probably failed to hold their position near the Don,' and asked, 'Where is your unit?'

'We are looking for it, Comrade Lieutenant,' answered the one with the beard.

'And where is your weapon?'

'It sank when we were swimming across the Don... We even had to leave our boots on that side. The river is wide...'

The flaxen-haired soldier kept his eyes fixed on me. Suddenly he said smiling: 'Comrade Lieutenant, I know you... Was it you who crawled into our trench across the neutral zone near Nyrkovo?'

Now it was my turn to be surprised. I recognised the signal operator, who had called 'Akula' in the trench. I was very glad to see him.

It appeared that Misarov's battalion suffered great losses defending Lisichansk. Misarov was killed. The remnant of the battalion led by Politruk Murakhovsky covered the retreat of our troops across the Don. They had to cross the river under the enemy fire when everyone else was already gone: the fascist tanks broke the defence and forced their way to the bridge.

I could not help thinking about Battalion Commander Misarov, Politruk Murakhovsky, soldier Birbier, and, of course, the blue-eyed nurse, Lyuda, who cleaned my bleeding knees and elbows. I kept thinking of her, dreamed of meeting her one day. I asked the soldiers if they knew Lyuda, the nurse.

'Of course we know her...'

'Is she OK?'

'She drowned in the Don...'

'How?'

'She ran into the water in her calfskin boots and with a sub-machine gun round her neck. The men shouted at her: 'Drop it!', but she didn't. Perhaps it dragged her to the bottom, or maybe she was shot...'

We gulped water from a bucket near the well. A woman came out of the house. She looked at us with sympathy, and came up to us. 'Sit on my front steps... I'll milk the cow, you can drink some fresh milk. Perhaps my boy is wandering like this somewhere...'

'Thank you, mother,' I said. 'We are in a hurry.'

The soldiers, who had not eaten anything for the last few days, asked me to wait. I knew that they could not find the way to the Manychsky canal by themselves. They did not have a map.

We were sitting in a yard in a porch. It was not really a yard - there was no fence round it. Opposite the well there was a small ramshackle barn; a pile of pressed dung could be seen behind it... I consulted the map once again. It was about thirty kilometres to the Manychsky canal. We could not get there in one night.

A girl came running from the street. She cried: 'Uncle, uncle, they are coming!...'

I jumped from the porch and looked round the corner. A column of German cars was entering the village. A Fritz was sitting on the hatch of the first armoured car near a machine-gun. I rushed back. 'Germans!' I whispered angrily to the soldiers. They ran behind the

102

dunghill and disappeared in the burdock. I dashed into the barn. A loud cackle of alarmed hens met me inside. I huddled near the door, and stood stock-still peering into a slit. How silly of me to wind up here! I should have followed the soldiers to the burdock! But it was too late to change plan: the leading car drove up to the well and stopped. I watched the Fritzes filling jerrycans with water, filling radiators, washing themselves. One of them even took off his shirt and asked another one to pour water on his back. Several soldiers were pissing at my hen-house. 'Are they going to stop here?' I thought. 'What then? First of all they will deal with the hen-house. The hens will go into a soup, and what about me? I have no retreat. I will discharge my pistol into the chicken-lovers and that'll be it.'

My legs grew numb. Trying to change the uncomfortable pose I moved carefully, and the hens began cackling again. I whispered angrily to the silly birds: 'Hens, hush, hush!...'. The rooster kept looking sideways at me with an unwinking eye and giving alarming crows. God, how I wanted to wring its neck!

After a short halt the German vanguard moved on. When the column disappeared behind the hill, I rushed out of my shelter. My soldiers came as if out of nowhere. 'All because of your milk...' I barked at them. 'Follow me!'

We ran across the road and hastened southwards. We went right through the steppe, with no road. The North Star helped me to keep the right course. We walked for a long time. The soldiers asked me to stop, but I was in a hurry. I knew that once I allowed them to lie down, I wouldn't be able to wake them up. I was wearing boots, and they were barefoot. I'd had my dinner today in Kagalnitskaya, and they had not eaten anything for the last few days. I had had enough rest, and they had not slept for several nights. I told them: 'We will have rest only at dawn. We must walk as far as possible from Kleist.'

I wanted to frighten them, but there came no reaction. Kleist was an empty name for them. They were stumbling, dozing in motion.

After some time I heard a noise: carts were creaking, horses were snorting, and somebody was talking quietly. We sat still on the country lane and listened. Somebody was speaking Russian. Glowing cigarette ends could be seen. I decided to find out where the people were heading, and walked towards them.

The carts were loaded with trucks. A score of civilians were following the carts, accompanied by a soldier. I took him aside: 'Who are these people?'

'Recruits.'

'Where from?'

'Mechetinskaya.'

'Where are you going?'

'To the assembly place in Konstantinovskaya.'

I explained to the officer that Konstantinovskaya was occupied by the enemy, and a German vanguard was approaching Orlovka. He did not believe me at first. He had also read the order with the words 'Not a step back!'

At dawn we came across a haystack. My soldiers fell down, and I knew that nothing could get them up now. I tried to talk them: 'Do you see that dwelling?'

'Yes...' they mumbled drowsily.

'Remember, this is Kalinovsky farm. Have some rest and go in that direction. Then cross the Manychsky canal...'

The soldiers fell asleep without listening to the end. I walked on alone. I was thinking about sergeants Nikolayev and Kladko again. Their first combat sortie was also their last. They followed me up to the target, did not fall a metre behind. Nikolayev perished before my eyes. Kladko stayed in formation until the end in spite of the pursuing fighters, and hit the bridge if not with bombs, than perhaps with his plane... The remnants of Misarov's battalion defended the bridge near Lisichansk to the last, and then swam across the Don. I thought about the two soldiers sleeping under a haystack... I was sure they would wake up, join some unit, and entrench themselves again at a new front. We just needed some time to summon up our strength.

I was walking southwards trying to reach Kagalnitskaya and my regiment as soon as possible. A group of Ils flew at a distance heading to the Don. I thought that it was probably guys from my regiment.

On a dusty country road I overtook a cart. A soldier was sitting inside. The nag was hardly moving, but the coachman offered me a lift. By that time I was totally exhausted, so I sat down near the soldier. 'Where are you going?' I asked.

'I am bringing shells for the battery.'

'Don't you have any cars?'

'We've left them on that side of the river.'

'Your horse is hardly breathing.'

'Well, we have no fodder. The grass is burnt, it's practically impossible to get hay,' the soldier tried to explain.

We were passing a barn. I said to the soldier: 'Take a bucket and go. There is fodder quite near.'

While he was away, I tried to drive away the flies that swarmed around the horse. Its withers were rubbed sore and tarred. It stood lifelessly ignoring the flies, its lower lip drooping... How many times had it been to the remote battery without food and rest? A job might know no limit, but there was limit to endurance. The sorrel would collapse in harness, and no force would be able to raise it. The same went for the soldiers that were sleeping like the dead under a haystack before a new fight.

My companion came back with an empty bucket. 'The watchman wouldn't give me any grain. He said he was not allowed to squander the reserves of the *kolkhoz*.* He threatened me with a rifle.'

I grabbed the bucket and ran to the barn myself. I had to threaten to the watchman with my pistol. As I was going back to the cart with a bucket of grain I heard him saying: 'Wish I'd fired a shot. You'd remember me!' Well, the old man was also defending his position.

I was running with my last bit of strength to the end of the village. A U-2 was going to land there. I arrived the last moment: the pilot was already about to take off. He was heading to Salsk. He had brought spare parts for a fighter which was concealed in a shed. His rear cockpit was empty, so he took me in. 'Look back carefully! The Messers give us no rest. If you notice any − tap me on the shoulder. We'll dive and run in different directions. Got it?'

'Got it...'

I only got to Kagalnitskaya on the evening of the second day. Major Kholobaev was striding towards me from the starting line. I wanted to report on arrival, but he wouldn't not listen. Instead he embraced me, clapped me on my back for a long time, and said: 'You will be in command of the third squadron.'

'What about Mospanov?' I asked alarmed. Mospanov was my squadron leader.

'We buried him yesterday. Messers shot him down above the airfield.'

*A collective farm.

After supper pilots and mechanics gathered near a sweet-scented haystack. I told them about my adventures. Some people were unknown to me: graduates from a flying school had arrived only yesterday from Uralsk. Among them were Ivan Ostapenko, Georgy Bondarenko, Victor Korsunsky, Vasily Bazhenov, Ivan Dudnick, Grigory Snopko… They laughed with the rest, when I told everybody about my taking shelter in a hen house, persuading the silly birds: 'Hens, please, hush, hush…'

Junior Sergeant Mikhail Talykov was lying closest to me. He had arrived in the regiment not long ago. I once had to tell him off for his recklessness and selfishness during a flight. He was my wingman at that time. Now he was appointed my second-in-command. In the war people got promoted quickly. But the war was merciless to them.

I lay flat on my back on the hay. The North Star winked to me happily from the sky. Tomorrow we would get a new mission. 'Not a step back!'

10

A RECKLESS WINGMAN

A leader at the front was worth his weight in gold. He flew the leading aircraft. He was the most experienced pilot in the group. If there were leaders in the regiment, then a unit was considered efficient. A leader could 'drag on his tail' as many young and inexperienced pilots as he wanted. Our young pilots were not only inexperienced but also half-educated, because they had taken a quick war-time training course. The first thing we had to do was to fatten them up a bit after the half-starving on the rations they'd had in the rear. Then we checked their pilot technique, and conducted the practice flights. Only then did we allow them to follow the leader in their first combat flight.

For young pilots a leader was a guide during the flight, and the best adviser on the ground. He could quickly assemble the planes, could lead the group along the agreed route, knew how to dodge ground fire and fighters, could spot the target between the trenches and shell-holes and could adapt the tactics of the attack to the situation. But before becoming a leader and grasping all the details, one had to spend much time following a more experienced pilot, and survive. If a leader was shot down, a military operation was likely to fail.

Wingmen did not have a good time either: they had to keep the formation. That was not an easy task. Other wingmen would often dash about, either diving or climbing above the formation. You had to keep a constant eye on your neighbours. There was practically no time left after this to look at the instrument panel, to see the bursts from the anti-aircraft guns, or notice the approaching Messerschmitts. A wingman did not have time to navigate and usually he did not know where he was flying. If a leader was shot down, and none of his wingmen were experienced enough... well, I've already described what could happen then.

But wingmen were all different. Once I got annoyed with my wingman during an operational flight. The six of us were attacking the enemy near Lisichansk. Beneath us German tanks were crawling along the bare steppe. One of the tanks was twirling round and giving out smoke. Behind the tanks I could see occasional files of German soldiers. Our troops must have pressed them from the front line. We arrived just in time! We reformed in line and dived one by one. We swept along the line of the German tanks, and opened the containers just above the ground. A fiery rain of burning phosphorus poured from the aircraft. Clouds of white smoke concealed the scene. We climbed again. The sky was pale, as if it had faded in the heat. Plumes of smoke appeared constantly near our planes: the anti-aircraft guns were shooting. But we did not pay attention. We formed a circle and began the attack. At the same time a dozen German Junkers-87s were circling not far away. We called the German dive-bombers *lapotnicks*,★ because their wheels stuck out from under the fuselage. One by one they banked and dived almost plumb inside the cloud of black smoke above the railway station at Jama. Messerschmitts were patrolling in couples above the Junkers looking for victims. We had come without escorts, and were perfect prey for them.

We carried out several attacks, and ammunition was running out. At that moment I noticed four enemy fighters approaching us. They must have been directed by radio. I ordered retreat, and turned to the front line. The wingmen followed me. To my amazement one of them suddenly moved away, and began diving again. What recklessness! We were forced to circle near the front line and wait for him just in sight of the Germans. He was going to be a certain prey for the fighters, but fortunately everything turned out all right. The fighters did not notice the Shturmovik. It rejoined the formation and we headed to the airfield.

We landed and I had to tell off Junior Lieutenant Mikhail Talykov for his wilfulness. He was a regular military pilot (before the war he had graduated from an air school), but he did not get chance to take part in military operations before the summer of 1942. A twenty-year-old guy was standing before me frowning and pursing his lips.

★ From the Russian *lapot,* a peasant shoe made of bast (lime-bark fibre).

Talykov had a broad face and a massive stubborn chin. He was watching the toes of his calfskin boots.

'Did you hear my order to retreat?' I asked him and was ready to hear all kinds of excuses. The usual excuses were that the transmitter was not tuned right, and the person did not notice, when the rest of the group left the target. But Talykov answered so unexpectedly, that I was taken aback.

'I heard...' he said casually, and glanced at me with his grey eyes.

'Why did not you reform immediately then?'

'My cannons and machine-guns were still firing!' he said rapidly, obviously sure of himself. His answer meant that it was my mistake to leave the target so early without letting Talykov use his ammunition up. The fact that we must save some shells for a possible scrap with the fighters meant nothing to him!

Still excited after the operational flight I shouted at him: 'Go!'

He saluted, turned sharply, holding his map-case, and went out stepping firmly.

I watched him for a long time. His calfskin boots were etched on my memory. Talykov was marching through the dried grass, raising dust. I tried to calm down: 'It's OK, he will calm down after the anti-aircraft guns and Messerschmitts deal with him. We all try to show off at first.'

I recalled my own first operational flight with Junior Lieutenant Ivan Bobrov as the leader. I made a fool of myself twice in the same flight. Immediately after taking off, still above the airfield, I formed up so close to the leader that he must have lost his breath on seeing me. I had happened to fly in close formation on a UT-1 during a fly-past before the war. At the front I learned that this was just for show. During an operational flight close formation was absolutely unsuitable, as it prevented manoeuvre. I knew that, but I still pressed near Bobrov. What was I doing that for? Just to make all the rest think: 'The one at the right was not born yesterday!' Later, as we were assaulting a motorcade, I made an unnecessary attack just to show off in front of the leader.

My conversation with Talykov took place at the beginning of June, 1942, a few days before an unexpected turn of events. We observed at first days the successful attack by our troops to the south of Kharkov, but then the group was surrounded, and an avalanche of German tanks and cars poured across the Donets Basin to the east. We were forced to change airfield very often: Pogoreloje, Shakhty, Kagalnitskaya... In five days we were already behind the Don, to the south of Rostov. I had little chance of seeing Talykov in those days: he had already become a leader, and we did not fly together.

Once Talykov entered our canteen together with several other pilots. Among them were some freshmen, who had just joined the regiment: Grigory Knyazhev, Nikolai Pismichenko and Victor Olenin. On that day Talykov had led them into their first sortie – he had become their 'godfather'. Talykov was impulsive as usual. He pulled his cap off, and flopped down on the bench. He seemed to be angry with somebody. His eyes were red from tiredness. He had made three operational flights that day – his group attacked the troops that tried to make a forced crossing of the Severniy Donets near Belaya Kalitva. Talykov dealt with his meal in silence, but when vodka got into his head, he began a lively conversation with his neighbours. He struck the table with his fist, and tried to make a point to the young wingmen. After supper he carried on in the dormitory: 'The more attacks you make, the more tanks and cars are lost by the Fritzes!' he tried to persuade somebody.

'Still fussing over his "theory".' I thought. 'Just like after our flight to Lisichansk.' But still it was a pleasure to see Talykov so self-confident and stubborn. He was now experienced enough, and had faced difficult situations, but that did not break him. He was still sure of himself and was severe in fighting. Talykov often came back without a single shell. His spirits boiled in him, but I was afraid that his hot temper would kill him in the end.

The advanced detachments of the enemy were already approaching Kagalnitskaya. On 29 July 1942 we were forced to shift to an airfield in the Salsk steppes. The airfield was bordered by a green fence of trees, but the shadow was not enough to protect us from heat. The sun was burning mercilessly, the hot air was still. Our light suits stuck to our bodies. The only cool place was the dug-out of the regiment's staff operational group. But it was impossible to stay there for long: dry soil poured from the ceiling in many places and got behind one's collar – and the place was full of mice. Major Gudimenko moved his folding table from one place to another, and blew angrily on the map, which was constantly getting covered with sand.

The mechanics found an iron tank somewhere and filled it with water. Back from an operational flight the pilots first of all pulled off their suits, submerged into the warm 'font' and only then hurried to report. That was the order established by the regiment commander Kholobaev.

When the drinking water was finished we quenched our thirst with warm stripy watermelons. We learned to smash them with our hands. The mechanics got them from deserted plantations.

From that airfield we flew to the north to attack the enemy columns behind the Manychsky canal. We also observed the enemy columns to the east from our airfield. It was not clear where we had to shift next. We had no communication with the headquarters of the 4th Air Army.

We received an order to attack an enemy column, which was moving along the road from Orlovka to Nesmejanovka between the Don and the Manychsky canal. By that time there were only six Shturmoviks left in the regiment. Two fighters from the regiment of Ibraghim Dzusov were going to escort us. There were only the very best pilots in that regiment, including Alexander Pokryshkin.*

We took off. I was flying ahead with my wingman Kudinov. To my right flew Mikhail Talykov with his wingman, to the left – Vasily Shamshurin with his wingman. We climbed right after taking off – thus we would spot the enemy column from afar. Behind the Manychsky canal we noticed a line of dust, which looked like a smoke screen. It was the road from Semikarakorskaya to Nesmejanovka. I knew those places well; it was not my first flight there. It was the place where my plane had been brought down five days ago, when I had had to walk to my regiment with the soldiers from Misarov's battalion.

We flew up to the road at a height of 600 metres, and could already see tanks, automobiles and armoured troop carriers. The leading automobiles stopped. The soldiers began to jump out and hide in the roadside ditches. The anti-aircraft guns were already firing at us… I made an additional turn in order to dive along the column, starting from the head. One by one we dived and dropped bombs in train.

---

* Pokryshkin was a three-times Hero of the Soviet Union, an ace with the second largest number of victories in the air among the Soviet Air Force (59).

Then we levelled out, turned left, and flew in a line along an arc in order to form a circle and attack. We could see the bursts from our bombs above the column. Now we hit from the side. I lowered the nose of the plane and targeted a lorry, aiming at its side. The missiles exploded just near the lorry. I fired a long burst from four guns. The lorry caught fire. It felt good! I rushed really low, and climbed again for a new attack. As I was enclosing the circle I looked up. There were six fighters above us already: two Yaks and four Messerschmitts. It was going to be a mess. Our 'hawks'* would have a hard time. We must also be on the alert. I was flying along the circle, and suddenly saw a Messer just ahead of me. It squeezed impudently into our circle and was aiming at the Shturmovik ahead of it. Hurriedly I pulled the trigger. Tracer bullets raced past the fighter. It climbed abruptly, but immediately started to dive at the next plane – Shamshurin's. 'Manoeuvre!' I shouted to him over the radio, but Shamshurin did not seem to hear me. The German plane was rapidly approaching the Shturmovik. A second – and it would shoot it down! I directed my plane inside the circle and pulled both triggers without even aiming properly. Tracer bullets flashed behind the Shturmovik. The fuselage of the fighter flared up. The plane was rapidly losing height. A smoking trail followed it. It was the first time I ever had to fire at a fighter, and how lucky I was! Meanwhile Shamshurin was flying on. I had to attack one more time, and then we could go home.

As I dived at the column I noticed the smoking lines coming after me from the ground. An Oerlikon was firing. I wished I could turn and fire a couple of volleys at it, but I noticed it too late. The anti-aircraft gun was already under my wing. I hoped that somebody behind me would notice and fire at it. I took aim at an armoured troop carrier, held my breath and was ready to pull the trigger, when... Bang! Something hit the engine. It stopped immediately, and my heart seemed to stop as well. Should I bail out? The altitude was too low, and there was only the enemy column below. All I could do was to fly across the road and land there. I glided over the column. The ground was approaching. 'Should I release the landing gear?' I thought. That was a big risk, but I had managed to survive in the same situation near Nyrkovo when I drove into the enemy's first

---

*Yakovlevs were Russian fighters; 'hawk' was a nickname for them.

trench. Perhaps I would be lucky again? The worst thing would be if I got into a ditch and turned over. If even I survived, the Germans would fish me out like a bird from a cage. But if I landed successfully, I could drive as far as possible from the column.

All those thoughts flashed in my mind in a second. I pushed the stick, and the wheels came out. The plane was already bouncing along the knolls. I set one hand against the instrument panel: thus I hoped I wouldn't bump my head and lose consciousness. The run was successful. I jumped out of the cockpit and saw my wingmen racing over me. They were heading to the airfield. They had surely heard my last command: 'Finish the attack.' 'Has none of them noticed me?' I thought bitterly. But then I thought that they could not help me anyway.

I looked around. I was not more than a kilometre away from the column. I could see the results of our 'work': a dozen cars and tanks were burning on the road. We hadn't wasted our time... Now my plane was standing in the bare steppe in full view of the enemy. German soldiers were running towards me from the road. I had no way to escape. There was neither a bush nor a mound around. The worst thing would be to get wounded. They would pick me up, and then cut five-pointed stars on my back. I thought it better to shoot myself at the last moment. Right now I had to blow up my aircraft, so that they would not get it.

I could hear the sub-machine guns firing. I threw off the parachute, hurled it under the petrol tap, and pulled the red ring. The parachute pack swept open. A bundle of white silk swelled out. The tap was blocked by a steel pin. I tried to pull it out. My hands were bleeding, and the tap would not turn. I punched, and finally a stream of petrol gushed forth. Now I only had to light a match. I felt in one pocket, in another one – there were no matches! I had left them by Talykov, when he asked me for a light before the flight! I thought about the flare gun. It was always charged. I jumped on the centre-section, grasped the gun and jumped down. I stretched out my hand, turned round so my face would not get burned, and fired. It blazed. I jumped aside, and fell face down on the ground. That was the end!

I took my pistol out of the holster and heard a low rumbling of some aircraft. Rather indifferently I looked at the road. The line of fascist soldiers was closer, but suddenly they all lay down, as if on

113

command. I heard the crackle of gun-fire, and in the next moment two fighters came out of a dive above the road. It was our Yaks! I was not alone! They zoomed and were ready to attack again. They were obviously trying to help me. I realised that I should seize the opportunity and run as far as possible from that place.

I was ready to run, when I noticed a German armoured car dashing towards me. I also noticed a Shturmovik hedgehopping towards me from the column. I stood up at full height. I wanted the pilot to see me, and was going to wave him farewell. He was flying at an altitude of ten metres. As he came closer I could see his helmet, his goggles, and his face, which was turned to me... I began to wave with my hands, and suddenly saw a big white '9' on the fuselage. It was Talykov! As usual he was the last to leave the target. The hothead... I waved to him, and he slightly swayed the plane from one wing to the other. He had noticed me! Or was it just an illusion?

Suddenly the plane zoomed and banked left. I thought that Talykov wanted to remember the place where I had landed and then report to the regiment commander. But then I saw the landing gear coming out. Was he going to land? I watched him in astonishment. The plane raced above the column and glided. I could even see the flaps lowering under the wings. Meanwhile the Germans came to their senses. The enemy column bristled with fire. A rain of tracer bullets was dashing towards the plane. The Shturmovik was landing inside a curtain of fire. It was a terrible sight. Luckily one could not see that inside the plane.

Talykov managed to escape by some miracle. Sub-machine guns kept firing. I fell down again and watched the risky landing. I had landed successfully, but what if Talykov got into a trench and damaged the landing gear? Would it be two pistols set against two temples? Talykov was already flying just above the ground. Suddenly the wheels knocked against a bump. The plane jerked, the engine roared. I thought Talykov would change his mind, but in the next moment the plane made a three-point landing and taxied on the ground.

The plane stopped a hundred metres in front of me. Talykov jumped out on the wing, waved to me, and leaned behind the cockpit. I rushed to the plane. A thought came to my head: 'How could I fit into the cockpit of a single-seat plane?' Meanwhile Talykov opened the inspection hatch in the fuselage. One of us could squeeze into it. 'Get in,' shouted Talykov pointing at the cockpit. He was going to dive inside the fuselage.

I felt exhausted after the run, so I told him: 'Take off yourself! Turn round facing the column, and go along your tracks on the grass.'

Talykov nodded and climbed into the cockpit. I got inside the fuselage. Before hiding my head I saw the armoured car approaching us, shooting. The engine started, the plane turned round and taxied. I prayed that Misha could keep on course. What if the Fritzes hit a tyre? Than we will spin on a rim and that's it - no more flying for us. We were speeding up. For the last time the plane jerked and hanged in the air. We took off!

The fuselage was shaking under me. Through the open cover I could see the tracer bullets flashing past. I huddled up. I was not sitting in an armoured cockpit. Each bullet could pierce the hatch through. I consoled myself that we were moving away from the column heading to the airfield. If Messerschmitts did not attack, we'd be fine.

I was pressed against the floor – Talykov was making a sharp turn. In the next moment I was lifted – the plane was diving. I heard the guns shooting. Talykov opened fire. Was it Messers? That was the worst that could happen in my position. Talykov was protected by the armour, and I was lying as if in a matchboard coffin. Michail could hold out until the airfield in a plane riddled with holes, but he would be carrying a pile of bones in the fuselage.

I felt acceleration again, and realised that Talykov was attacking something. I became angry: while he was hovering about, Messerschmitts might spot us. Had he forgotten about me? I wished I could shout at him, but he would not hear. I could not tap him on the shoulder either, as we were separated by a solid armoured plate. Meanwhile Talykov was diving again.

I grabbed the metal pipe which connected the control column with the elevator, and began to shake it as hard as I could. The plane, and of course the control lever in Talykov's hands, began to jerk. My actions had effect: Talykov levelled the plane out.

The engine was running smoothly. I peeped out carefully and looked down. Behind the aircraft the enemy column was burning in many places. My own plane was smoking a bit further on, and next to it the German armoured car was burning! So that was Talykov's aim!

115

I looked up in the cloudless sky. A pair of Yaks was guiding us from above.

Six planes took part in the operation, and only four of them returned. The pilots reported: 'The leader was shot down...'

'And where is Talykov?' asked the commander.

Everyone shrugged his shoulders. He did not return, which meant that he was also shot down. They were going to write in the death reports: 'On 29 July 1942 during the attack on the enemy column in the district of...'

But in fifteen minutes number 9 landed. The engine stopped, and everything fell silent. I heard Kholobaev's strict voice: 'Talykov! Why have you fallen behind the group again?'

'I had to land...'

'Where did you have to land?!'

'In the target area...'

There were no more questions: I emerged from the fuselage hatch. Talykov helped me to get out, and we hugged. Then we were lifted up by dozens of hands. I could see Talykov's boots rising to the tops of trees.

At night a storm raged. The sky blazed with blue lightning. Pilots gathered in the dug-out lit by a dim oil-lamp. Major Gudimenko bent over his folding table. He was filling in an award paper on Talykov. Mice were rustling; sand was pouring from the ceiling. Chief communications officer Nudzhenko ran up beaming. 'We've established connection with the headquarters of the 4th Air Army! They named the new airfield. The ground echelon can move.'

The rest had to wait until dawn. We could neither take off nor land at night. We packed the transmitter, and a small column drove eastwards. In the middle of the night somebody heard the roar of engines and the clanging of tank tracks. We sent mechanics to have a look. It appeared that a column of German tanks was moving eastwards a kilometre from the airfield. We turned the noses of the Shturmoviks towards the forest, and placed the ammunition boxes under the tails, so that the guns could shoot at the ground targets. We had to spend the rest of the night sitting in the cockpits.

We took off at dawn carrying our mechanics in fuselage hatches. Recalling my last flight I felt really sorry for my passenger – mechanical engineer Sergej Temnov.

11

THE CROSSING

The Southern Front units were forced to move from the Don to the foothills of the Caucasus. We settled at the airfield at Novoselitskoye to the east from Stavropol. There were only two aircraft left in our regiment: numbers 8 and 9. Number 9 and its pilot were celebrities. On 29 July Mikhail Talykov had managed to get me away inside the fuselage under the Germans' very noses. Number 8 was mine. All the 'horseless' pilots and mechanics were sent to the assembly point at Achaluki not far from Mineralnye Vody.

It was a hot midday. Misha and I had just returned from a sortie. After reporting on what we had seen, we hurried to get some rest in the shade. We took off our belts with their heavy pistols, unbuttoned the collars of our wet blouses, and fell flat on our backs. There was not a cloud in the sky. We enjoyed the quiet moment. Only at the front could you learn the real value of such quiet minutes. When we had some free time between operational flights we tried not to think about the war. I did not want to guess how much longer Talykov and I were going to fly or which of our planes would be shot down first.

But it was impossible to suppress such thoughts. I remembered what I had just seen during the sortie. As far as one could see all the roads from Salsk to Stavropol were wrapped in smoke. The enemy was advancing. And the road from Stavropol to Nevinnomyssk was crowded with carts and lorries jammed with packs, bundles, and other stuff. A stream of refugees was moving along the road. I could see many children. Most people were carrying branches over their heads. The carts and lorries were also covered with branches. Looking at the sky and the rustling leaves I thought how defenceless those people were. The Germans were already approaching my native land.

Misha must have had the same thoughts in his mind. He asked

117

suddenly: 'Do they believe they can camouflage themselves from Messerschmitts with those branches?'

Well, I suppose they did. They were following the soldiers' example.

Somebody brought a box, turned it upside down, and made a table for us. A girl from the aerodrome service battalion brought two bowls full of hot rich borsch. We supped a couple of times – we couldn't eat. The girl was already putting chicken before us. As the only two pilots in the regiment we got enough food. But the meal was interrupted by a messenger: 'To the commander! Urgently!'

We dropped our spoons, grasped the belts and map-cases, and hurried to the dug-out. The regiment commander was already coming towards us himself. He was angry for some reason, and did not start speaking at first. He looked at both of us intently, as if it was the first time he had seen us, and said quietly: 'Our troops have blown up the bridge over the Kuban near the village of Prochnookopskaya to the north of Armavir. The enemy has managed to restore it. Budenniy himself has ordered to use air-power and stop the enemy tanks. This task...' Kholobaev made a pause, and then raised his voice 'this task is given to our regiment!...' He said it as if there were not only the two of us, but at least a rank of pilots facing him. 'Six fighters will cover you. You must destroy the bridge at any price!' He made a gesture, as if he had a sabre in his hand.

As we took out maps and measuring equipment, thoughts were flashing through my head: 'How on earth can two Shturmoviks destroy a bridge? This is not a pontoon bridge, which can be damaged by an air-blast. Here only a direct hit can help. This task can be completed by no less than a squadron. Perhaps the person who gave this mission to Kholobaev does not know that there are only two pilots left in our regiment? Or maybe he does, but the situation does not leave any choice. We have to fight to the last plane, the last tank, and the last soldier. There are no impossible missions now... You must carry out your mission, or die. "Not a step back!" '

'Go!'

Talykov strode to his plane, which had many patches on its wings. He looked angry. He must have been offended by the harsh words of the commander. We taxied out to the take-off. Kholobaev was already there. Without waiting for the starter's signal, he pulled off his cap, and waved with it: 'Clear off!'

We were flying very low above the wheat fields. As far as one could see there was nothing except the quiet yellow sea. Red flames were moving along the sea in many places, leaving black tracks behind them. People must have set the crops on fire so that the enemy could not use them. From time to time I spotted the islands of villages and ponds. Something that looked like white clouds was drifting along the blue surface of the ponds. The dark shadow of the plane would glide across those clouds, and flocks of snow-white ducks and geese would scatter in every direction in panic. Blessed Kuban! The war had been here already.

A village was burning far ahead, as if a steamer was releasing smoke from its funnels. There we must turn to Prochnookopskaya. We turned left and began to climb. I could already see the river, and a narrow strip across it: the bridge. We were still ascending on the over-loaded Ils, and a black cloud of defensive fire was already hanging in the air before us. The closer we were to the bridge, the more bursts surrounded us. Inside my helmet I could hear the abrupt commands of our fighters: they were dealing with Messerschmitts. We were already on the battle course, we could not manoeuvre. I only hoped that the Germans did not shoot us down before we began to dive... The bridge was approaching very slowly, as if we had slowed down.

It's time! The plane banked, and lowered its nose. The river bank and the target glided across the glass. The air whizzed, the plane was shaking. The bridge was approaching rapidly. There was only one thought in my head: 'To hit, to hit, to hit!'

I pushed the button, releasing the bombs, and at the same moment heard a blow, as if a balloon had burst by my ear. The plane jerked. I levelled out, turned, and shot a quick glance back. There were splashes of water, and Talykov's aircraft making a steep turn. Inside the helmet I heard a fighter's hoarse voice, and the bitter words: 'You missed.'

We were flying back. My plane had a hole in its left wing. That was the reason the plane jerked when I released the bombs – an anti-aircraft round hit me. The engine was working all right. Talykov was flying to my right, wing to wing, but my heart was heavy. Our mission failed.

On that warm August night I was lying next to Talykov on the hay, covered with a canvas bag. Guns were firing at a distance. A fascist reconnaissance aircraft flew past, howling monotonously. A blue ray of a searchlight stopped vertically in the sky, as if listening to something. Then it moved idly, swallowing the stars. Somewhere close hammers were knocking: our mechanics Temnov and Loginov were patching up our planes. Talykov had been hit in the tail.

'I wonder, where are the rest now?' said Talykov. The rest were our 'horseless' pilots and girls who had joined our regiment as armourers before we began to retreat from Donbass. And also the eight sergeants, the graduates of Voroshilovgrad flying school, who had joined us near Rostov. Where were they? We had not enough cars to transport them from one place to another. So they had left on foot straightaway from Kagalnitskaya. The commander of the second squadron, Major Hushper, who was also a freshman in the regiment, led the group. Their destination was the village of Achaluki. We had not heard from them for fifteen days now. Misha asked about 'the rest', but I knew, he was thinking about the grey-eyed girl, Kseniya. I felt pretty sure that she was also thinking now about her 'knight' as she walked along some dusty road. I had noticed her many times washing his undercollars and handkerchiefs. Oh, those girls…

They had joined our regiment in June 1942. There had been a telephone call from the division headquarters: 'Send someone to the assembly point. He can choose sixteen girls for the regiment.'

Kozhuhovsky thought that he misheard, and asked to repeat: 'Did you say "girls"?'

'Yes, girls…'

'What are we going to do with them?'

'They will become armourers.'

The chief of staff was nervous. It was unprecedented! Before that we only met female typists or communication officers in the headquarters. To make a woman a mechanic, or an armourer – that was something new for the air force. How could they raise 100 kilogram bombs, or dismantle, clean and install guns that weighed 70 kilos?

Kozhuhovsky sent Jakov Kvaktun, commander of the third squadron, to the assembly point. 'Choose stout ones – understand!

Kvaktun was ready to follow the chief of staff's instructions, but failed. He began to pick the tallest girls, but the short ones followed them without any command. All the girls from Astrakhan firmly declared: 'We will all go to the same regiment. We will not part!'

The sixteenth girl was Tosya Tabachnaya. She was as tiny as

Thumbelina. Kvaktun was not going to take her, but the other fifteen girls started rattling like magpies. Kvaktun saw bitter tears in Tosya's eyes and gave in.

All the pilots and mechanics cast quick glances at the lorry in which the girls arrived. They were wearing calfskin shoes, knee-length skirts and military blouses. The girls unloaded their baggage and disappeared inside a barn, which had been prepared. Our 'professor', Maxim Ivanovich Shum, couldn't help noting: 'Nice figures.'

Kozhuhovsky went inside the barn. Sergeant Shergin was already there. He had brought a large pot of millet porridge, put it on the floor in the middle of the barn, and ordered: 'Come on, help yourselves!'

He got his spoon out of his bootleg, and began to eat. The girls looked embarrassed. Kozhuhovsky looked at the scene, and could not restrain himself: 'A kindergarten...'

He went out. Later he reported to the regiment commander: 'With such waists... they won't be able... they won't be able to work.'

But it appeared that our chief of staff drew the wrong conclusions. The members of the 'kindergarten' not only managed to perform their duties, but also greatly raised the spirits of the aircrew. Even Boris Evdokimovich Ryabov noticed that. Men's vigilance during sentry duty increased rapidly. If girls were sent on sentinel duty, there were always plenty of volunteers ready to join them, so the level of vigilance doubled, while the number of violations rapidly decreased.

One of the girls, Chernova, was once standing sentinel. She noticed a trespasser crawling towards her. Instead of crying 'Halt! Who is it?' and shooting in the air, Chernova fired a shot without any warning. Fortunately there was no victim, because what she thought to be a trespasser turned out to be tumbleweed. A funny story once happened to the smallest armourer, Tosya Tabachnaya (everybody called her 'our Tabachok'*). A guard commander did not find her near the plane, when he was relieving the guard. 'Could she have deserted?' The commander cried: 'Sentinel!'

'What do you need?' came a thin voice from somewhere.

'Where are you, Tabachnaya?'

'I'm here,' she answered and crawled out from under the plane hood on the warm engine.

---

* *Tabachok* is a diminutive form of *tabak* – tobacco.

'Why did you go there?'

'It's warm, and there are no mice. I'm very afraid of mice...'

Tosya Tabachnaya could not master the rules of subordination at first. Once she was on duty in the headquarters. The regiment commander came up to her, but instead of saluting she was just staring at him. The commander shook hands with her, and identified himself: 'I am Kostya Kholobaev...'

'You are lying, you are not Kostya...'

'And who am I, in your opinion?'

'You are the regiment commander...'

Such things happened, but only in the beginning...

The girls' arrival greatly influenced the pilots' appearance. And not just the pilots! Our 'dark force' (technicians and mechanics) looked different now. Everybody was wearing white undercollars now, and our bed-sheets were quickly diminishing. The amount of quilted jackets also decreased. Evil tongues blamed our girls for getting the wadding out of the jackets. My squadron leader Yasha Kvaktun even noted philosophically: 'This is how quantity changes into quality.' One of the girls, Klava Kalmykova, was a tailor. She made excellent breeches for me from a trophy coat. Many men in the regiment looked jealously at them.

The Komsorg Nina Alekseeva, the most timid girl, had a beautiful lyrical soprano voice. Her performance of *'V zemlyanke'* was, in our opinion, far better than that of Klavdia Shulzhenko, a well-known Soviet singer whom we had had an opportunity to listen to in Timashevskaya village. And the grey eyes of Kseniya Emelianova!.. But I was not going to prevent Misha Talykov from dreaming about them. He was now tossing and turning next to me on the hay...

'Where are the rest now?'

A scarlet strip of sky appeared on the horizon. Soon we were to fly in that direction carrying our mechanics in the fuselages. I could hear Misha breathing regularly. I also fell asleep.

On the next day Kholobaev told us: 'The mission is the same. The enemy is conveying tanks to the other side and advancing towards Maikop and Tuapse. The command demands that the bridge must be destroyed!' He thumped the table with his fist, puffed out and concluded: 'To put it plainly, the bridge weighs on your conscience... If you miss now, you will have to fly again and again... You will be provided with extra cover – twelve fighters will guard you. There will also be a controller with a camera; he will record the results. While they are getting ready, you may go and think it over.'

We went to our tree. Misha sat on the ground, placed his elbows on his knees, propped his cheekbones up on his fists, and stared at the map-case before him. I also felt uneasy. 'The bridge weighs on your conscience...' Was it a reproach for our sortie yesterday? 'You will have to fly again...' If only there would be anyone left to fly...

'Which way shall we go?' I asked Talykov, meaning the route.

'It doesn't matter which way we go. We must destroy it.' He turned his head abruptly and looked me in the eyes: 'If we miss this time, I will turn back and crash into it with my plane...'

It felt like a blow in the breast. Talykov meant what he was saying. He was able to do that; he had proved his determination on 29 July near Nesmejanovka... What could I say? If I tried to dissuade him, he would only grow more stubborn, and would only become more firmly set on his decision. And how would I look in such situation? The wingman was ready to do everything, and the leader was concerned for his own skin. I pretended not to hear what Misha had said, and concentrated on the task. 'There is always time to die... But is there a chance to outwit the enemy? What can we do to remain unnoticed? The elementary truth of the tactics says: never repeat what you've already done... What if we approach the bridge from the other side?' And then it dawned upon me: if we did that, the sun would be behind us! And if we kept descending exactly on the line between the sun and the target, the blinding sun would prevent the anti-aircraft gunners from noticing us. The sun was already high in the sky, but we could gain more altitude and begin to descend in advance. Yesterday we could not suppress the anti-aircraft fire, because we were not high enough, but now it could be different!

'I'll fly ahead and will shoot at the farthest side of the river, and you stay behind and shoot at the opposite side. We'll suppress the anti-aircraft guns, and aim at the bridge.' I said.

Talykov also had an idea: 'We will drop bombs from the altitude of 200 metres or even lower. Yes, it will shake a bit from the air-blast, perhaps some splinters will hit the planes, but we will destroy the target...'

123

And so we took off, followed by four fighters from behind and four fighters high above. They were our guards. The other 'hawks' raced past us and disappeared in the sun. Their task was to clear a path through the enemy fighters, or engage them in a fight until we came. We made a big detour towards Kurgannaya village, and left Armavir at our side. The crops were burning there already, and German tanks were crawling through every village. They had advanced considerably since yesterday. We started to climb a way off Prochnookopskaya, so when we turned and headed for the target, the sun was right behind the plane's tail. It was not yet time to descend, when something flashed ahead of us. A twin-fuselage reconnaissance aircraft, a Fokke-Wulf 189, raced past us. I looked at our fighters, expecting them to start the hunt, but fortunately they did not pay attention to it. The guys knew their mission was to guard us, and flew in complete silence. None of them yielded to temptation to increase his military score and get a 1,500-rouble bonus.

The bridge was slowly approaching. Enemy troops could be seen on both sides of the river. We glided smoothly, aiming at the target. The anti-aircraft guns kept silent. Well... it's time! I launched the missiles to the farthest side. Cannons and machine-guns began to fire, but the bridge was already in my sights. I put my finger on the bomb-releasing button, and checked the altitude. It read four hundred. I was ready to release the bombs, but remembered: 'Drop lower!' I waited for several more seconds, pressed the button, and felt a heavy strike from beneath. It felt like I was sitting not on the parachute, but on a bare board, and somebody had struck it with a sledgehammer. My plane was dashing towards the steppe riverbank. I zoomed. Tanks and cars raced below the plane. I heard some noise in my helmet, and the familiar hoarse voice said: 'Well done, humpback,★ you hit it right!'

'Roger... roger...' I answered calmly, though I felt like screaming with happiness.

Behind me number 9 banked from right to left making a graceful S-turn. I knew how glad Talykov was and appreciated it. The engine was working smoothly... We were going home.

★ 'Humpback' was a nickname for the Shturmovik Il-2 at the Russian front.

12

THE CAUCASUS

We moved from Novoselitskoye to the Kurskaya airfield, and were now to the east of Mineralnye Vody. There were still only two planes in the regiment: numbers 8 and 9. After the bombing of Prochnookopskaya I made ten sorties together with Misha.

It was 8 August 1942, and the heat was unbearable. The armoured parts of the Shturmoviks were red-hot. Each time I taxied to the start the water in the cooling system started to boil, and the engine was smoking. The planes, loaded with bombs, could only take off at the very edge of the airfield.

We used to fly wearing nothing but underwear and light flying suits, but it still felt like we were sitting in a tank, even if the window was open. When we came back from a flight we taxied to the dispersal area near the forest. Kholobaev was already there, holding a water hose. 'Come on, guys, get undressed! Quickly!'

We pulled off the suits, and allowed the squirts of water to beat on our backs, heads and bellies, washing away the tiredness and tension. We laughed and could really forget for several minutes what we had just gone through during the flight. After that we reported on the mission accomplished. Our staff 'office' was situated quite near the dispersal area. The head of staff's deputy, Major Gudimenko, had made a table and some chairs from shell-boxes, and used to sit there with a map and other documents. After we reported on what we had managed to set on fire, or hurt, and how many Fritzes we had killed, there came time for the customary question: 'What did you see?'

That was an endless procedure. Vasilij Tarasovich marked all our military information on the map, compared it with the results of the previous sortie, and took notes in the military operations register. And we knew that while he was keeping us busy with that stuff, four mechanics were again loading our planes with bombs, missiles, shells and cartridges. As soon as they were ready, the commander would set a new military task for us. We had already made two flights on that day, and were exhausted. We dreamed of lying in the shadow under the plane's wing, and relaxing a bit.

'What did you see on the road?' Gudimenko was asking us in a polite, official tone.

'Tanks, cars, artillery...' I was answering casually. 'There is a horde...'

He wouldn't leave me alone, though he knew everything from my previous report. 'Where is the head of the column?'

'Approaching Mineralnye Vody...'

'Will you please show it more precisely,' he gave me a sharp-cut blue pencil, which we used to mark the enemy position on the map. I stuck the pencil into the spot where we had seen the enemy leading units, and pierced the map. Gudimenko frowned displeased, and took the pencil back. He placed a paper-case under the map, and drew the conventional sign – a blue arrow.

'And where is the end of the column?'

I felt irritated. We had seen no end to the enemy columns since we retreated from the Don. The Kleist tank army was moving in an endless stream. 'The road is crowded as far as the horizon...' I answered indifferently, trying to conceal my irritation, and annoy Gudimenko.

'How many tanks have you seen?' Gudimenko went on, bending over the map and making some notes.

'It's hard to tell. I did not count...' I turned and began to roll a cigarette.

'There are lots of them!' Talykov cut in hastily. He obviously forgot that 'lots' or 'few' were empty words for Vasilij Tarasovich. He needed numbers, if not precise, then at least close to the truth. He had to report to the higher command.

'Please, let's try to estimate together,' Gudimenko said in a begging tone, seeing that we were annoyed. His tone made me feel sorry for him. I knew he would sit late at night, writing a final report, then encode it, and try to connect to the division headquarters. And if they made some mistakes in decoding, they would keep him awake until the morning, while everybody else, including us, would be sleeping...

We noticed a U-2 flying low above the ground. It landed and taxied to the forest. Our division commander Getman got out of the cockpit smiling. It had been a long time since we saw him, so we were really glad. 'Guys, you are so tanned! Well, how are you doing? Tired?' His warm words seemed to carry the tiredness away.

'Not really...'

Getman was already giving instructions to Kholobaev, and his smile gave way to official tone: 'Load the trucks immediately, and move to Achaluki. You must hurry, and slip through this road.' He showed the way on the map. He looked at our loaded planes and said: 'Since the aircraft are ready, attack the column one more time, guys, but don't come back here. Fly to Achaluki, you'll be waited for. Be careful, the airfield is difficult to spot from above. Watch the flares.'

We took off heading for Pyatigorsk, and climbed so that we could locate the enemy column from afar. The tops of Beshtau and Mashuk were turning green as we came closer. In the distance I saw a column. I thought that it must be our troops retreating to Pyatigorsk, but we had to check it. I looked at Talykov through the side window, and he swayed from one wing to the other – he had also seen the column. The enemy could not have advanced so far! I was flying now above Mashuk. Suddenly an anti-aircraft gun fired. The plane jerked; puffs of black smoke surrounded me. The enemy! My feet pressed the pedal, and Mashuk glided to the side. 'What am I doing? Level out! The target is ahead of us!' I looked at number 9 – it was flying a bit behind me, ready for the attack. I thought, how good it was to have a wingman who did not following me like a dormant burden. Flying with Talykov I could forget that there were only two of us against an endless enemy column...

The guns were firing, the cars were burning on the road, the enemy soldiers were rushing about. I headed to Achaluki, but had to wait for Talykov, who noticed a car and dived...

We hedgehopped past Prokhladnaya village towards Achaluki. I saw red flares, and fire burning beside the white panels. The duty officer must have been too zealous, and the dry grass had caught fire from the flares. We had little fuel left, so we could not wait for the fire to go out. Number 8 followed by number 9 landed and taxied on the ground, quenching the flame with propellers.

In the evening the regiment drew up in two ranks. Dremlyuk was holding the banner on the left. Talykov and me were standing before the rank facing the rest.

The regiment commander was reading out the order that described the attack on the bridge in Prochnookopskaya, and expressed thanks to Talykov and me. We answered simultaneously: 'We serve the working people!'

We were going to celebrate the end of the second 'round' in Achaluki with a special dinner, so besides the usual porridge we were going to have some wine. A small barrel waited for us near the door.

Before dinner the head of the division's political department came to see us in a U-2. 'What's in the barrel?' he asked, poking it with the heel of his boot.

'Wine.'

'So that's how you understood order number 227? Are you celebrating the victory?' Without waiting for the answer he took out a revolver, shot the barrel and was gone.

Thus our barrel was executed. But we did not lose all the wine, because the hole was rather high. Some smart guys collected the red liquid from the puddles with spoons and filtered it through bandage. We had enough for a small company.

Konstantin Kholobaev sat on the floor, and everyone else gathered around him. A can filled with wine circled the men. It did not yet come back to the commander, when the door opened, and there came... Sergeant Lenya Bukreev! Two weeks had past since the day, when he flew to bomb the crossing on the Don, and had not come back to Kagalnitskaya. He was believed to be dead, and now he came just in time for the dinner!

On the next day Talykov and I ferried number 8 and number 9 to another airfield, and handed them over to the 103rd Regiment.

The commissar drew our regiment up. 'We are sent to reform. We'll restore our strength, and go forward. Now – only to the west!'

Guards Major Nikolai Zub

Junior Lieutenant Mikhail Talykov

Senior Lieutenant Ilya Mospanov, Donets Basin, summer 1942

Major Nikolai Galushenko

Above: Senior Lieutenant Vasily Emelianenko tells Chief of Staff Major Fedor Kozhuhovsky how he was shot down above the Artemovsk airfield

Vasily Emelianenko at the Hutor Smely airfield, May 1942, Donets Basin

Junior Lieutenant Konstantin Averianov and Boltik

Armourer Alpatov loads the 23-mm guns of the Shturmovik, 1942

Il–2s in the air, 1944

The Il–2 Shturmovik, 1944

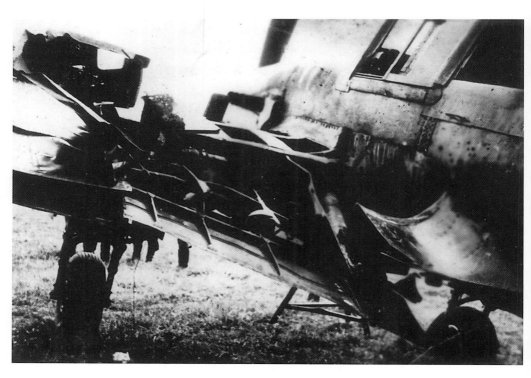

Although severely damaged this Shturmovik still managed to return from its mission

The remnants of the Junkers 86K shot down by Vasily Emelianenko on 9 January 1943 above Kagalnitskaya village

The squadron receiving its first mission. Point 3 airfield, Grozny, January 1943. On the left is Ivan Chernets in his fur boots

The show flight for the Commander of the Special Littoral Army, General Petrov. Shooting at tanks and cars after the bombing, 18 December 1943

Vasily Emelianenko
and Junior Lieutenant
Mikhail Talykov, 1943

Majors Nikolai
Galushenko,
Konstantin
Kholobaev, and Vasily
Emelianenko.
Timoshevskaya
village, 1943

Konstantin
Kholobaev and Vasily
Emelianenko.
Timoshevskaya
village, 1943

Above: Relaxing at the piano, August 1943

After the mission: (far left) Vasily Emelianenko, (third from left) Ivan Ostapenko. Timoshevskaya village, August 1943

Nikolai Sednenkov and Vasily Emelianenko. Timoshevskaya village, August 1943

Aeroclub instructor Vasily Emelianenko on the left, 1935.

Vasily Emelianenko on the wing of his Shturmovik, August 1943

General Nikolai Naumenko, Guards Lieutenant Vasily Emelianenko and the regiment commander Konstantin Kholobaev (in front, with his back to the camera). Breakfast after the attack on the Stalino airfield, 4 June 1942.

Ivan Ostapenko (left) and Vasily Emelianenko by the Il-2

The division commander, Colonel Getman (centre, wearing a Cossack hat), and other officers at the two-day conference on pilot technique for division and regiment commanders, 1944

Above: Training freshmen.

The band of the third squadron: Emelianenko (*balalaika*) and Ivan Chernets (guitar, vocals)

Below: Captain Emelianenko inside the Il-2 cockpit, August 1943

A German self-propelled gun, probably a Stug III, moving along the road

The single-seater Il-2

A German anti-tank battery, probably Pak43

Attack on enemy depot

Shturmoviks attacking targets on the road

Bombing a train. The view from a Shturmovik

The same incident as the above photograph, taken from another perspective

Shturmoviks attacking a road

Maintenance works at the airfield

13

AT THE SEA

We all needed rest, but we were not allowed to stay in Achaluki for more than a day. The 1st Kleist tank army was approaching Nalchik, Prokhladnyy village and Mozdock, trying to force our troops back to the mountains. The enemy was driving the exhausted 37th Army to the wooded foothills of the Caucasus ridge. The 9th Army, led by General K. A. Koroteev, was hurriedly entrenching near the rough Tereck, so that it could cover the avenue of approach to the Military-Georgian road and Grozny from the north.

On 12 August 1942 we started to move eastwards along the dusty Alhan-Churt valley, which was blocked on two sides by the Terski and Sunzhenski ridges. Rows of bandaged soldiers were retreating to the rear, while columns of infantrymen with rifles and sub-machine guns were marching to the front line. We also saw soldiers carrying long thin-barrelled guns in pairs – those were the tank destroying units.

The irrigation canals were filled with oil instead of water. That was a new kind of anti-tank barriers: the canals could be set on fire...

Some of us managed to get a lift, but the majority had to travel on foot. We moved in silence, lost in gloomy thoughts. Many people hoped that the winter defeat of the German troops near Moscow, Tihvin and Rostov was a turning point in the war. Hitler had lost about thirty divisions there, and were pushed back 400 kilometres. 'We'll go only to the west now!' we used to think. But the situation changed unexpectedly. The fascists managed to occupy the whole Crimea peninsula, forced their way to Stalingrad, and to the foothills of the Caucasus. And there was still no second front in Europe...

The war brought me back to familiar places. I remembered how I hurried to the front from Bujur-Nus. Now the Germans occupied

145

the Crimea, and the war seemed to drag on for ages. The enemy was forcing his way to Nalchik – the town of my youth, where I first started to work as an instructor in an aeroclub. We were now heading for Derbent – an ancient town which my mother had often described to me. My heart ached from memories: I could not imagine the war would reach the places which I used to think of as the edge of our land. Now I had a chance to see Derbent, to see the blue sea, which my mother told me about...

The regiment assembly point was in the outskirts of Gudermes, near a deserted barn. Swarms of mosquitoes and midges were buzzing in the air, and we did not at first hear the noise from a German reconnaissance aircraft flying above us.

'It flies to Baku,' concluded Talykov, after he consulted the map.

'It may be Tbilisi,' someone objected.

We did not know where we would be sent from Derbent, and one of us expressed an idea which had not come to our heads before: 'They can now send us to England through Iran.'

'What for?'

'To open the second front! They must be frightened to hell, so we could show them an example...'

'He might be right!'

'Only our clothes are worn out. We do not look up to the mark.'

'That's no problem; we'll get new uniform.'

The idea of sending Soviet pilots to open up a second front seemed to us quite credible. We began to dream about the day when the war was over. We realised, of course, that that day was not coming soon, and tried to be sensible in estimating the time.

'We will have to win the lost territory back, so it will take us as long as it took to move east,' said Fedya Artemov.

But somebody corrected him: 'It's only up to our boundaries, and it will take one more year to get to the very heart...'

'I wonder, will there be a parade on Red Square?'

'Come on! Of course, there will be! Both on the ground, and in the air! Shturmoviks will hedgehop above Red Square...'

'No, you can't hedgehop there – the Kremlin towers are high!'

'We can climb a bit higher!'

'And we will strew flowers from the bomb hatches,' said Talykov with conviction.

After the discussion about the parade everybody fell silent for some reason. Some might have fallen asleep, but the majority were watching the crimson smouldering coals, propping their chins up on their hands.

The picture in our minds was rather colourful: a sunny day, Shturmoviks racing above the ancient towers of the Kremlin, an endless stream of people pouring into Red Square, red banners fluttering in the wind... People would wave to us from the ground, and we'd be strewing fresh flowers on the crowd... Each of us must have thought: 'Who will be lucky to fly above Red Square on that sunny day?'

The next day those who had travelled on foot arrived. They had walked from Rostov for 700 kilometres, they survived many bombardments, and spent nights in the open air in fields. They arrived with their feet rubbed sore, many had no boots on, but nobody was lost. Together with them arrived a lorry heaped up with haversacks and damaged trunks. Among them were the belongings of those who had been killed. We wished we could send the things to their relatives, but we did not know where to direct them. Many towns and villages, where the families of our fellows had lived, were occupied, and we did not know, where they had managed to escape.

Major Hushper, who had been in command of the second squadron, which did not exist any longer, and later led the group from Rostov, addressed Kholobaev: 'The possessions of the dead men are a burden.'

'Do you suggest that we throw them away?'

'Why? We should give them to those whose outfits are worn out.'

Somebody objected: 'They're the clothes of corpses...'

'Did you said "corpses"?' Kholobaev was outraged. 'They are our comrades, who fell in action! We should be proud to wear a blouse that belonged to Mospanov or Boiko! Yes, we will give them out. Today!'

In the evening shoes, blouses and sweaters were sorted into piles near the barn. The regiment was set up in one formation, and examined by the commander and the head of staff. They stopped in front of our 'professor', Shum, whose boots were wound round with wire, but which were still gaping at the toes.

'Shum, three steps forward!'

Maxim Ivanovich Shum had received the boots of Ivan Bobrov. He fell back in rank, and the commander moved further. Fedya Artemov was trying to conceal a hole in his blouse with his hand.

'Drop your hands. Are you a pilot or not?' the commander reproached him.

Artemov had received the blouse of Ivan Boiko, our lost friend. Fedya returned to his place with tears in his eyes, carrying the folded blouse in both hands. We were all recalling the day when Ivan Boiko returned to the regiment after the forced landing in Donbass with his head bandaged up and a broad smile on his face. He had hardly managed to cross the front line, had hit a pine-tree with a wing, and his plane spun round. Ivan was sent into hospital, but soon ran away and returned to the command post. He unwound his bandage, so that he could put his helmet on, and hurried to the commander: 'Give me a mission! My head doesn't ache.'

On 16 July he flew to reconnoitre enemy positions near Millerovo and did not come back.

The blouse was the right size, but the badge of rank was wrong: Boiko had been a lieutenant, and Artemov was a junior lieutenant. Fedya had to remove one square from the faded tabs. Two rich blue spots on the faded material were a blessed memory of our lost friend.

The details of Ivan Boiko's death came to light twenty-five years later. I opened *The Soviet Russia* of 22 June 1966 and saw a photo of two smiling pilots. There was a caption under the photo: 'On the right, Lieutenant Boiko; perhaps our readers know who the person on the left is?' A farmer in the Rostov region kept that photo for many years. As an eight-year-old boy he witnessed an air fight between one Shturmovik and six enemy fighters that surrounded it. The Shturmovik managed to escape the smoking tracks dashing towards its tail for a long time, and fired a burst at one of the Messerschmitts. The German fighter caught fire, but soon the Shturmovik also went down and disappeared behind a hill. The boy ran there and saw the plane standing in a forest clearing. The pilot was lying face down not far from the wing. It seemed as if he had sheltered from the hot sun in the shadow of an oak, relaxing after the fight. His blouse looked as though it had been stitched on to his waist with a sewing machine. At night the boy's father buried the pilot secretly on a high hillock. In his blouse pocket the man found a photo which was published in a newspaper a quarter of a century later.

I called the paper immediately: the pilot on the left of Boiko was the young me...

We went to Derbent by train. I was in the seventh heaven lying on the upper berth in the freight train. The car was rocking me to sleep like a boat on the waves, and I felt I could sleep for ages. But suddenly the car began to jerk, and somebody pushed me. I opened my eyes with difficulty, and saw my neighbour, Petr Rudenko.

'Get up quickly! The commander is calling!' he shouted.

'Where are we?' I asked half asleep.

'In Makhachkala.'

'But we must go on to Derbent!'

'That's none of your business! Get up quickly, the commander is waiting!' Petr hurried me up, pulling his blue plywood trunk and dark-blue overcoat with a 'hen' on the left sleeve. The 'hen' was a pilot's emblem: two spread wings, a star and crossed swords in the middle. It was originally embroidered in silver thread, but that had gone black long ago.

The commander de-trained the six most experienced pilots, and the train moved on. We found some of our mechanics, who had been trying for two weeks to send seven Shturmoviks to repair shops, but could not find a free truck. The engines on all the planes had to be changed.

Kholobaev told us: 'Someone managed to fly here on these planes, so we must manage to fly to the repair shops in them. It's less than an hour's flight. We won't go through the mountains or above the open sea, but we'll fly along the coastline. If your engine stops, land without releasing the landing gear on the sand, or shallow water. Got it?'

'Is the sea shallow?' Petr asked astonished.

'It is shallow near the coastline,' the commander smiled.

He liked the pilot's Ukrainian manner of speaking, and also tried to use some Ukrainian words.

The taciturn pilot Junior Lieutenant Petr Rudenko was only twenty-two. He had married before the war, and used to write long letters to his wife, Olya, in Murtusovo village in Konotop region. After we learnt that Konotop was occupied by the enemy, Petr had become even more taciturn. Life had never been rosy for Petr. He had worked since he was sixteen at Konotop electromechanical plant, studied in an aeroclub at the same time, and graduated from Serpukhov Military School. It had not been easy for him to become a pilot, but once he mastered it, he never lost his skills.

He was a brave person, but too direct. He did not use any tricks to outwit the enemy, and returned in a damaged plane more often than the rest. However, he did not care about the holes in the wings... Rudenko had made a hundred sorties by that time – a record military score in the regiment, but he was a wingman longer than others. Now he was promoted to be the deputy of the squadron commander. Rumours were spread that he was recommended for the highest decoration, and we all waited for him to become the Hero of the Soviet Union.

Rudenko was a very thrifty person. At the front you could never know whether you'd be alive in ten minutes, but Petr still set aside every rouble, and did not allow himself any extras. That's why we were really surprised in Makhachkala.

The commander allowed us to have a walk through the town, but asked us to come back early, and have a good rest. We were to take off early next morning. We were strolling along the streets, trying to find 'Triple eau-de-Cologne' for shaving, but in vain. Eau-de-Cologne had vanished from shops long ago as a luxury object. We saw endless queues near the shops – people trying to get some bread. So we went to the wharf to have a look at the blue sea and bathe. But all we could see was a crowd of many thousands of refugees. Women with children, old men and women were waiting for several weeks for a steamer to evacuate them across the Caspian Sea. The sea was not at all blue. Oil, pieces of paper, melon rind and other garbage were drifting along the surface.

As we went back we realised that Petr Rudenko was missing. He returned in the evening with a small trunk.

'I bought a gramophone!' he declared proudly.

'What do you need it for, Petr?' we were interested. A gramophone was a strange and rather expensive thing in war time.

'It can play at parties.'

'But we have Yurchenko playing the *bayan*!'*

---

* The *bayan* is a Russian folk instrument similar to an accordian.

'He can't play this...'

Petr opened the lid, put on his only record, turned the handle, and we heard the familiar sounds of 'Rio–Rita'.★

'I met Olya at a dance party, when this song was playing,' he said.

At dinner he told Kholobaev in everybody's presence: 'When I die, present this gramophone to the bravest pilot...'

On the next morning we took off. Following Kholobaev we circled above the airfield to gain more altitude and headed to the south. We had to fly high, so that we could glide on the shallow water if the engine stopped. Soon we were flying between the dark gloomy canyons of Dagestan on the right, and the quiet blue sea on the left. You could not tell where the border was between the sea and the cloudless sky, they were of the same colour. Every few minutes we had to check the water temperature. Soon the indicator reached red – the engine was overheating.

Ages seemed to pass before we saw a chain of limed houses, the remnants of an ancient fortress and a mosque. That was Derbent – we had covered half the distance. The town slowly slipped behind us, the mountains receded from the coastline, and a gold disk rose from behind the horizon. The temperature in the cooling system was now beyond any limits, and the armoured glass was splashed with water. During the next twenty minutes I was waiting nervously for the engine to pack up, and could not enjoy the scenery. Finally I saw the airfield. We landed one by one without circling. We did it!

The commander looked very proud, as if he had won an important battle. 'We'll have a bite, bathe in the sea, and take a train!' he said.

The airfield canteen was small, and we had to stand in a long queue. The sun was blazing. Clouds of sand drifted on the ground, getting everywhere, including in our mouths. Salt stood out on our blouses. My body itched from mosquitoes or other insects which had appeared during our several weeks wandering through the Donets Basin and the Salski steppes.

We had our meal, and hurried to the sea, which was very clean at that place. Rudenko headed our group carrying his gramophone. He was the first to undress, and his body was white as paper. Only his hands and neck were tanned. Petr got into the water, scooped a

★ 'Rio Rita' was a popular song from a movie of the same name.

handful, supped it and spat angrily: 'Damn! It's bitter...' He thought for a minute, ran to the beach, picked up a stone, took his clothes, immersed them in the water, and weighted them down against the bottom with the stone. 'Lice will croak here!'

Petr cheered everybody up. We floundered about in the water like boys, dived, laughed, and then lay naked on the beach warming in the sun. Soon everything fell silent. Only Petr kept playing his record. We dozed listening to 'Rio-Rita', and soon all the sounds seemed to be carried away by the wind to the sea...

Fedya Artemov was the first to wake up. 'We're burnt!' he shouted.

Everyone jumped to his feet in alarm: where was the fire? And then we burst out laughing: our backs and legs were scarlet. Kholobaev's shoulder blades were blistered. Petr was standing naked by his gramophone. His favourite record had melted in the sun; its edges were hanging from the disk like a pancake from a plate. We got dressed quickly and went to the railway station. Rudenko bought a bottle of sour milk and oiled our backs, but it did not help much. In the train we could neither sit nor lie. We had to stand by the windows and could not stop looking at the blue sea. A steamer could be seen on the horizon; a long smoking trail was dragging behind it...

14

A JUMP OVER THE CASPIAN SEA

It was the season of grape picking, but there were not enough people in Derbent for this. Men had gone to the war, and women were either digging anti-tank ditches or working in hospitals. We were sent to reap the harvest. We worked in the vineyards and could eat our fill: one bunch in the basket, one in the mouth. But we did not have chance to enjoy it for long: it was declared that pilots were to go to Kujbyshev to the aircraft factory of S.V. Ilyushin. Some of the mechanics were to accompany us.

We racked our brains over the new problem: how to get there? The enemy had blocked all the nearest railroads, and German aircraft were bombing steamers that tried to cross the Volga. There was only one way left: across the Caspian Sea. But a steamer could only sail for 600 kilometres to Gurjev, and then we had to go by train.

Kholobaev came to us late at night a bit tipsy from the young wine. 'We start tomorrow! Don't take much stuff with you, but take the parachutes. We'll fly a 'communal grave'.'

Young pilots stared in surprise, but the more experienced ones knew that 'communal grave' was a name for an outdated four-engine giant – the heavy bomber TB-3. It could carry a big crew, and in accidents eleven people died at once.

In the morning we got into the giant bomb bay, and those who were left had to squeeze inside the thick wing. The engine started and the plane took off. We were sitting in a closed box and could not see anything. The giant plane was shaking so much that even our skin shivered. The plane would ascend on a rising air current, and then fall abruptly, so that we were tossed about. Many people felt sick. We wondered if we were flying above mountains. We found a crack in the floor and peered through it. The view was not encouraging: very

153

close to us we saw the high crests of waves. After that everybody fell silent. After five hours of flying we saw sand through the crack. People began to move; some smoked into their fists. In the evening we landed on a grassy airfield. We refused dinner and fell down to sleep. At dawn our restless commander woke us up.

'Get up! You have not come here to sleep! Have your breakfast and go to the factory airfield. We'll ferry the aircraft.'

We picked the dry lumpy millet porridge in the canteen. Starvation rations behind the lines.

At the factory airfield we saw several lines of brand-new Shturmoviks. We could choose. Our mechanics thoroughly examined each plane. 'Professor' Shum was in great demand: each of us wanted him to check the engine of the chosen plane. We were also granted a dual-control plane: the long-awaited training plane UIL-2. Now we could check the flying technique of the freshmen.

There were ten experienced pilots among us, including Petr Rudenko, Mikhail Vorozhbiev, Vladimir Zangiev, Mikhail Talykov, Leonid Bukreev, Eugene Ezhov, Nikolai Dorogavtsev, Vasily Shamshurin… We also had graduates of Vorosrhilovgrad Air School: sergeants Ivan Ostapenko, Georgy Bondarenko, Petr Tsyganov, Grigory Snopko. They had joined our regiment in Kagalnitskaya, but had not made a single operational flight yet. We were to assign about twenty freshmen to the regiment, train them, and prepare them for a thousand-kilometre flight to the front.

During the first half of September we flew from dawn until night, checking, choosing, training the pilots. Kholobaev paid special attention to radio communication. He said: 'The man who does not listen to commands from the ground is a definite candidate for the next world. I don't want such men in my regiment!'

But accidents still happened. Once sergeant, Snopko, a blond, good-natured guy, was returning from a training flight. He was going to land, but forgot to release the landing gear. We tipped him off by radio, but he did not respond. We set up red flares, and made him fly another circuit. The situation was repeated several more times: Snopko was stubbornly trying to land without the landing gear, and we were setting up several flares at once. The exhausted pilot stopped paying attention to the warning signs and was going to land. As he glided Major Hushper took a risk: he ran to the landing strip and raised his hands. We hoped that the pilot would notice his squadron leader, and fortunately he did. For the fifth time Snopko stopped descending and climbed. Hushper fell on his back, raised his legs, and began to slap them with his hands. The pilot finally grasped our message, and understood that he had forgotten to release his 'legs'. Thanks to that his flight did not end with any damage.

Kholobaev was furious, and wanted to dismiss Snopko from the regiment, but after he talked to him, he changed his mind. Grisha Snopko became the pride of our Guards family later, but he always remembered that incident.

Sergeant Ivan Ostapenko was in the third squadron under my command. The round-faced phlegmatic Ukrainian appeared to be a great joker. Other pilots and mechanics could listen for him for hours, and the evening silence was interrupted regularly by bursts of laughter. He always talked about himself, but you could never tell where reality intertwined with fiction in his stories. He imitated either the brave soldier Shveik, or the favourite hero of the soldiers, Vasya Terkin.* Ostapenko was a great storyteller, and I knew the value of people who were able to cheer everybody up. I was glad to have him in my squadron.

But on one occasion he barely escaped dismissal. Kholobaev often checked the pilot's reactions to the commands from the ground at that time. Most of the planes were equipped only with receivers (the transmitters were installed only in the squadron commanders' planes), and the only way to check the pilot's attention was to ask him to perform some simple trick. If he did – he had heard.

Number 25 was flying above the start line.

'Who is it?' Kholobaev asked me.

'Sergeant Ostapenko.'

The commander took the microphone: 'Number 25, if you hear me, wave your wings!'

Ostapenko kept flying in one direction. Kholobaev said angrily: 'Your favourite can only tell stories, but in the air he is a fool. I'll dismiss him from the regiment, let him study in the brigade...'

'Konstantin Nikolaevich,' I asked the commander, 'he walked with

---

* Shveik, a clumsy soldier of World War I, was the hero of popular novels by the Czech writer Jaroslav Gashek. Terkin was another fictional character, the hero of Ivan Tvardovski's front-line poems, a cheerful and lucky Russian infantryman.

our regiment all the way from Rostov. Let him land, and then decide: perhaps the radio isn't working.'

'A bad dancer always finds an excuse! Let's see how he lands.'

'He lands perfectly, you'll see...'

And what do you think? Ostapenko, who had always landed well, came too close to the ground this time, smacked it with his wheels, and the aircraft jumped several times.

'You can tell the bird by the way it flies... Walking is not flying. Send him to me!'

Ostapenko came up to the commander, and saluted.

'Did you tune the radio before the flight?'

'I did.'

'Did you hear my command?'

'I did.'

'Why didn't you obey?'

'I couldn't, comrade commander,' answered the sergeant calmly.

'For what reason, I wonder?'

'You ordered me to wave the wings, but it's impossible: they are fixed at the fuselage. If you had ordered me to swing from one wing to the other, it would have been different,' the sergeant explained with an ingenuous expression.

'Why did you make a poor landing?'

'I knew you would be angry, because I didn't carry out your command, so I was nervous.'

Those who were standing nearby chuckled, and Kholobaev burst out laughing.

We were to fly to the front on 20 September. It seemed to me that there was no problem. All I had to do was to gather my squadron (twelve planes), fly for an hour and land for refuelling. We'd make one landing by the Elton lake, one near Astrakhan, one near Makhachkala, and the last one near Gudermes – that's it. And the flying conditions were favourable: there was not a cloud in the sky, and visibility was perfect. We were not going to fly over dangerous places, so there would be no Messerschmitts, and no anti-aircraft guns firing. A pleasant trip, in my opinion. Meanwhile, Kholobaev devoted a whole day to getting ready for the flight.

We were busy planning the route, and the commander rushed between the squadrons. Petr Rudenko led the first squadron (he had been promoted), Major Hushper led the second, and I was the leader of the third. Once again Kholobaev appeared as if out of nowhere, grabbed the map, and began to interrogate Ostapenko: 'What's the compass course on the first stage of the flight? The track time? What are the main reference points?' The sergeant was answering excellently, and I was glad for him.

Judging by his questions, it seemed our commander was afraid that we might lose our bearings. I could not understand how we could get lost on this route. The Volga and the only railway in the steppe were very reliable reference points. Besides, each squadron would be accompanied by a leader: the Pe-2 bomber with a navigator aboard. The squadrons would take off one by one at thirty-minute intervals. But the commander was still nervous. He ordered Major Galushenko, who had just been appointed our regiment's navigator, to accompany Petr Rudenko.

Nikolai Kirillovich Galushenko was an excellent pilot, and more experienced than any of us. He had been a voluntary pilot in China in 1937, and flew an SB bomber. The regiment commander wanted Galushenko to secure the first squadron. Petr took offence, but the commander was probably remembering the incident when Rudenko barely escaped trial a year ago. He was returning from a mission and fell behind the group, got lost, and had to land in the steppe. He asked the way, took off, but got lost again. It was evening by now. Rudenko landed by a village to ask the way, and somebody told him that the Germans were close. Rudenko put some firewood inside the cockpit, poured petrol over it, and set fire to it. He returned to the regiment on foot. Petr got into lot of trouble that time: the rumours about the Germans being close appeared to be false, but the plane had been destroyed. So the commander decided to keep him away from any 'accidents' this time.

Early in the morning my squadron took off. We set the course following the leader. Ostapenko was flying to my right. Looking past him I could see the wide ribbon of the Volga and the yellow Zhiguli.

The first landing: the refuellers quickly did their job. Rudenko's squadron landed after us, and Hushper's squadron landed when all my planes were already refuelled. We took off. Everything went on exactly to schedule.

In the air again: the Volga turned to the right and disappeared. We wouldn't see it until Astrakhan now. My native Nikolaevka and destroyed Stalingrad were left far behind. We were flying above the flat steppe. Trains were crawling along the railway to the front. Finally we saw the white, salty lake, Elton. Kholobaev landed first, and directed the rest from the ground. I stretched my legs, and saw my deputy Fedya Artemov hurrying towards me.

'One plane is missing!'

'Nonsense! Everybody flew to the airfield. I checked it myself.'

'Number 25 is missing!'

Ostapenko! We climbed at the engine and looked around.

'What's that dust?' Artemov pointed with his hand, shielding his eyes from the sun.

'Probably a car. What else can raise dust in the steppe?'

'Isn't it a plane taxiing?'

'He could not have landed so far away...' Kholobaev ran up to us pointing at that direction with signal flags.

'Do you see, where your *hohol*★ managed to land?'

Ostapenko taxied for a long time hitting marmot holes with his wheels. The water in the engine started to boil. Mechanics gathered around the plane checking the landing gear and the engine. It appeared that the sun had blinded Ostapenko just before the landing, and he lost the T. He turned, noticed something white ahead, and landed there. On the ground he found out that he had taken a gully caked with dried brine for the landing cue...

The sergeant stood before me frowning. 'Now they will take me to pieces,' he said in a sad voice. I thought he was talking about the plane, and tried to calm him down before the next take off, though I felt like telling him off: 'There's no need to dismantle it, there's nothing wrong with the aircraft.'

'I don't mean the plane, I mean myself. I am to blame for the accident.'

The next part of the route was really difficult: half way there we were to fly over desert. We had to follow the compass to the south, and then along the coastline to the west. We had to make a big detour in order to avoid the enemy aircraft operations zone. Before we took off each of us received a corked bottle of water.

★ A common name for Ukrainians in Russian.

'It's emergency stock. I forbid you to drink it!' declared the commander.

Everybody guessed when the water could come in handy. We took off in the same sequence, following Kholobaev. The aircraft jerked in the hot air streams. Wherever you looked there was nothing but yellow sand. During twenty minutes of flight I did not see a single bush. I could not help listening to the engine, and thinking about the water bottle.

Finally I saw the blue Caspian Sea and a white lace of foam along the coastline. We flew for a long time along the deserted coast, until we saw the Volga's mouth and numerous islands. Astrakhan was coming into view from the side.

The third part of the route was eventless. While the mechanics were refuelling the planes, the pilots received life jackets. It was the first time we'd seen them.

'Here are the air hoses,' explained an officer from the flight department.

We looked at two long rubber tubes. When you put the vest on, they reached your mouth.

'These are the valves that close the openings of the hoses when the vest is inflated...'

'How do you inflate it?' asked Fedya Artemov.

'I was just going to show you... You take the ends of the hoses in your mouths, inhale through the nose, and exhale...'

'Is it possible to get inside the cockpit, when it is inflated?'

'Comrades, you aren't going to inflate it in the plane, are you? You do it after you've left the plane and the canopy has opened. But you must do it before you land on water...'

Fedya Artemov was the first to try: he put on the vest and began to blow. His face became red from strain but the vest swelled slowly. Finally Fedya grew really stout. He made a wry face, bowed, held out a begging hand, and began to mumble: 'Lard, lard, lard...' Everybody laughed, thinking about our nice chief of staff, who was probably still gathering grapes in Derbent. It was good to laugh, but we realised that we would not have time to inflate the vests, because we would be flying too low above the sea. We did not feel like laughing any more. To make things worse, Kholobaev was dashing along the runway, looking at his watch every minute. Thirty minutes had already passed, but we could see no sign of the leader and Rudenko's squadron. A single Shturmovik whizzed low above the airfield, zoomed, banked, made a circle and landed. Judging by the style that must be Galushenko. But why was he alone? Where was the first squadron that the regiment's navigator was supposed to guard?

We watched Galushenko facing Kholobaev. The commander was gesticulating like a madman, and Galushenko was standing to attention. The last squadron had landed now, but Rudenko's planes still did not appear. Kholobaev stayed in Astrakhan, and sent Galushenko to accompany my group.

We flew to Makhachkala without a leader, but yellow Hawker Hurricanes guarded us from behind and from the sides. It appeared that the Germans were aware of the air route to the Caucasus above the sea, and had sent Messers to hunt for our planes. Major Galushenko was flying apart from my group. We approached the coast near Makhachkala, and Galushenko descended until he was hedge-hopping. Flocks of ducks were rising in the air before his plane's nose. I had never seen such amount of gamebird in my life! Soon I heard Galushenko's voice: 'Something is wrong with my engine. There is a smell of burning; I guess it's the electric wiring.'

'What do the instruments show?' I asked him.

'The water temperature is rising...'

'We are approaching the airfield. Land first,' I advised him.

When I was descending I saw Galushenko's plane lying on its fuselage at the far end of the airfield. Galushenko had forgotten to release the landing gear in his hurry. He was going round the plane cursing himself with the worst words, but it didn't help. Our mechanics lifted the plane up, and changed the propeller. They checked the engine, but could not find any problem. Nothing could really burn there. We wondered what could have happened. Sergeant Shergin climbed on the engine, thrust his hand into the air inlet of the water radiator, which was situated behind the propeller in front the glass canopy, and pulled out – a burnt duck! How could it have squeezed in there through the three-bladed propeller rotating at a speed of two thousands revolutions per minute?

Petr Rudenko got into trouble. Galushenko thought that he could leave him on his own as far as Astrakhan, since a leader would be accompanying him. The leader was to take off in the last turn, but his engine broke down and he never took off. Rudenko flew alone, swerved from his course over the Volga's mouth, and got lost. The fuel ran out, and the pilots from his squadron landed separately in different places. Rudenko landed on a deserted island in the Volga's estuary. The soil was too soft, and the plane turned upside down. Fortunately the squadron commander got off with bruises and the plane was also safe. We found everybody, and they flew to the assembly point.

The flight was over. Thirty-six Shturmoviks were ready for the battle, but Galushenko was downgraded, and became the commander of the first squadron, while Rudenko became a flight commander. It was rather unpleasant: we had learnt to fight, and then stumbled on an even surface.

15

WE RESTORE OUR STRENGTH

We landed in a broad valley near Gudermes. The last Shturmovik was still taxiing in when we saw a German reconnaissance aircraft in the sky. The regiment commander followed it with his eyes and called all hands on deck: 'Camouflage the aircraft!'

We began to carry hay and sheaves to cover the propellers, wings, and fuselages. Everybody did his best, and soon you could not distinguish a plane from a haystack even at a close distance.

We settled in a deserted village, Isti-Su, which was an hour on foot from the airfield. Volodya Zangiev, who was an Ossete,* translated the name of the village as 'hot water'. There was indeed a stream of almost boiling water running down from the mountain. The water smelled of rotten eggs. A wood-lined hollow had been dug into the ground near the stream. It could be filled with water, and when it cooled a bit, a dozen bath-lovers could submerge into it slowly and enjoy the healing water. Even our young hearts pounded after this!

Enjoying the sulphur spring we thought that tomorrow we would probably get an order to fly to a front airfield somewhere close to Mozdock and Nalchik. The head of the reconnaissance unit flew to our regiment in the evening with a map. He told us about enemy air and ground forces in our section of the front, mentioning lots of numbers, listing the numerical strength of the units. We marked the military contact zone and the places where the fascists' air force was based on our maps. The commander seemed to be informed of every single detail. It looked like he had seen everything with his own eyes. Our reconnaissance was not wasting time. He was not supposed to

* A native of Ossetia, near Georgia, i.e. not far from Gudermes.

say anything about our own forces, but in the end he said encouragingly: 'Our forces are getting ready to smash the enemy!'

We thought that the rearranged regiments of our 230th Ground-Attack Aircraft Division were also a force, and not the smallest one.

We spent several days in Isti-Su, but the order to fly closer to the front line did not come. Instead we were ordered to continue training, practising group co-ordination and shooting. So we flew from dawn until night, using as much fuel and ammunition as we wanted.

After some time there came an order to hold a conference to exchange battle experiences. A conference in wartime was an unprecedented event! It seemed that we were not doing so badly after all, if they were not in a hurry to bring us into action.

Kholobaev defined the subjects of the presentations, and distributed them among the pilots. Fedya Artemov revolted unexpectedly: 'I am a poor orator, comrade commander! As soon as I step out to the platform, I'll start to stutter...'

'So don't perorate! Just speak naturally about the attacks on the Artemov and Konstantinov airfields which you performed with Mospanov. Everything as it was: from take-off to landing. And show it on a plan. It does no harm to use your brains, and it will be interesting for the young pilots. And forget about the platform. We are not going to bother about that stuff. An ora-a-tor...'

The number of presentations was rather large: pilots were going to speak about manoeuvres against anti-aircraft guns, about air fights between Shturmoviks and Messers, about battle formation, attacks on crossings. Only Petr Rudenko did not get a subject for presentation. He was getting ready for a meeting of the youth of the Northern Caucasus. Later we learnt that he made the shortest speech at the meeting: 'We have been fighting and will be fighting against Hitler until we win!' He left the stage followed by a storm of applause.

For me Kholobaev chose the rather delicate subject of shooting and dropping bombs from the aircraft. It was easier to demonstrate than to explain. The shooting was no problem: you lowered the nose of the aircraft, located the target through the crosshairs, descended nearer the ground, and fired. If the tracer bullets missed, you could easily change direction with the help of the rudders. It was a pure pleasure to shoot from the Shturmovik: you could see the results.

Bombing was quite different. Nobody bothered to develop sights for the Shturmovik until the end of the war and even after it. That's why each of us had his own shooting method. We dropped bombs by eye, trusting our own feelings. We called it 'booting'. Some smart guys even invented an abbreviation for the non-existent sights – TB-42 meant 'tarpaulin boots of 1942' – by the end of the war we were on TB-45. Everyone coped as best he could, and on the whole we dropped bombs on target.

To compensate for the missing sights the Shturmovik was covered with different kinds of markers and pins, just as the bottom of a ship is covered with shells. We used the markers to determine the time we began to dive. Then we had to bank at an angle of thirty degrees, and immediately begin to count off the seconds for the delay, much as photographers used to count off the time of exposure. moreover, we had to keep an eye on the altimeter, because we had to drop bombs from the right height.

As soon as factory markers and pins appeared, somebody wrote instructions on their use. It was obligatory to learn the instructions and pass a test on it. There was only one thing the instruction did not take into consideration: how was it possible to perform the whole procedure in a few seconds during battle with anti-aircraft guns firing at you?

I asked Kholobaev: 'Should I stick to the instructions, or tell them about the 'boot'?'

'Tell how them you do it but don't mention the 'boot' to the young guys! To make them believe, show them everything on the training ground.'

During the conference we discussed and argued about many things, many of which we had not bothered to think before. We remembered the tactical methods used by our famous experts – Major Nikolai Zub, and Senior Lieutenant Ilya Mospanov. Fedya Artemov didn't stutter when he spoke about his sorties to the enemy airfields.

Before the demonstration flight I asked the commander: 'How would it be if I broadcast my every action so everyone can hear?'

'Will you have time to do that?'

'I'll try...'

The head of our communication service Nudzhenko mounted a

loudspeaker near the ground station. I also asked him to set the transmitter switch on the control column, so that I did not have to reach down to the floor each time I wanted to use it. Nudgenko arranged it so, and now my plane had an extra cable and a shift knob, which was fixed on to the control column with insulation tape. You pressed it when you wanted to talk, and released it when you wanted to listen. Excellent! When Jakov Ivanovich Maltsev, the chief designer's deputy, visited us later, he examined the extra knob, which was already installed on all the leaders' planes, and said: 'That's a practical improvement. We will apply it in the factory.'

My demonstration flight was successful. The correspondents called it 'a lecture from the air', and later that form of teaching became commonplace. After the flight Kholobaev came up to me, took off his Parachute Master badge, and fastened it on my breast. 'But I haven't jumped enough times!'

'Take it. Perhaps you'll need to make another hole in your blouse soon...'

At that time none of the pilots who had gone through the long run of fighting from the Donets Basin to the Caucasus had a single decoration. Even Talykov did not get one, though he had already been recommended for the Order of Lenin in June 1942, when he saved me from the Germans. Artemov and I did not get a decoration either, though we had made more than fifty sorties each. To be honest, everyone who deserved one was just waiting for a decoration. We hoped to get them before we entered the third 'round'. Sometimes we would begin to discuss it:

'I've heard that the high commanders are pocketing all the decorations.'

'Who is talking such nonsense?'

'I've heard it myself from the clerks. They know everything...'

'The decorations are probably kept outside the division.'

Everybody dreamed of the day when he would 'make a hole' in his blouse. It was important to receive a decoration while we were alive.

September passed, but we were still training in Isti-Su. The young pilots learnt to shoot and bomb on target, could keep formation not only flying in line, but also during manoeuvres, and had mastered attacking targets with the whole squadron. It was an inspiring sight. Twelve Shturmoviks lowered their noses in unison, and launched ninety-six missiles in a single smoking track. Hosts of tracer bullets shredded the targets, and when the planes came out of a dive, black spots rushed down. The ground quaked, a cloud of dust hid the sun, and a crushing echo resounded from the mountains. The Shturmoviks climbed again for a new attack. The regiment commander gave an order through the microphone: 'Attention! Enemy fighters!'

The pilots responded to the command, and the leader moved forward. His plane banked, the wingmen formed a line following him, and in a few seconds there was a merry-go-round in the air. That kind of battle formation was devised to defend the planes from Messerschmitts. We called it a 'ring-buoy'. A single-seater Shturmovik was defenceless from behind, but if a Fritz tried to attack it, the plane flying behind him could stop him with frontal fire.

'The attack is repelled. You may land,' the commander said in the microphone, got into a car, and drove to check the work of the first squadron.

It was really beautiful. Misha Talykov was the first to break the silence: 'Now we are ready!' And he tapped his heels together.

I thought: 'Yes, this is not a regiment with nothing but two Shturmoviks any more.'

The regiment was ready to fly to a front-line airfield, but quite unexpectedly we got a new order: the 7th Guards would be a night regiment. That was news! We had never heard of Shturmoviks flying at night. Now we would have to spend time learning again. There were few pilots in our regiment who had flown at night and they had all flown only U-2s.

In the evening we were discussing the new order excitedly.

'I don't understand, what's the use of our flying at night?'

'There will be fewer casualties. Think of the girls from the Bershanskaya regiment. Many of them have already made 300 operational flights on U-2s at night. And they don't have any armour! And how many Shturmoviks do you know that have made at least fifty flights?'

'Farewell to hedgehopping. We'll have to fly high, in order not to hit a mountain in the dark.'

'And if we fly high, we won't be able to shoot. All we can do is to drop bombs with TB-42...'

'And our group co-ordination will come to nothing...'

'Why?'

'How are you going to keep in formation in the dark? Even infantrymen step on each other's heels in the night marches.'

'You can see your neighbour's navigation lights. They're mounted on the wing tips and the tail.'

'If you must know, they are turned on during take-off and landing only. If you fly with navigation lights on, the German anti-aircraft gunners will be really grateful to you: they won't even need the searchlights. It's easy to spot a night Shturmovik through the lights...'

'Guys! How can we find targets at night?'

'We'll have to use the flares.'

'And where should we fix the demolition bombs?'

No-one could answer that question. We got really confused.

Next day about fifty 'bat' lamps were set on the airfield forming a night starting line. We didn't have a searchlight to illuminate the landing runway. A pilot from a night regiment flew on a U-2 to train us. We flew from dusk until dawn for several nights, and the process of relearning was going amazingly fast. And what a pleasure it was to fly a U-2 at night! The air was still, and the plane glided smoothly as if in sour cream. Everywhere was in complete darkness. Only the instrument panel slightly flickered, and the two rows of lamps shone dimly on the airfield. It looked like a city street at night. It was unusual to see it: all the settlements were blackened out now, and cars drove with their lights off at night. You could not help thinking of the peaceful days preceding the war.

We were standing on the runway watching a plane flying above. Three lights were moving in the starry sky: red, green, and white. If it weren't for the sound of the engine, you might take them for the shooting stars. It was sergeant Ostapenko. He was performing an independent flight in a circle.

'Your *hohol* is doing his best,' the commander said approvingly. He inhaled deeply, and the cigarette illuminated his face and wrinkles round his lips. At that very moment we were blinded by a bright light, the air blast hit us, and we fell down. The commander was the first to jump up. 'Turn off the lights!' he cried. Everybody rushed to carry out the command. Now we could hear a distant rumble from a German night plane, which was hurrying to cross the front line before dawn. The sky was already clearing in the east. Our mechanics

167

filled up the shell-hole. Nobody was hurt, and the planes were all safe as well. We drove to the village dozing.

'The Fritz has also bombed 'with a boot',' I heard Ivan Ostapenko's voice.

The period of flying U-2s was over. It was time to fly Ils at night. Who would be the first to try? Kholobaev wanted to do it himself, but unfortunately he was suffering from a stomach ulcer in those days. He couldn't do without a hot-water bottle. He summoned Major Galushenko and asked him: 'Have you ever flown an SB at night?'

'Yes, I have.'

'Will you fly an Il?'

'I will,' he answered with confidence. 'Only I'd like to perform the first flight at dusk, so that my eyes can get used to the dark gradually.'

'All right. You'll fly the dual-control plane, and take Major Hushper in the rear cockpit. Two majors are better than one.'

It was not dark yet, when the UIL-2 taxied to the runway and took off. It circled the airfield and did a perfect three-point landing. Again it took off, climbed, and flew aside to wait until it was dark. We did not have to wait long. Darkness was crawling fast from the mountains. We could no longer see the Shturmovik, then it roared above the airfield. We spotted it by the glare from the exhaust rather than by its navigation lights. It was a surprise for many of us.

'It can be spotted even when the navigation lights are off,' somebody said disappointedly. 'With U-2 it was different.'

'On a U-2 the five cylinders and exhaust stubs are placed in the manifold. Here fire gushes out of twelve cylinders,' explained a mechanic.

The plane circled the airfield and began to descend slowly. The roar changed as the pilot reduced throttle. The flame was even brighter now. We listened intently, waiting for the moment of contact, but the engine started again very close to us. The pilot made a new circle, and tried to land again, but in vain. He climbed again and transmitted: 'The glare is blinding me. I can't see the lamps. I'll keep trying...'

Ostapenko asked Kholobaev: 'How did you attack Bobruysk airfield in the dark then?'

'Are you continuing the conference?' the commander pulled him up. He did not tell the sergeant that they had in fact taken off in the dark that time, but landed in bright sunshine. Galushenko managed to land at the fifth try only, and he still missed the guiding lamps. Fortunately, there was no ditch there, and our only dual-control plane was safe.

Kholobaev stopped the flights, and 'phoned the division command. They called up the air force, and prohibited night flights 'until special orders arrive'. The engineers were told to devise flame dampers. They decided to lengthen the exhaust stubs, but it was not an easy task and required much time. For that reason we did not become night pilots.

On 4 October we had a holiday – the first anniversary of the day our regiment was decorated with the Order of Lenin. The day before the anniversary Kholobaev received a telegram. He looked through it and threw it away. 'Kozhuhovsky!' The chief of staff jumped up in surprise. 'I must urgently fly to the Air Force Headquarters. Be on the alert!' and he threatened Kozhuhovsky with his finger.

The commander flew away on U-2, and our head of staff went to the dispersal area. His voice could be heard from afar: 'Keep on alert!'

'We are always on alert, comrade Lieutenant Colonel,' answered the regiment engineer Timofey Tuchin.

'Check everything again!' He looked at a plane and noticed a shameful sight: 'Who hung a gas-mask on a gun?'

'It impedes the work...' said someone's subdued voice.

'Whom does a gas-mask impede?' Fedor Vasilievich got even more irritated. A mechanic scrambled out of the fuselage hatch. 'The gas-mask must always be with you! Put it on!'

Kozhuhovsky inspected the dispersal area for a long time, but did not have time to put everything in order before a messenger ran up to him across the field. He brought a short telegram: 'I fly. Kholobaev.' Fedor Vasilievich fussed about with double energy, waiting for his stern commander.

Kholobaev flew in, got out of the plane smiling, and clapped Kozhuhovsky on the shoulder: 'We are allowed to celebrate the regiment's anniversary before we go to the front!'

We were getting ready for the celebration, and Indian ink, pens, paints, brushes and paper were in high demand. We had no red paint, but we found a way to make it from red flares. It appeared that there were plenty of painters and poets among the crew. Kozhuhovsky examined the work, and was attracted by a man with fleshy ears and a gas mask, depicted in the humour section of the mural newspaper.

'My ears and my gas mask...' he mumbled. 'Well done, guys! Make everybody laugh...'

In the middle of the fuss a lorry drove up to Isti-Su. Two men got out of it. They were wearing uniforms with military decorations. One of them had a strange gait: his legs remained straight, and the toes of his boots were bent up. The other one had many scars on his face and his arm was bent at the elbow. Kholobaev and Kozhuhovsky dashed towards them. They embraced and stood for a long time, rubbing their eyes with crumpled handkerchiefs. They were Shahov and Smurygov back from the Astrakhan hospital. Not a year had passed since the day when Shahov's plane crashed in the forest near Krasny Shahtar. Even less time had passed since the day when stretcher-bearers carried Smurygov to the dead soldiers. Practically no men who knew Shahov and Smurygov were left in the regiment by now, but many new pilots ran out to the street. Without any order they fell in rank, welcoming the veterans, whom they had seen in photographs and heard a great deal about.

The sun was shining, so the grand meeting took place in the open air. Smurygov and Shahov sat at the top table with the command and Mikhail Talykov. The Guards Banner with the Order of Lenin was placed behind the table. The walls were covered with slogans, pictures and significant data showing how many operational flights the regiment had performed since the beginning of the war, how many bombs had been dropped, how many shells fired, what enemy forces and equipment destroyed. There were no numbers, however, showing how much we had to pay for it...

Artemov was the first summoned to the table after the report on the military actions performed by the regiment was over. An Order of the Red Banner was now glittering on his blouse, which he received after Ivan Boiko's death. Then came my turn to receive the same decoration. We all waited for Talykov to be summoned, but his name was not even in the list.

The next day we were ordered to fly to Point 3 near Grozny. Now we were ready indeed! We were armed not only with new aircraft, but also with battle experience.

16

POINT 3

The place where we came to from Isti-Su was marked on the map as a state farm. Now it was our airfield, named Point 3. Our Shturmoviks were standing in caponiers under camouflage netting near the Terski ridge. At the other side of the airfield stood the LaGG-3 fighters from Romantsov's regiment. They would accompany and cover us against Messers in all flights. Not far from the airfield there were three barracks, a wilted acacia, and a rusty trough with ten taps as a washstand. There was also a new 'office area' with plank beds for the crew, and a long table with telephone sets behind a plywood partition. That was the place, where we would get our military orders.

One of the barracks was called 'the nunnery'. Our girls – armourers, waitresses, cooks and nurses – lived there. We were not allowed even to cross its threshold. The stern typist, Maria Brodskaya, whom we called Mother Superior, was held in awe by everybody including the staff commander. She knew and remembered the names of all the men who began the war in the regiment, including the lost ones. She would witness the end of the war in the same regiment.

Victor Shahov was allowed to fly. I trained him on a UIL-2. The flights cost him a lot. The artificial limbs rubbed his legs, which had been amputated a bit below the knee, until they bled. In the evenings I used to bring him a basin with cold water. Victor immersed his stumps and relaxed.

'You see, my heels still itch... Perhaps that's the reason I have problems with co-ordination?' he joked.

Shahov pressed the pedals too hard at first, and could not hold course without my help. But after a while he adapted, and things went better. Kolya Smurygov spent all the time on the runway with

171

us, but he could not fly. His fracture had knitted badly, and pain prevented his pushing the throttle. Kolya was very upset. He was appointed the adjutant of the second squadron.

'I give you leave,' the commander told him. 'Go home for a month. Your arm will heal and you will fly!'

One of the rooms in the 'nunnery' was separated from the living rooms and had its own entrance. We used it as a dance-hall. One of the mechanics, Yurchenko, played his *bayan* in the evenings, and pilots danced with the girls. Our girls looked different now. Once they went to Grozny and came back with their hair curling like young sheep. It was impossible to stay in your barrack at night. Even Petr Rudenko came to the dancing hall with his gramophone, and played 'Rio-Rita', which he had bought again in Grozny. It became very stuffy in the room after a swift foxtrot, and everybody went out to take the air.

A full moon hung above the Caucasus ridge in those days, and lit every corner. Couples could not hide anywhere, so everybody stood by the entrance in awkward silence. Boys were smoking non-stop, and girls did not know, what to do with their hands. Everybody tried not to stand in the bright moonshine, only the pilots with orders put their breasts under the silvery light.

I looked at the wasp waist and slender legs of Masha Odintsova. She was our most dashing armourer, and always had a way with words, but now she was standing silent with Fedya Artemov, as if she had lost the gift of speech. Could that possibly be connected with the Order of the Red Banner glittering on my deputy's breast?

I came up to them and turned so the moon lit up my breast as well. Fedya finally broke the silence: 'It's so good in the fresh wind…'

'It's time to go to bed,' I said. 'Kholobaev will wake us before dawn tomorrow. He'll check the regiment's alertness.'

Fedya and I went to our barrack, and Masha went to the 'nunnery'. She too had to wake up early tomorrow.

'Wake up!'

The person on duty gave the command in an undertone, but the iron beds began to creak and shake at once. Someone lit the 'lamp' – a flattened shell filled with petrol and salt. The washstand was already clattering outside. It was dark and chilly. The moon hid behind the mountains, and the fog was so thick, that we could not even see the 'nunnery'. Fedya Artemov stepped into a puddle and cursed quietly. The rest were laughing:

'Fedya hit the wrong tempo!' they were referring to yesterday's dances. We washed ourselves quickly, put on the warm flying suits, took our pistols, helmets, and map-cases, and hurried to the canteen for an early breakfast: tea with bread and butter. The hot tea was perfect in the morning, especially after the vast amount of tobacco we had smoked at night.

'Help yourself,' the waitress was fussing around. She was running from one table to another pouring more tea. A lorry was already honking by the window – the commander hurried us. We ate as we ran, leaving the canteen and getting into the lorry.

'Is everyone present?' Kholobaev asked from the cabin.

'Everyone!'

The lorry jerked and drove to the dispersal area. The white shroud of fog was impenetrable. We drove up to the first caponier, waited for one of the pilots to get out, and moved on, making short halts near each plane.

My mechanic Temnov reported on the plane's status. I believed my careful assistant, but the instructions obliged me to control everything myself. I checked the fuses of bombs and missiles, the amount of fuel and oil, and many other things.

I got into the cockpit, turned on the transmitter, and heard the commander's voice: 'Start up!' The deafening roar from thirty-six engines swept across the valley. We waited for the next command, and soon it came: 'Fire!' Cannons and machine-guns started firing almost simultaneously. The bright tracks from tracer bullets cut the fog layer and glittered in the sky. After that everything fell silent. The lorry gathered the pilots one by one, and drove us to the office.

'The regiment must be on the alert today!' the commander declared. 'Third squadron stay here and wait for a mission!'

My pilots got into bed. I could name almost all my guys by their boots sticking out: Fedya Artemov, Misha Vorozhbiev, Kolya Sednenkov, Vasya Shamshurin. The rest were sergeants, Ivan Ostapenko among them. He wasn't in the mood to talk that morning. I guessed he must be nervous, since it was going to be his first sortie.

Two telephone sets were standing on the table. The green one rang often, but we did not pay attention. But when the black one buzzed, men began to stir in their beds. 'Is that command calling?' The person on duty was speaking quietly into the receiver: 'The fog hasn't cleared away yet…'

It was already time for the second breakfast. The pilots took their plates and went out of the stuffy place to get some fresh air. The fog was rising a bit above the ground, and both the valley and the mountains were hidden from view. No flying conditions yet…

After breakfast everybody cheered up. Ivan Ostapenko was telling a new variant of the story of how he had managed to get into the Guards Regiment from the Air School:

'I was practising banking and noticed a plane with yellow cantilevers following me. I felt hot all over: a Fritz! How on earth did he get to Uralsk? And was he going to shoot me down in the hinterland? I was frightened as hell, and banked so sharply that I was hanging on the seat-belt headfirst. The engine began to stall. I throttled down, and thought: 'That's the end, Ivan Petrovich!' My plane's nose was already lowered and I was aiming at the ground. Fortunately, I was still rather high… As I was trying to understand what was going on, I saw the horizon line again. Then I realised that I had rolled right over! I landed more dead than alive, and saw the plane with yellow cantilevers landing after me. It appeared that a student pilot from the neighbouring airfield had got lost and was following me. His Il had yellow cantilevers. I did not want to tell the instructor, that I had performed a forbidden manoeuvre out of fright, so I said I did it on purpose. The head of the school, General Kravtsov, put me in the garrison jail for ten days, but I was still a hero. Rumours were spread that a second Nesterov★ had appeared in the school. Two days before the end of the punishment I was summoned to the head of the school. I thought that was the end of my flying career. I entered the office and saw the head of the school, the head of the political department, my instructor, and a colonel from the Air Force, whom I did not know. I wanted to fall to my knees, but remembered that it was not allowed in the regulations.

' "Comrade General," I said, "forgive me. I won't commit a single

★ Nesterov was a famous Russian pilot of World War I who was the first to perform the loop and use the ram attack.

violation in the air. I will justify your confidence…"

'The colonel grinned and said: "Comrade Ostapenko, do you mind going to the front?"

'I thought: "Is he joking? Who can possibly refuse to go to the front?" Our instructors put away money from each salary into a common fund, and then an article would appear in the newspaper: "Aircraft bought on personal savings". Instructors would raffle it off, and the lucky one was allowed to go to the front despite being on reserve. My instructor must be looking at me with jealousy.'

' "I long to go to the front!" I answered.

' "That's good, Ivan Petrovich," he said, "your wish will be fulfilled. We need men who can fly in more than one direction. You may go and serve your term of punishment!" '

At this point in the story Ostapenko inhaled and said: 'So now I think that if it hadn't been for that incident, I would never have got into the 7th Guards!'

Everybody laughed heartily.

The mist was rising higher and higher; blue gaps appeared in the cloud. A triangulation tower could already be seen at the top of the Terski mountain ridge. So we would not have to wait long now. It was good to listen to Ostapenko's stories, but I felt I had to repeat the battle formation to the wingmen. At the end of my short speech I once again warned the young pilots: 'Remember: the most important thing in an operational flight is sticking together!'

I looked at sergeant Ostapenko and could read his mind: 'How many times are you going to repeat the same thing? It's all been clear for ages. And you may be sure, I've learnt to hold the formation. Well, yes, I haven't performed an operational flight myself yet, but still I've seen others taking off many times… And as we were marching from the Don I've experienced real fear. Just let us fly - and I'll show you that I was not born yesterday, squadron leader. I will smash the Fritzes as much as the famous Talykov or Artemov!'

The person on duty ran out of the office: 'Crew, to the commander!'

It was as if a whirlwind swept off the men of the third squadron. Artemov and I were by the entrance before the rest of the team. We could hardly keep from running, our pace was unusually springy. Though our commander did not tolerate slowness, I always held myself back not only in movement but also in word when it came to discussing a military task. It did not stop me from being nervous of course; I had enough butterflies in my stomach. But I had to conceal my nervousness from the wingmen. The men must believe in you on the ground at this point. So I tried to look calm. As we were entering the office, thoughts were swirling in my head: 'Where will they send us? To Mozdock, or to the Elkhotovsky gates? It would be better to lead the sergeants in their first flight in a relatively quiet region, with less flak and no Messerschmitts.'

The commander struck his hand impatiently on a map spread on the table: 'Orders! Take seats, quickly!'

Everybody began to look at the maps. Everyone was smoking, except for Vorozhbiev, who was a non-smoker. You would inhale, and hide your hand immediately under the table, so that the rest could not see your fingers trembling from strain and fear. The commander was rushing: 'To the south of Mozdock, Voznesenskaya... on the actual Terski ridge... Has everyone found it? It's near the mark 703. Does everybody see it? About ten kilometres to the north our troops are repelling enemy infantry and tanks on the mountainsides. That's where you must strike. Yemelyan!' he addressed me. 'Be careful, don't hit our own troops! Do you understand?'

'I do,' answered I.

I looked up and saw all the crew staring at my left hand, in which I held a cigarette. I deliberately didn't hide it. I leaned on the table with my elbow and relaxed my forearm and hand. Thus my fingers were not trembling. That was my old trick. It always calmed people down. 'If the leader is not nervous, we will all be back safe.' Let them think this way, while I worry about other things: 'How will we locate the target?' Point 703 was marked on the map, but nobody was going to draw numbers on the ground for us. The battle would be fought on the bare slopes, and everything would be mixed up for sure. How should we distinguish our troops from the enemy's? And what if the young pilots dashed aside from an anti-aircraft gun and hit the wrong target? It's easy to say: 'Don't hit our own troops!...'

A lorry brought us to the dispersal area, and I watched Ostapenko jumping out near his plane. His mechanic, Nikolai Bublik, was waiting for him. Bublik had seen off more than a dozen pilots both in their first, and the last flights.

We completed the mission successfully and did not lose any aircraft, but Shturmovik number 25 was the last to land, and its canopy was broken. An ambulance car dashed towards it from the runway. The nurses grabbed sergeant Ostapenko, who got out of the cockpit with his face stained all over with blood, and put him on a stretcher. Tosya Tabachnaya was wailing nearby: 'My God! What are you waiting for? Take him to the hospital!'

They put the stretcher in the car, and drove away.

We were sitting in the office again, and the commander was facing us. Everything was just as before the flight, but Ostapenko was missing. Nobody talked about him at that moment. The regiment commander asked me: 'How did it go?'

'Not bad, I guess...' It was difficult to evaluate your own actions. 'Everyone did his best.'

'What does it mean "not bad"?' Suddenly he became angry. It grated on me.

'You should have seen the mess yourself...' I realised that I said the wrong thing and added: 'Our troops should at least mark the front line with the flares! There were no signals.'

'I will see, if there is a need... And don't make excuses! Whether they've set up flares or not, the leader is still responsible!'

'If we did something wrong, I'll bear the responsibility...'

'Are you sure, you did not hit our troops?' the commander kept on interrogating. He was angry.

'I don't think so.'

'Can you guarantee it?'

'I can't guarantee, but I am sure...'

The commander began to interrogate the wingmen, but did not learn anything new. We went out of the office and lay on the cool autumn ground. I had to hold a debriefing, but did not feel like talking. The sky was clear now, the sun was shining, and the green mountains could be seen perfectly. We were to fly again soon, but now without Ostapenko. Where was he?

Shahov stumped towards us looking very depressed. He had been ready to perform his forty-seventh sortie that day, but we had a call from the headquarters of the 4th Air Army.

'I forbid Shahov to fly!' said the Corps Commander. 'If he is shot down, the Germans will shower the whole world with leaflets:

Russians are so desperate, they are already making people with artificial limbs fly...'

When Shahov learnt this, he went behind the caponier so that nobody could see him and wept. It was the second time he had cried at the front: the first time it was when his friend Nikolai Sinyakov burnt down, the second time was now.

'You'll be a staff officer,' the commander tried to console him.

Shahov watched the first squadron taking off. The Shturmoviks from the third squadron were getting ready for a new flight. Fedya Artemov was watching Masha Odintsova dragging a hundred-kilo bomb to the plane.

The head of staff's deputy Gudimenko ran out of the blindage waving a piece of paper and shouting: 'Confirmation!'

He gave me the telegram and I read: 'The commander of the 9th Army expresses his thanks to the Shturmoviks working at 10.20.' Now I was not just sure, I could guarantee!

Suddenly we saw Ostapenko going out from behind the barrack, and could not believe our eyes! He was walking towards us with a broad smile on his face. How could it be so? He had been carried on the stretcher with his face bleeding, and now there was not a scratch on it.

The smiling Ostapenko told us what happened to him in his first sortie. When he got in the cockpit and put his feet on the pedals, they were trembling. The elated mood vanished. Unexpected thoughts were running through his head: 'What if I fail to form up and lose the group? How will I locate the target? It won't be training targets marked with white lime! What if I fail to notice it?' Fortunately, he did not have time to think, that his first sortie could well be the last, because he heard a familiar voice.

'They are starting!' Bublik was tipping him off.

Ostapenko looked around and saw the propellers of other aircraft rotating already. With his left hand he opened the compressed air valve, but his right hand could not find the starter button. Bublik pressed it himself, and the engine fired.

Ostapenko taxied to the runway and took off. In the air he kept his eyes fixed on the planes before him, since he was afraid to lose them. It seemed to him that he circled above the same place for too long. He looked down and did not see the airfield. The leading flights had already set the course, and Ostapenko fell behind. He pushed the throttle, and the tails of the planes flying ahead of him began to approach rapidly. Then it seemed that somebody pulled them all up by a string. In his helmet Ostapenko heard the familiar voice of the squadron leader: 'Number 25, stop dancing and take your place...' The remark calmed him down and he thought how easy it had seemed to hold the formation during the training. He joined his flight and flew further.

Soon he heard the commander's voice again: 'Get ready for the attack! Aim to the left. Begin the manoeuvre!' The group ahead of Ostapenko moved left, then right, some planes were jumping up, some down. Ostapenko hardly had time to watch his neighbours, and there was no time to look at the target. Meanwhile the leader was giving a new command: 'Manoeuvre! Manoeuvre!' His plane was moving off, followed by black puffs of smoke. 'That must be smoky exhaust,' Ostapenko thought. He noticed that his windshield was growing dim, but he was not worried. He had a clean rag in his pocket, and he remembered students in the Air School wiping the glass in the air. He took the rag and reached out for the window. At that moment a black cloud appeared before his very eyes. The plane jerked, and the pilot lost his breath for a second. Wind was beating in his face. There was no windshield left. At first Ostapenko did not realise what had happened. His only thought was 'Stick to the rest!' The Shturmoviks were already lowing their noses, getting ready to dive. Ostapenko pushed the column forward and heard the command: 'Drop!' Bombs were pouring out of the hatches. He found the releasing button and pressed it.

The Shturmoviks were now circling above the ground and firing. Ostapenko was also pulling the triggers. His plane was shaking feverishly; something was smoking and burning on the ground. The wind was blowing hard, and now Ostapenko realised that safety goggles were not there for appearance only. Fortunately he did not know yet that the goggles would also protect the eyes from fire. 'One more attempt!' said the leader's voice inside the helmet. Ostapenko had long since lost count of the attempts. Neither could he determine the right direction, from which he had to attack. His mouth was parched, sweat was showering down his face, and he had to wipe it every few seconds with his left hand. Suddenly he heard:

'Assemble!' It was time to form up, but he could not see a single plane. He turned his head and saw white tracks swishing the air. A plane with crosses on the fuselage raced past him. Ostapenko pulled the triggers aiming at the Messer, and suddenly noticed a group of Shturmoviks. He caught up with them and formed up. The group was heading to the east. Soon they crossed a ridge and flew above a valley. A big town was coming into view. It was Grozny.

Ostapenko saw the airfield, but... it was not our airfield! The group was already landing. It would have been a really nice end of his first operational flight, if he had landed in the wrong place! The sergeant looked around desperately, and, thank God, saw his barracks at the foot of the mountain in a distance, and planes circling above. He was terribly glad. He landed and was taxiing to the dispersal area, when he saw Nikolai Bublik giving him a sign to stop the engine. Ostapenko did not understand what was going on, but obeyed. He got out of the cockpit quickly, took off the parachute, and was ready to jump down from the wing, when the nurses grabbed him. It appeared that he had cut his fingers with the broken glass, and later smeared the blood all over his face trying to wipe sweat from it. The sight was rather horrible.

The next day the local newspaper published an article about the feat of sergeant Ostapenko, who 'being heavily wounded in the head and bleeding all over managed to pilot his damaged plane to the airfield and made a perfect landing'. Ostapenko sent the article to his instructor in the Air School.

17

OVER THE NOGAJSK STEPPES

The front line was still bounded by the Tereck, and we were stuck at Point 3 for a long time. At the end of September the fascist troops managed to capture a bridgehead near Majsky, but the command did not seem to bother much about the enemy enclave, and we were not sent there. Instead we often flew to the Mozdock region. Despite the heavy losses the 1st German Tank Army kept on ramming our defence lines from the north. The reports from Sovinformburo* were rather alarming: severe fighting was in full swing in the Stalingrad region. Though we were more than 200 kilometres away, we still considered Stalingrad our closest neighbour. We had to work hard in our region to prevent the enemy transferring reserves from the Caucasus to Stalingrad.

Our reconnaissance aircraft discovered that there was a big gap between the enemy forces in Stalingrad and the Caucasus. The command decided to station the 4th Cossack Cavalry Corps led by Lieutenant General Kirichenko in the gap, so that they could strike the rear of the Kleist's tank army. The Cossacks had to fight in the vast Nogajsk steppes to the north from Grozny. In our free moments we studied the region, where we would have to fly. We took a 'dumb' map without legends, and tried to remember by heart the strange-sounding names of tiny settlements, salty lakes, and rivers. We had to learn everything, since it is not always possible to consult the map during the flight.

Deputy of the Air Corps for intelligence Ivan Philimonovich Radetski came to instruct us. He unfolded his map on the table and bent over it.

* A Soviet news agency.

181

'I'll describe the situation in the Nogajsk steppes,' he paused. Someone asked immediately: 'Shall we start from the front line?'

'There's no front line, comrades.' Radetski answered.

'How is it possible to wage war without a front line?' asked Fedya Artemov. He asked it as a joke, because he remembered too well, how we had fought without any front line on our maps, when our troops were retreating from the Don to the Caucasus foothills. Perhaps he expected Radetski to joke back, but he only coughed and continued.

'The enemy has occupied the following settlements −'

The pilots quickly took blue pencils.

'Mark: Abdul-Gazy, Achikulak, Makhmud-Makteb, Berezkin... That's where the enemy cavalry has settled.'

'Do the Fritzes also have cavalry?' someone was surprised.

'According to the reports of all the reconnaissance units there are up to 400 cavalrymen, an infantry battalion, and thirty tanks in Achikulak. In other settlements there are small infantry sub-units.'

Radetski said nothing more. We were seriously alarmed. What if we mixed up the enemy cavalry with our Cossacks? We had learnt to distinguish the enemy's blunt-nosed lorries from ours, but how should we distinguish horses? Our only hope was for the forward aircraft observer, who was sent to the Cossacks with a radio station. He could help us, if he would see us.

Several days later a big van brought the division navigator Vasilij Krivoshein to our airfield. Mechanics set up a tall antenna next to the van. Krivoshein gathered the pilots and began to explain: 'This is a radio station. It can lead you to your airfield from any place.'

'Can it also lead us to the target?'

'No, you must find the target yourself.'

'That's something at least.' we thought. 'After the attack you often can't work out straightaway which way to fly.'

Krivoshein proceeded: 'Your plane's receiver will be tuned to the station frequency. When you fly back, don't forget to turn it on. Then you won't need to do anything: you'll just have to keep the needle in the middle of the scale. That's all. Got it?'

'Got it,' we answered, but somebody asked: 'Does the enemy have such kind of stations?'

'Of course...'

'And what if they tune up to the same frequency?'

'Then you may pay them a visit,' the navigator smiled.

The pilots murmured, displeased, 'We'll fall into the beast's clutches with this radio station!'

'Don't worry, comrades,' the navigator was calming us down. 'Our frequencies do not coincide with the enemy's. And besides you can distinguish your station by the music.'

'What music?'

'We'll play some popular record. It will be a music password for our station.'

After he said that Petr Rudenko started: 'We'll play "Rio-Rita"!' he suggested, and everyone burst out laughing.

On 2 October the cavalry corps led by General Kirichenko moved from Gudermes to the north-west along the Nogajsk steppes. They marched at night only and managed to cover 150 kilometres. In the second week of October the Cossacks smashed the enemy garrisons in Abdul-Gazy and Berezkin in a sudden attack. They watered their horses and rode to Achikulak. When the Germans found out about the cavalrymen, they began to transfer reserves and our regiment was ordered to assault the German troops near Achikulak. It was almost 200 kilometres away. Fighters from the Romantsov regiment were unable to accompany us as far as the target. The most they could do was to protect us from the enemy covering forces near Isherskaya, since there was no way to avoid that area.

The third squadron took off. Two pairs of fighters were covering us from behind and from above. We were heading for the north-west. We crossed the Tereck and were flying above the sand-dunes as low as possible.

'Messers to the left. We start approaching.' The voice of the fighters' leader, Vasya Fedorenko, sounded calm, as if nothing special was going on. But we knew it would be a mess.

I looked to the left and saw four black points against a white cloud.

'Roger, roger.' I answered to Fedorenko counting in my head. Four of our fighters against four enemy fighters, that would be one to one. If they managed to keep the Messers busy even for five minutes, we would be thirty kilometres away, and they would have a hard time trying to catch up and find us.

'Number 3, cover me! I'm attacking,' I heard Fedorenko's voice again. So it had started already.

There was nothing but sand beneath us. After a twenty minutes' flight I noticed about a hundred dismounted cavalrymen near the dry river Kura. When they saw us, they began to throw up their *kubankas*.* They had really gone a long way! Now I saw the village of Berezkin, won back from the Germans, and relaxed: we were flying the right course. Achikulak should come into view in ten minutes.

We began to climb. This would make it easier to spot the target, and, besides, our bombs had delayed-action fuses and we could not drop them too low because of the air-blast. Perhaps the leading aircraft observer would notice us and help us find the target.

I saw a big settlement ahead. White ducks were swimming peacefully in a pond. Many German lorries were standing around. Puffs of black smoke could already be seen near our planes. 'What should we attack?' I was thinking. 'The lorries? We can't bomb the houses, can we?' We flew above Achikulak. How I wished I could hear a tip from the radio from that aircraft observer! But the radio remained silent. Suddenly I saw a big herd of horses. Many of them were saddled, and soldiers were running nearby. Some of them mounted the horses and galloped off in different directions. That's the target! Captain Radetski had informed us correctly: there were up to 400 cavalrymen.

'Attack!'

We dived one by one, and our hundred-kilogram bombs exploded beneath. I levelled out, banked and began to climb again. The roof of the stable crashed down and caught fire. Horses were rushing about, trampling down the cavalrymen. Anti-aircraft guns were firing, but it was not as bad as near Mozdock. We were ready for a new attack, but there was nothing left by now. Soldiers and horses lying by the burning stable were no danger now. But some groups escaped and were galloping along the field. The Shturmoviks raced in different directions following them.

'How will I assemble the group?' I was worrying. The guys were carried away by the pursuit, and I knew we had just barely enough fuel to come back. I climbed and began to circle to the side of Achikulak. 'Group! Group!' I kept ordering looking sideways and trying to spot my wingmen. At a distance I noticed a long strip of dust. An enemy column was moving to Achikulak from the west. That

---

* Cossack hats.

would be a nice target for the group who followed my squadron. The wingmen finally caught up with me and we headed home. I turned on the receiver and heard the familiar foxtrot. The audibility was perfect. It was hard to believe that we were so far away from our airfield!

Again I saw the Kura and Berezkin, but the Cossacks must have galloped somewhere further to the north. Twelve Shturmoviks flew in the opposite direction. Major Galushenko was leading his squadron to Achikulak. I told him about the column I had seen. 'Roger,' answered the leader. My guys held the formation, and I felt relaxed.

Our regiment had to fly to the Nogajsk steppes many times. The Cossacks were pleased and presented us with a huge cask of Kizlar wine with an inscription: 'To the Guards Pilots from the Guards Cossacks'. General Kirichenko himself ordered it to be delivered to our airfield.

We were sitting by the command post waiting for new orders. It was a sunny October day, and the air was amazingly clear. The blue mountain slopes with white snow tops could be seen in a distance. Fedya Artemov was admiring the view: 'God, it's so beautiful!'

Fedya was a very positive person. It seemed he was not at all upset by the fact that he had failed to lead the group that day.

'It's high time you became a leader,' I had told him yesterday. 'We always fly together, and it's exhausting for both of us. Let's take turns: one time I will lead the squadron, the next time you can. I'm tired, and you don't look well.'

Fedya always flew to my left, that was his favourite place. He often flew so close to me that I had to drive him away. I was afraid that if a shell hit one of us, we would both be shot down. And who would be a leader then? I did not say that to Fedya, of course, but I made another important argument: 'You know that Galushenko and Rudenko take turns leading the first squadron, and there are actually three leaders in the second: the squadron commander, Talykov, and Smirnov!'

Fedya answered frankly: 'I'm afraid to lead.'

'But why?'

'I don't think I can assemble the group after the take-off, and lead them to the target.'

'It only feels like that. You've made half of a hundred sorties. You can do it. Let's try tomorrow. You will be the leader, and I will fly on your right and look after you. If anything goes wrong, you'll take your usual place, and I will lead.'

But the attempt failed. After the take-off he turned too early. The circle was small and the last planes had to catch up with the rest of the group. Fedya noticed that and slowed down sharply. The rear planes began to approach too fast. It all happened so quickly that my comments by radio were in vain. Fedya had to occupy his usual place.

'Let me fly as a wingman once again, and then we will change,' Fedya told me.

So we were sitting by the command post enjoying the scenery. The sun was shining above the Caucasus ridge. Suddenly the blue sky was covered with black blots. We heard flaps. Fedya shouted: 'They're diving!' Nine dark spots were racing to the ground. One of them blazed and fell like a fiery drop followed by a line of smoke.

'It's shot down!'

Fighters were taking off from our airfield. The bursts from anti-aircraft guns were accompanied by the rattling of machine-guns. The nimble fighters hovered behind the German bombers like wasps. We saw a new smoking track and two white canopies hung in the air.

'One more!'

The bursts exploded very close, and we bent down in surprise. Twin-engined Junkers were hedgehopping above our airfield. There were only six of them by now. They did not bother about the formation and were making off for the Terski ridge one by one. Our LaGG-3 caught up with the last one, fired a burst, a second one... and the left side of the bomber caught fire. The plane banked sharply, hit the ground with a wing and tumbled... That was the end of it!

Black smoke was curling meanwhile above Grozny. It hid the mountains and the sun and was drifting to the valley. The black shroud covered our airfield soon. It became so dark that we could not see our barracks. The pitch darkness lasted for three days. A huge smoking cloud stretched for 200 kilometres as far as Makhachkala. Flights were out of the question. Only cars dared to drive cautiously with their lights on. Soot was everywhere, even our faces were black. We stayed in the barracks and thought: 'The Fritzes must have abandoned the idea of capturing Grozny oil.'

18

THE CRUCIAL FLIGHTS

On 25 October 1942, seventy enemy bombers destroyed the headquarters of the 37th Army near Nalchik. The command was lost. Hundreds of German tanks moved eastwards from a small bridgehead near Mayski village. Units of the 37th Army retreating to the Caucasus foothills were suffering heavy tolls. The only flight route now was towards Nalchik. We attacked the German tanks and infantry near Erokko, Chikola and Dur-Dur. Our troops were gathering by Ordzhonikidze in order to block the main route into Georgia.

On 1 November enemy aircraft bombed Ordzhonikidze, and on 2 November fascists troops broke through the outer line of the fortified area and their vanguard moved up to the suburbs of the town. On that day I led my squadron to attack tanks near Alagir. We managed to set three tanks on fire and were hedgehopping back. We were flying above a valley with nothing but maize fields beneath. Suddenly I noticed a tank track on the ground. 'How could it get here?' I thought, and immediately noticed another track. And then… I saw a tank camouflaged among the corn-cobs, another one… I looked around – there was a host of them! For several minutes I flew above the maize fields breathing heavily and seeing more and more tanks… They were lying doggo like cockroaches in holes. Obviously they had gathered there for a fatal strike. As soon as I landed I reported: 'In this area,' I showed on the map, 'I spotted loads of tanks.'

'What do you mean by loads?' the commander looked at me in disbelief. 'Can you define it more precisely?'

'Yes, I can! There are no less than a thousand!' I said with confidence. I had been unable to count them, but what I saw shocked me.

'Who else saw the tanks?' the commander asked the wingmen.

They looked confused, and I realised that they all had been busy watching the neighbouring planes and did not see anything else. And I did not broadcast anything, because I was afraid the Fritzes could hear me and I wanted them to think they hadn't been seen yet.

The commander said, 'Go have a nap,' and tapped me on the shoulder. I took that friendly gesture for an evident hint that he did not believe me. I was furious.

'Comrade commander,' I said in an official tone, 'I ask you to call the headquarters of the Air Army immediately. I will report to General Naumenko myself!'

The commander of the 4th Air Army General Naumenko sent a reconnaissance aircraft, and my report was confirmed. For the next three days our Air Army attacked the 13th and 23rd Tank Divisions of the enemy, which had been secretly transferred from Mozdock to the valley for a fatal strike on Ordzhonikidze. Meanwhile enemy units were forcing their way to the town. They managed to make a narrow passage along the steep mountain slopes, but the 11th Guards Rifle Corps did not allow them to widen it.

On 6 November the enemy advance was stopped. In those days our regiment was fighting under the greatest strain. A squadron used to take off as soon as another one landed. On that day my squadron made three operational flights. It was already evening, and we did not expect any more tasks. Fedya Artemov cheered up, expecting a good dinner. For several days we had not had any lunch. It was brought to the airfield, so that there were no delays with take-offs, but we did not have time to eat it. That's why in the evenings we gobbled up dinner *and* lunch. We also received our hundred grams for the flights. We had lost three men by that time, but their rations were still delivered. The commander distributed them as a reward.

After dinner we usually went dancing. Fedya was thinking, of course, of the slender Masha, so he had several reasons to cheer up.

'Tomorrow we'll celebrate the twenty-fifth anniversary of October!'★ Fedya said. 'I'm short of money unfortunately. I asked one guy to lend me some, but he refused.'

'Why?'

'He said: 'How will I get my money back, if something happens?''

★ The October Revolution of 1917.

'Who said that?'

'A guy from the depot. Doesn't matter.' Fedya did not seem upset.

'A scoundrel!' I found some cash in my pockets and gave it to Fedya to buy some perfume. 'Don't be gone for too long in the evening, we've got a dress rehearsal.'

We were rehearsing a small play for the celebration. There were only two characters in it: a fascist general who lost his trousers near Ordzhonikidze and his adjutant. I had talked Major Galushenko into playing the general, but nobody wanted to play the adjutant. The general was too harsh. Fedya agreed to play this role only after he was told that it was a Komsomol order.

At that moment we saw a flare and knew that we had to make a fourth flight to Gisel today.

We were flying above the Sunzhensk valley. The wooded mountain slopes glided to the left. There were lots of anti-aircraft guns near Gisel, but we had learnt to approach the target not from the valley, but from the mountains. It was more difficult to spot the dark-green Shturmoviks against the dark mountains. I moved closer to the mountains making Fedya move as well. We were flying at an altitude of more than 1,000 metres. The anti-aircraft guns kept silent. I could see the target already, and was going to begin the manoeuvre.

Suddenly there was gunfire. My plane jerked, and something flashed to my left. I looked there and saw a Shturmovik tumbling chaotically with one wing missing. It crashed down to the forest on the mountain side and a fiery pillar rose to the sky.

'Artem! Artem!' I screamed and turned to attack the guns. The wingmen dashed after me. We dropped the bombs and fired until the guns were destroyed. Then we began to shoot at the lorries, but Messers attacked us, and we had to defend ourselves. We were circling at a low altitude, and the Messers were trying to outflank the planes one by one. Tracer bullets raced past me. I yawed and saw a Messer dashing past. Vasya Shamshurin, who was flying behind me, had driven the enemy fighter away. Well done! I noticed strips of cloth fluttering on the rudder of Vasya's plane. The Fritz must have hit it in the tail. At that moment I noticed our fighters flying above. ' "Little ones",★ cover us, we are under attack near Gisel!'

★ Another common name for Soviet fighters during the war.

The fighters rocketed down, and the Messers zoomed and headed to the mountains. We finished the attack and flew home – Point 3.

As soon as I stopped the engine a lorry drove up to my plane and the commander got out of it. 'How did you accomplish the mission?'

I threw off my parachute, jumped down from the wing, and stood facing the commander with my teeth clenched. 'Fedya Artemov...' I could hardly utter the word, 'was shot down.'

I turned round and walked to the barracks.

Boots shuffled on the grass behind me. 'Messers or anti-aircraft guns?' the commander wanted specific information.

Without answering I pulled my helmet off my head, and threw it on the ground. The goggles smashed. The barracks became blur, and inside my head I was hearing: 'Tomorrow we'll celebrate the 25th anniversary of October...'

Low clouds hid the green mountains. It was raining constantly, and the valleys were covered with mist. Our troops regrouped and were surrounding enemy units at Gisel. The Germans resisted desperately, and managed to hold a narrow pass near Dzuarikau where the only road was. I had few experienced pilots left in my squadron. My friend Volodya Zangiev had been shot down the day before above Khataldon. Together with sergeant Pismichenko he was covering my group from Messers. All the fighters had been sent to cover Ordzhonikidze, and two of our Shturmoviks were doing their job. Zangiev was fighting above his native village, Ardon, and managed to shoot down an enemy fighter, but then his plane was hit, caught fire, and fell in the enemy area. Misha Vorozhbiev had not returned the day before. Now we lost Fedya Artemov... The only person, who was now fighting his second 'round' was Junior Lieutenant Vasya Shamshurin. Strange as it might seem, he had not even been promoted to flight commander. But he was glad he did not have to give orders to anyone. He always looked embarrassed when he listened to his mechanic's reports. The commander often told him off for 'the lack of exacting demands from subordinates'. Vasya always treated his mechanic and armourer casually. The commander was unable to make him behave more officiously.

'Why is he so harsh with me?' Vasya wondered.

Shamshurin could not be called handsome. A wedge-shaped face, a wide forehead, a boxing scar, and a lock of straight hair. He talked little, but liked to listen to the others. He stood out among the pilots for his quiet but infectious laughter.

Flights, flights, flights... Everyone was exhausted, but there was no end to it. The enclave occupied by the enemy troops was blocked almost from every direction, but there were hosts of Germans there! And we were not just physically exhausted, we had also lost many people. Some freshmen arrived of course: Zlobin, Papov, Chernets, Fominyh. Some of them could only pilot fighters, and we had to retrain them.

The weather was awful. Because of heavy clouds we had to fly just above the ground, and thus were a target for everything that was able to shoot. Each time we came back, our planes were riddled with bullets, and the mechanics hardly had time to patch them up. But in our turn we set on fire dozens of enemy lorries and tanks, and hundreds of Nazis were mown down by machine-gun fire.

It was 8 November. We had a mission to destroy enemy hardware in the outskirts of Dzuarikau. We took off and hedgehopped towards Stolovaya mountain. The weather improved a bit, and the sun shone through the breaches in the clouds. We crossed the front line and were approaching the target, trying to avoid the bursts of anti-aircraft guns. I could see a road and small white houses at the foot of green mountain slopes. In the outskirts of Dzuarikau all the gardens were packed with lorries. The Fritzes must have been getting ready to break the encirclement. That was our target. Ostapenko was flying to my left, Shamshurin to my right, Talykov and Ezhov behind us.

'We approach the target...' I warned the wingmen.

Ostapenko moved closer immediately, but Shamshurin stayed behind for some reason. There was an inscription on his plane's fuselage: 'Avenge Mospanov!' Suddenly I saw fire under it. It was spreading fast towards the tail. The lower petrol tank, which was under the pilot's feet, must have been punched.

'Shamshurin, you are on fire! Go back!' I radioed, trying to sound calm.

He swayed from one wing to the other, meaning that he got it, but kept flying forward. I could not understand what he was doing. The front line was not far away. The flame was already approaching the cockpit. Shamshurin pushed the canopy back, put his left hand on the windshield, rose a bit from his seat, and looked forward. He had his goggles on. What was he waiting for?

'Bail out!' I shouted. He sat down, sped up, and was now ahead of us. His plane was coming down followed by the fiery tail. Shamshurin was firing short bursts at the lorries. The ground was already close. It was time to stop diving!

'Level out! Level out!' That was all I had time to shout before the Shturmovik loaded with bombs hit the very centre of the enemy machinery and exploded.

'Attack! Attack!!'

One by one we dived into the flame and smoke.

The German tank divisions were making their last attempts to escape from the trap. They tried to force their way to the Suarskoe canyon near the village of Mayramadag, but met heavy resistance from the seamen, supported by attack aircraft from the air. The enemy failed to break the defence. On 11 November we got good news: the Gisel grouping of the enemy was crushed! That was our first serious victory in the Caucasus.

Our neighbours in Stalingrad began to surround the enemy mass of 330,000 on the Volga. Now we were all convinced that we would start moving to the west soon. But the victories cost us a lot. Our regiment suffered a new bereavement: Petr Rudenko did not come back on the day when the enemy group in Gisel was finally defeated. He was killed in an unequal aerial combat with enemy fighters near Mozdock. His dark-blue overcoat was hanging on a nail, and his gramophone was standing on his empty bed. I remembered his words: 'When I die, present this gramophone to the bravest pilot...' In my mind I went over the names of those lost in the last days. All of them had fought heroically, but I would have presented this gramophone to Vasily Shamshurin. His fiery ram attack near Dzuarikau brought him everlasting fame. Who could have expected such tremendous store of courage from that shy guy?

We had a meeting with all the regiment present. The commander read out the order to confer the rank of the Hero of the Soviet Union to Petr Ivanovich Rudenko, and the request to confer the highest degree of battle honour to Vasily Grigorievich Shamshurin posthumously.

We celebrated the New Year of 1943 at Point 3. Everybody was in high spirits. We had our reasons: the enemy was retreating to the west pursued by our forces. Besides, Misha Vorozhbiev, who was thought dead, came back to the regiment. His plane had crashed near a target at the beginning of November. A shell exploded inside the cockpit, and a splinter hit Misha in the eye. When he came to his senses, he felt someone rummaging in his pockets. He half-opened his only eye – the left one – and saw a Fritz, who had already taken off his watch. The decision came in a second: Misha grabbed the marauder below the chin with his strong fingers and strangled him. For seven days Vorozhbiev crawled along the steep slopes licking hoarfrost from branches. He managed to get to Tashkent and was sent to Professor Filatov's eye hospital. Now he returned to Point 3 with an artificial eye and declared that he wanted to fly. He was allowed to pilot a training aircraft, and later he trained the freshmen.

The New Year party took place in a barn. We hung a slogan: 'The day will come soon when the enemy will face fatal strikes from the Red Army!'

Nikolai Galushenko and Mikhail Vorozhbiev received their first high awards: the Order of the Red Banner. Mikhail Talykov also got this award. I was presented the Order of the Red Banner and the Order of the Patriotic War. It was the first time we had seen this order, and it was passed from hand to hand. Everyone wanted to have a look at the silver rays and the sabre crossed with a rifle. Misha Talykov examined the order for a long time and said: 'It's a pity they haven't depicted a diving aircraft here. It looks like the infantry and the cavalry are the only fighting corps.'

'Come on, you've forgotten to mention the artillery and tank units. A plane, a gun, and a tank would not fit here anyway,' I said. I turned to Vorozhbiev, who was grinning.

'Let me fix it on your blouse, Vasya.'

Meanwhile the home-made curtains rose up, and the show began. Amateur singers, dancers, poets, and magicians entertained the audience. Our sketch was the highlight of the programme. Major Galushenko was at his best. The commissar of my squadron, Yakov Kvaktun, who played the adjutant instead of Fedya Artemov, was a great foil to the stern general. The show lasted until long after midnight. When it was over, the regiment commander rose on the stage and declared: 'Tomorrow we'll be getting ready to move to a new airfield in Galyugaevskaya!'

That was New Year news! We were to fly 100 kilometres to the west. It would be our first airfield on the territory won back from the enemy since the beginning of the war.

Farewell, Point 3!

19

A SPECIAL MISSION

On January 5, 1943, we landed on an airfield not far from Mozdock. It had been raining a lot, and the wheels were stuck in the mud. It was difficult to believe that not long ago Messerschmitts were taking off from that airfield to hunt our fighters, and anti-aircraft guns had met us with heavy defensive fire. Now we found there a cemetery of German planes. We examined curiously the punched fuselages and wings, the warped propeller blades.

The Fritzes left an intact billet for us. Its walls and ceiling were covered with veneer, so soil did not pour down the backs of our collars there. The Germans had also taken care with decoration: the walls were covered with all kinds of pictures.

Next to the airfield there was a village Galyugaevskaya. It was almost reduced to ashes. Black cats prowled between the remnants of the houses. We met a scrawny old man who lived there. With his white beard and long white hair he looked like a hermit.

'Hello, Grandfather!' We gathered round him, longing to ask about life during the German occupation.

'Hello, children,' he took off his hat and looked at us with his faded running eyes. We offered him cigarettes and bars of chocolate, given to us by the regiment doctor Boris Cot. The old man took the presents eagerly. He examined our warm flying suits with curiosity.

'And they have spread rumours that the Red Army has no ammunition and is dying from hunger: "*Kaput, kaput*"... but you look great, and even have some sweets...'

The old man told us that the Germans had driven all the residents out of their houses, and they had had to live in cellars and holes. And before the Germans retreated they drove almost all the natives,

195

including girls, away to dig trenches, and burnt down the houses.

The enemy was retreating. It was the perfect time to attack the Fritzes from the air, but the weather was awful as never before. The clouds were hanging low. The constant drizzle would change into snow from time to time. The planes were covered with icy crust. The fog hid the horizon, and we could see no further than the end of the airfield. The infantry was having a hard time as well. Lorries got stuck in the mud on the roads. Soldiers had to go on foot carrying mortars and boxes of shells on their backs. They also had to help the horses to drag out guns from the mud. And the enemy was gaining distance. The Germans had a serious advantage: the only railroad from Prokhladnyy to Caucazskaya via Mineralnye Vody was in their hands. They loaded the carriages with the loot, entrained and were off. The track-destroying machine followed the last train. This monstrous device was able to tear sleepers in two and twist the rails. We could have stopped the trains if we destroyed the locomotives, but the weather did not give us a chance. Nothing was more dangerous than to get iced over. According to the pre-war rules, it was a non-flying weather. But the war had its own laws.

The division commander arrived at our regiment. He gathered the pilots together. We kept silence waiting for him to speak.

'The commander of the Northern Forces General Maslennikov has charged the 7th Guards regiment with a military mission of the highest importance,' he began.

'What kind of a military mission can be discussed in such weather?' the pilots were thinking to themselves. It grew very quiet.

'The commander wants the disruption of the railway line between Mineralnye Vody and Nevinnomyssk at any price. At least one plane must try to get up to Mineralnye Vody and damage the railway lines.'

We realised that one of the most experienced pilots should try first. And by that time there were so few of them left in the regiment, that you could count them on the fingers of one hand. We wondered whom the division commander would appoint for the mission. But instead he asked: 'Who will fly?'

An awkward pause followed.

'Let me try, comrade colonel!' said Major Galushenko. It did not take him long to make the decision. It would have looked embarrassing to volunteer after him.

'Very well, comrade Galushenko. You may start getting ready.'

Galushenko saluted and made for the door.

Mechanics and armourers were fussing around the plane under the supervision of the chief engineer Mitin. They fixed 100-kilo bombs with delayed-action fuses and missiles. Then they began to pour hot water on the wings, and hack off the melting icy crust with wooden screwdriver handles. Mitin had an idea to lubricate the propeller blades, the edges of the wings, horizontal stabiliser and fin with engine oil. During the flight those places got covered with ice first of all. The mechanics rubbed the plane with oily rags, and the pilots stood nearby watching these unusual preparations anxiously. Galushenko walked around the plane checking everything himself and did not look at us. He was busy.

It was no wonder that Galushenko volunteered to fly first. He was an unsurpassed ace in aerobatics on a Shturmovik, and he was the best in the 4th Air Army. He often demonstrated techniques that none of us even dreamed of. The command did not restrict Galushenko. During training flights he would make dozens of steep turns and zooms, then he would descend sharply almost to the ground and pass out of sight. In a few seconds the audience would see the Shturmovik racing towards the airfield at maximum speed. He would fly at minimum altitude up to the T and then rocket up. The heavy Shturmovik would climb easily until the speed was almost zero. It would seem to be high time he levelled out, but instead the pilot would spin the aircraft round on its longitudinal axis and keep on ascending inverted. Then he would lower the nose smoothly, dive sheer, reduce the angle slowly and aim at the airfield. The G-forces were enormous. The plane would descend very fast, and it would seem that the pilot wouldn't be able to level out and would hit the ground. But he always managed to estimate the distance so precisely that he could level out exactly at the same point where he had started to climb.

The ability to manoeuvre despite critical G-forces allowed Galushenko to become the first pilot in the regiment to shoot down a Messer. He already had two personal victories over the German fighters. Once he was attacked by eight enemy fighters and had to avoid shots from the deadly 'flock' for about ten minutes. He returned to the airfield with only one hole in a wing. When he got out of the cockpit, the lapels of his waistcoat were full of biscuits. An emergency ration box had been torn off the seat back because of the G-forces, and its contents had drifted through the cockpit.

I watched the preparations and thought that even aerobatics could not help him today. He had to be very good at blind-flying. Meanwhile Galushenko put on a parachute and got inside the cockpit. The propeller began to rotate, and the plane moved forward unwillingly.

The Shturmovik took off at the very edge of the runway, and disappeared in the haze. We peered into the white mist, expecting him to come back in a few minutes, but Galushenko did not return. We stood in the drizzle smoking, and waited for forty minutes, praying that the plane did not get iced over. Ages seemed to pass...

'He's coming!' several people shouted at once. We saw the aircraft descending, and then it landed. As it was taxiing, we noticed the bomb-fuse locking cables hanging freely under the wings. It meant that he had dropped the bombs, and that he had managed to reach Mineralnye Vody.

Galushenko got out of the cockpit, jumped down from the wing, and walked towards the division commander. As he reported his voice sounded a bit unnatural: 'Comrade Colonel, the railway lines are destroyed. Here,' he showed the place on the map. The pilot's face was covered with goose-pimples, and there were blue circles under his eyes.

The colonel asked him: 'Are you cold?'

'It was hot in the cockpit, and now I'm frozen,' the pilot smiled embarrassed.

'Let's go indoors. You can report there.'

The flight had not been easy for Galushenko. At first he followed the railroad, then he hedgehopped at the altitude of a telegraph pole. After some time the windshield began to get iced. Visibility was extremely poor, and he had to watch the ground from a side window. His biggest fear was that he would crash into a water tower or a chimney-stack. He even felt like turning back, but managed to resist the temptation. When he crossed the Kuma river the weather began to improve suddenly, and the windshield began to thaw out.

Galushenko flew past Mineralnye Vody and found the railroad. The unexpected question was how to damage the railway lines with delayed-action bombs. The railway embankment was high, and the bombs released from a low altitude would fall flat, bounce off, roll down and explode there. Galushenko noticed a drain tunnel which crossed the railway embankment and had the idea to drop the bombs there. He made several attempts, dropping only one bomb at a time and making corrections for the rebound. Finally one of the bombs exploded exactly under the embankment, and it sank. On his way home Galushenko noticed a column of retreating German infantry-men at a distance. He zoomed, banked and approached the enemy form behind. He combed the column with four guns from the back to the beginning and back again.

Finishing the report Galushenko said: 'I've never seen such a mess as I've left on that road.' and he shivered.

I could imagine the masterly manoeuvre, which the pilot had performed in a matter of seconds. Of course the Germans had no time to scatter from the road.

Wet firewood was crackling and sputtering in the iron stove. Heavy sleet was coming down behind the window. There were no more flights that day.

In the morning the weather improved a little. I was summoned up to the regiment commander:

'A special task from General Maslennikov' he said. 'The reconnais-sance has reported that the enemy has concentrated many steam locomotives at the Nagutskaya station and is making up trains to evacuate. You must prevent it.'

I looked at the map. Nagutskaya was a small station to the west of Mineralnye Vody about 200 kilometres away. The enemy fighters were still based in Mineralnye Vody, so we would have to pass round the town. According to the map a small river, Mokry Karamyk, flowed to Nagutskaya hidden behind a row of hills. If we flew above it all the time, we would be able to approach the target unnoticed.

'It would be better to send two planes at least.' the commander said. 'Take Sergeant Tsyganov as a wingman. He can hold the forma-tion rather well, and he drops bombs on target.'

Petya Tsyganov was a twenty-year-old boy who had joined our regiment not long ago. When he learnt that he was chosen to carry out such an important task, he beamed with joy.

'You will repeat everything after me. Got it?'

'Got it,' Petya nodded.

We took off and hedgehopped above the railroad following Galushenko's yesterday example. Soon we got into a snow fall and had to descend very low, but we could hardly see the ground even so. 'What if the wingman gets lost?' I thought and felt sorry that I was not flying alone. Fortunately the snow stopped soon. I saw Tsyganov, flying confidently to my right. 'Well done, Petya!' I said in the transmitter, and the wingman swayed from one wing to the other. We still had to sink to the tops of telegraph poles from time to time because of clouds. I reckoned that Mineralnye Vody must be to our left. We crossed the Kuma river and suddenly it was another world: it was a bright day with no clouds and good visibility. Now we had to be careful, because the enemy could spot us and send fighters from Mineralnye Vody to intercept us.

We were flying above the steppe trying to hide behind the hills. Soon we reached a deep gully, which at summer was the river-bed of Mokry Karamyk. We flew above it as if in a trough heading to Nagutskaya. We decided to approach the station from the west, so that we could hide behind the steep bank of the river after the attack. The estimated time was up. I saw a settlement to my left and a railway station not far from it. That was Nagutskaya! I could see no locomotives behind the station buildings. Was it possible that the Germans had already driven them away? Or could it be a mistake by our reconnaissance?

We turned left to cross the railway and climbed for about fifty metres. I could already see the embankment. I looked up and suddenly noticed a twin-engined plane flying at the same altitude heading to Mineralnye Vody. It was approaching from the right and our courses were to converge soon. I took it for a fighter-attack aircraft, Messerschmitt 110. That was a very dangerous meeting. 'Should we descend and remain unnoticed? If it starts hunting us, we won't be able to attack the station,' the thought flashed through my head. The German plane was racing forward without noticing us. Without much thought I put my fingers on the triggers, peered at the sights and fired! The tracer bullets darted forward. The fiery track hit the left side of the enemy aircraft. The plane jerked and began to yaw leaving a smoking tail behind it. Its back side was now in my sights, and I had time to fire one more burst. The plane caught fire and disappeared under my wing. We were flying above the railway already. To my left I could see the station, two freight trains, and a long row of locomotives. 'Turn and attack the locomotives!' I ordered Tsyganov.

We began a shallow dive. I fired eight missiles on a locomotive, and it disappeared in a smoking cloud. Tsyganov was not missing either. I levelled out and pressed the button releasing the bombs.

We were flying low heading to a row of hillocks. The river bed of the Mokry Karamyk was behind it. The ground was covered with snow, and it was difficult to spot the hillock where we had to zoom, so I kept my eyes fixed on the ground. I was in the best spirits. We were coming home unhurt, we had delivered an unexpected and precise blow, and we had shot down a Fritz! Petya was flying to my right. I could imagine how glad he might be. The special task was complete!

The hillock was already close. My plane zoomed and immediately dived in the gully. Now everything was simple. I looked to my right, but did not see the wingman. I looked to my left, and did not find him either. 'What's up?' It was not a good time for playing hide-and-seek. I had to climb and circle above that place transmitting: 'Form up immediately! I'm waiting for you.' But Tsyganov did not appear. I thought that he had decided to get to the airfield ahead of me to surprise everybody. 'I'll deal with him there', I thought and headed to Galyugaevskaya. When I was approaching the airfield I saw a plane landing before me. 'That's Tsyganov!' I thought and did not feel angry any more. I taxied to the dispersal area and first of all asked my mechanic: 'Who landed before me?'

'Galushenko. He was testing a new plane...'

The special task was complete, but my wingman had disappeared mysteriously.

Several kilometres' distance from Galyugaevskaya we found the crashed plane of the Hero of the Soviet Union Petr Rudenko, who had been killed two months ago. We also found his body, which the fascists had thrown in a gully. We buried Petr with all the regiment present. We did not have an orchestra, but a Shturmovik circled above the cemetery for a long time howling monotonously. When the coffin was lowered into the grave, the aircraft dived steeply, raced above our heads with a deafening roar, and zoomed. That was Major Galushenko bidding farewell to his deputy... Farewell, Petr! We must go further to the west!

We had to catch up with the infantry, so we often changed airfields. We moved to Sovetskoye, Georgievsk, and then – Nagutskaya! Exactly where we had attacked locomotives with Petya Tsyganov several days ago. We were standing by the twin-engined plane that I had shot down. It was not a Messerschmitt 110 as I had assumed, but a Junkers-86K, which we had never seen before. Its left engine was burned out, but the right one was safe. I took a badge as a souvenir. The head of the regiment's air gunnery, Boris Lurie, who had arrived to the regiment from the Zhukovsky Air Force Engineering Academy, walked round the plane for a long time counting the shell-holes. There were thirty-three of them. He shrugged his shoulders and said: 'According to the laws of probability it's impossible to shoot at an object moving along a course intersecting with your own and hit it so many times...'

'Theory is one thing, and practice is another,' I answered. 'I was so close that I could see the patches on its wings.'

People from the neighbouring village came up to us. We asked them: 'Do you know, when this plane crashed?'

'Of course, we know. We've seen it with our own eyes... It was 9 January. Two of our planes were flying from that direction, and this one was cutting across their path. The one that was flying ahead began firing, and this plane caught fire! The Germans drove up to quench it. They pulled out three burnt bodies, and the forth Fritz crawled out himself with his legs broken. And our planes dropped bombs above the station and turned back flying very low. The one that was flying behind hit a hillock. It still lies there in the bushes.'

We drove to the hillock. The Shturmovik was lying in a depression hidden under thick bushes. Petya Tsyganov was buried on a hill not far from it. We put a little red pyramid on the grave. Farewell, Petya! We must go further to the west. To Stavropol...

20

CHIEF OF STAFF

It was in the early spring of 1943 at the Kuban in Novotitarovskaya. On that sunny day pilots were waiting for dinner in depression. There were just a few of us left in the regiment, and there had been new casualties in the last days: German Romantsov and Nikolai Nikolaevich Kuznetsov had not returned from a military mission to the Chushka inlet the day before. Before the war Kuznetsov worked for many years as an instructor in an Osoaviachim aeroclub. He was reserved, and had real difficulties in persuading the command to send him to the front. He had a big family.

On that very day an accident happened during my operational flight, and now I was sitting on one side with Kolya Galushenko, who had just come from Nevinnomyssk. I was sitting and recalling the details of the unfortunate flight.

Problems had already begun before the take-off. Unexpectedly our regiment commander decided to include Petr Kolesnikov in my group. Kolesnikov was a strange person. On the ground he was a normal man, but in the air he was not himself. For no obvious reason he would start dashing aside and driving his neighbours away. The regiment commander wanted to transfer him to the communication aircraft, but Kolesnikov got seriously offended: 'Do you consider me a coward?'

I was against his joining the team, but had to give in finally. I placed him on my right. As the gunners were also not willing to fly with Kolesnikov, he was given a single-seater plane. Before the take-off I was telling Kolesnikov: 'Look to my side only, hold the distance and interval. Don't pull the throttle lever too hard... Don't turn around too much, the most reliable fighters will be covering us. Pokryshkin himself will be in the team. The fighters will find and drive the Messerschmitts away.'

Petya was nodding in consent, but grew pale. On the ground he understood everything, but as soon as we took off I realised that I could not keep him in the middle of the formation. All my instructions by radio were in vain. His plane was either flying above the rank, or descending far below. As we were approaching the target I actually had to lure him out of the middle of the formation until he was in last place. 'Let him stay there', I thought and relaxed. Things seemed to settle.

We had finished the attack on the enemy column and were hedge-hopping back. Turning back I saw that Kolesnikov had fallen behind. I began to climb so that he could see us better. The plane caught up with the rest of the team. It was flying much lower, but then began to ascend steeply. Instead of taking the last place in the row it was aiming at his previous position between Zlobin and me. I kept on saying: 'Take the last place!' but Kolesnikov seemed to become deaf. Before my very eyes the Kolesnikov's plane hit the Shturmovik piloted by Ivan Zlobin and carrying the gunner Nikolai Muhin. Both planes blew up and fell in the outskirts of Baranikovskaya.

And it all happened after we had successfully completed our mission, and crossed the front line.

Now I was sitting depressed with Major Galushenko, who had just arrived with a new plane. Galushenko was trying to console me: 'Cheer up, Vasilek!★ Look around, they are all upset. Don't make the situation worse.' Suddenly he tapped on his map-case and whispered to me: 'The battalion commander in Nevinnomyssk sent a piece of lard for Kozhuhovsky. Let's eat it ourselves in his presence with all the guys!'

Major Fedor Vasilievich Kozhuhovsky was our Chief of Staff. At that time he was about forty, but looked even older because of his stoutness. He was a good-natured person and an excellent officer – under his supervision the headquarters worked like clockwork. He had a defect in his sight, which he concealed: he was practically blind at dusk.

'We'll offend the old fellow...'

'We'll keep a piece for him, don't worry. Nobody will be offended. A friendly chat is no worse than a dinner!'

Galushenko made a serious face and ordered: 'Air crew, to me!' He

★ A diminutive of the author's name, Vasily – it means 'cornflower'.

went to the headquarters. Everyone came into the room, and sat down. The men fell silent: 'Is it going to be a mission?' The last person to enter the room was Major Kozhuhovsky – the game began.

Galushenko moved a table to the middle of the room, took two chairs, asked me to sit down, and said loudly: 'Now we will show you…' he nodded at me, sustained a long pause in dead silence, and finished unexpectedly: 'We will show you how a man eats lard!' And he got the piece out of his map-case. Everyone burst out laughing. Fedor Vasilievich fidgeted uneasily in his seat.

Galushenko made a short speech about the usefulness of lard and began the show. Accurately and slowly he cut the piece into morsels, then divided garlic into cloves and removed the peel. Everyone's mouths were watering. After he had finished the preparation, he took the first morsel, pressed it round his lips so that they glittered, and then put it into his mouth with a garlic clove. The second morsel was for me. Before swallowing it I rubbed the roast rind with garlic. Galushenko commented upon my actions: 'That's another way a man may eat it, friends.'

He was giving out tiny helpings ignoring Kozhuhovsky. Then he began to complain loudly that he must have miscounted and somebody was not going to get his portion. Fedor Vasilievich looked worried. He was the last to get his helping. When he swallowed the lard Nikolai Kirillovich delivered him the fatal blow: 'Comrade Chief of Staff, will you please write out a receipt…'

'What receipt?'

'That you have received the lard passed to you by Major Galushenko.'

We had a real fun that day, and we remembered it for a long time! Kozhuhovsky was laughing with the rest. Nevertheless, later we found out that he sent a circular to all the neighbouring airfield support battalions and asked them to deliver the lard only through reliable persons.

21

THE GROUND
AND THE SEA

We were based at an airfield near Kropotkin. Talykov came up to me. 'Look! We are pursuing the Fritzes in the same places, where we were retreating the last summer!'

Indeed, we often set our courses through the same districts where Misha and I had piloted the only two unhurt Shturmoviks half a year ago.

I looked at the map. It was less than 200 kilometres to Rostov now. I also saw Nesmejanovka, where I had been shot down last time. I said to Misha: 'As soon as we move closer to Rostov and have a day off, I'll ask the commander to give me a U-2 and we can fly...'

'Where to?'

'To the place where you saved me.'

'That's a good idea!' Misha stamped with his heel. 'We'll see what's left of your Il.'

But our regiment was unexpectedly directed away. We had to pursue the Fritzes that were retreating to the Taman peninsula.

In March we were already near Krasnodar. The Germans wanted to prevent our Air Force from moving forward by leaving all the airfields in awful conditions. They blew up the concrete runway and all the offices at Krasnodar airfield. The local residents helped us a lot there. Dozens of men and women carried broken bricks from the ruins, filled up the huge shell-holes and rammed them. For the first time since we began to advance we could taxi on a solid surface and take off without difficulty. I remembered an incident at Point 3, when my wingman Senior Sergeant Ilya Mikhailov came back from an operational flight with two bombs left. Kholobaev did not punish the young pilot, but advised me instead: 'Next time you carry his two bombs to the target yourself in addition to your usual load.'

206

I remembered for a long time carrying an extra 200 kilos and trying to take off from wet ground. It was all different now. In Krasnodar I managed to carry one and a half times more weight than usual. Major Galushenko and Mikhail Talykov followed my example.

We had to fly not only above the ground, but also over the sea to attack German landing craft, tanks, ships and boats. It was extremely unpleasant to fly above the water in a land aircraft! The armoured Shturmovik could sink in a matter of seconds. Junior Lieutenant Petr Vozgaev was the first who experienced that, I guess.

It happened when we were flying to attack Temryuk – a large German base on the Azov Sea coast. Something was wrong with the engine of Vozgaev's aircraft and he flew back rushing to reach the coastline. But the engine stalled and he had to glide on the water. Hardly had the pilot jumped out to the water than the cockpit sank in a whirlpool. Vozgaev could swim pretty well, but the heavy flying suit was dragging him to the bottom. The pilot began to look around helplessly, and was very surprised to see the tail of his Shturmovik sticking out of the water. He swam back, clutched at the stabiliser, and hung there. He was up to his neck in water and it was cold. Vozgaev was growing numb and did not have much hope left but he heard the roar of Shturmoviks. Two planes were circling above him. He recognised Talykov's plane and was glad at first, but then he thought there was no help they could give him. It was impossible to land on water anyway. And they were attracting attention of the enemy...

Vozgaev managed to wave one hand: 'Fly away!' but the planes kept circling. 'How long am I going to hang like this?' he thought. 'I should take everything off and swim. Perhaps I will warm up a bit in motion.' He tried to take off his boots and suit with one hand, but in vain. He had cramp in his legs. Vozgaev looked at the coast and saw an enemy boat racing towards him from Temryuk. 'What now? Should I take my pistol and commit suicide? But it's under water. It will misfire for sure.' Meanwhile a friendly boat was approaching him from the opposite direction. It was further off than the German one, but it was moving fast. 'It can't come first,' Vozgaev thought. In the next moment he heard some shooting. The two Shturmoviks were diving at the German boat. The boat began to make sharp turns and slowed down.

Our boat came up to the sunken aircraft. The sailors grasped the pilot under the arms and went back at full speed.

Vozgaev returned to the regiment in a few days and told us: 'First of all they undressed me and rubbed me with alcohol, and also gave me some to drink. In general, I can say that Il-2 is the second worst floating object,' Vozgaev concluded.

'And what's the first?'

'A flatiron.'

Soon after that incident we were given life vests. Major Galushenko was the first to receive one.

'Will you please sign here, comrade Major,' the storekeeper gave him a docket. Galushenko looked at the gear. It was exactly the same as we had received in Astrakhan before we flew over the Caspian Sea. He threw the vest away.

'Take it back to the store!'

The storekeeper was confused. He thought he had done something wrong.

'If you don't like the red colour, comrade Major, I can give you a yellow one...'

'What's the difference? And you want me to sign for it? Take it away!'

That conversation took place in private, but on the same day Nikolai Kirillovich was summoned up.

'Will you explain the reason for your open disregard for the life-saving equipment?'

'Why are you so interested in that?' Galushenko asked.

At that time pilots were not afraid of such 'conversations', because they risked their lives every day anyway. As a result the most self-willed ones did not receive decorations which they long deserved.

'You are setting bad example to the rest.'

'There's nothing wrong if they don't take this stuff. Try and inflate such a vest with your mouth! It's the same as if you tried to do it with the tyre of a lorry. Naval pilots have self-inflating vests. Why do we get this old rubbish?'

Galushenko's words had an effect. We received life vests without inflating hoses. Instead there was a box in the vest's pocket. The box had tiny holes in the bottom and was filled with powder. If some water got inside, a chemical reaction would begin, and the evolving gas would fill the vest. If you dived, you'd be pushed up to the water surface like a cork.

'If I'd had one of these vests on, and if it hadn't been for the freezing water, I would have reached the coast myself,' said Petya Vozgaev.

'It's still better on a boat,' Talykov objected. He was rather gloomy in those days. The grey-eyed Kseniya had been seriously injured recently by a bomb splinter. She was in a base hospital.

14 March was a dull and chilly day. Talykov and I hid from the wind behind a high caponier. Our armourers had broken off some pieces of TNT from the inside of a bomb and made up fire where we could warm our hands.

We sat on the boxes smoking. Misha was writing a letter. It was comfortable near the fire, and we felt like talking.

'Now we'll definitely move to the Crimea,' said Talykov. 'Our troops will drive the Fritzes from Taman across the Straits of Kerch and there we are.'

Talykov mentioned the Crimea, and I remembered the cypresses in Bujur-Nus and my trip to Simferopol together with my friend pilot.

'Have you ever been to the Crimea?' I asked him. His answer surprised me:

'Yes, I have! I was sent to Yevpatoria after I graduated from the Air School. I was there when the war began.'

'Me too...'

'Soon we will get to familiar places...' Talykov said dreamily.

At that moment we heard someone calling from the command post: 'Talykov!'

'I'm here!' he rose.

'To the commander!'

After several minutes Talykov went out of the building heading to his single-seater plane. He was wearing a leather jacket and canvas boots made out of a parachute case. His map-case was knocking against his leg. Talykov was followed by his wingmen. I asked Lenya Bukreev, who was the last in the line: 'Where to?'

'To Temryuk... To attack the crossing.'

Temryuk was situated on a hill not far from the coast of the Sea of Azov. The main road from the Straits of Kerch to the German defensive Blue Line passed through it. The bridge, which we had destroyed many times and which the Germans still managed to restore, was crossing the Kuban river, which flowed through the western part of Temryuk. There were lots of German anti-aircraft guns around it. They were based in the hills, and it was impossible to approach the bridge unnoticed either from the coast or from the sea. Damned Temryuk... During the last few days we had lost Viktor Olenin, Nikolai Protalev with his gunner, Boris Maximchuk, and Petr Vozgaev there. We preferred to approach Temryuk from the coast. Perhaps that's why Talykov decided to make it from the sea on that day.

The Ils were flying just above the surface of the Sea of Azov. The pilots could already see the coastline and Temryuk. After about a one-minute flight to the coast, the enemy artillery began firing. Water was splashing up and Talykov zoomed. The waterspouts were very dangerous. It was a certain death to touch one even with the edge of a wing. The planes ascended surrounded by black puffs of smoke and soon began to dive, releasing the bombs. It was time to level out, but the leading aircraft was still descending. It was flying lower and lower swaying from one wing to the other. It seemed that it was heading to a two-storeyed house near the town park. Some flashes could be seen in the yard of the house. There was possibly an anti-aircraft gun there. The leading Shturmovik reached the yard and disappeared inside hitting the trees with the wings. The group flew back without the leader.

The piece of TNT which we had ignited with Talykov was burning out. I took the letter that Misha did not have time to finish, and read the wobbly lines. '... My dear parents, brother Aleksey, and sister Dusya...' After he complained that they did not write him often enough he wrote, '... The impudent Fritzes used to fly in flocks like birds of prey, and now they fly separately trying to escape our fighters. I'm still flying my immortal bird...'

It seemed to me that it was my turn now. I wished we did not have to fly on day, but immediately heard: 'Air crew are summoned to the command post!'. Slowly I went down the steep steps thinking of Mikhail Talykov running up them in his canvas boots an hour ago...

We were rather cramped at the Krasnodarsk airfield. Regiments of Shturmoviks, bombers, fighters and reconnaissance aircraft were all based at the same airfield. The LI-2 transport aircraft which flew to the Crimean partisans at nights also used it.

We moved to Novotitarovskaya not far from Krasnodar. There was an impassable mire there, but we managed to fly somehow. There were less than ten pilots and planes left in the regiment, but we had already lasted for half a year starting from Point 3. Our regiment could have become unfit for action long ago, but our mechanics managed to find and restore more than thirty damaged Shturmoviks during that period.

We had many freshmen in the regiment. Almost none of the pilots who had joined us at Point 3 were left now. Petr Kolesnikov crashed into the aircraft of Ivan Zlobin. Both of them were killed. We had lost Petr Vozgaev, Sasha Zakharov, Nikolai Kuznetsov, German Romantsov and our best singer, Ivan Chernigin. The newcomers had yet to be trained to pilot the Il-2. We trained them in our regiment training centre, led by Misha Vorozhbiev. He almost never left the cockpit of his dual-control plane in those days. That's how we managed to keep going.

The sun was already warming everything up, but the pilots were depressed. Even Ivan Ostapenko stopped telling his stories.

'The regiment is due to be sent for reformation.' the commander said to Galushenko and me. 'But don't mention it to the rest. They must not relax. Can you hold out for another couple of days?'

'We can,' answered Galushenko.

There were two leaders left in the regiment. Nikolai Nikolaevich Galushenko and I took turns leading the combined group.

That day I had already made an operational flight. We attacked a column on the road from Kurchanskaya to Varenikovskaya. We did not expect any more military tasks that day, but in the evening we got an order to attack trains at a railway station Krymskaya. Galushenko led the group and did not come back.

The leader's deputy Ivan Ostapenko reported:

'He landed on the fuselage here,' he showed a large wooded area on the map. 'He crossed the front line. A smoking tail followed the plane, but there was no fire. I heard his groans by radio.'

The commander ordered a pilot from the communications aircraft to fly there on a U-2.

'Let me?' I asked.

'Go!'

When I reached the area the sun had already set. I circled the dark underwoods for a long time, but could not spot the Shturmovik. I was already going back, and decided to fly above a country road. On the road I saw a cart. The driver was lashing the horse, but it was hardly moving. I circled above. The cart stopped, and the driver was waving his hands to me. I landed near the road, and found Galushenko in the cart. His leg was bandaged tightly above the knee. His boots and trousers were covered with blood.

'What happened?'

'A shell went through the seat and through my leg.'

The driver and I helped Galushenko into the second cockpit of my aircraft. We flew back in the dark and landed by the hospital. Fortunately the driver of the field ambulance had turned his headlights on.

The wound was serious. An Oerlikon shell had gone through the muscles of the left leg above the knee. The surgeon examined Galushenko and found that the bone was unhurt, but the wound was full of shreds of plywood and steel ropes.

'Anaesthesia...'

'Some alcohol would be better.'

'Give it to him!'

'It's not enough, doctor...'

'Give him a full glass!'

During the operation Galushenko was trying to make jokes: 'Make it smooth, sisters. I want girls to love me no less.'

'We are doing our best...'

The next day the commander declared: 'We are sent for reformation.' It was 26 March. Our third 'round' was over. We had to get ready for the fourth.

22

'FILTH'

Once again we had to fly to the Volga to enlist new pilots and get new planes. This time the first squadron was led by the regiment commander together with Kolya Smurygov. His arm had healed, and he was appointed the head of the regiment's air gunnery. Smurygov beamed with happiness.

We received new insignia: shoulder straps with stars and Guards badges. Our chief of staff Fedor Vasilievich Kozhuhovsky left the regiment. His health became worse, and he was transferred to a rear unit. And we were to have some rest and go back to the front.

We were based near the Kuban village Timashevskaya, and were mastering the new twin-seater Shturmoviks. They had an extra cockpit for the gunner. The gunner sat there facing the tail of the plane. His task was to repulse the attacks of Messerschmitts from behind. Special courses were organised to train former armourers and mechanics. None of them had had flying training before. They did not know the complicated rules of shooting at aerial targets. We made up a song about a young air gunner taking the melody from a popular film 'The Youth of Maxim'. The word 'young' was used only for rhyming. Many gunners were old enough to be the pilots' fathers. And we also had one girl among the gunners, Sasha Chuprina.

Although one gun could not be compared to four Oerlikons, our losses were greatly reduced. The fascist pilots were now afraid to approach our planes, and fired from considerable distances. Unfortunately, the rear cockpit had much less armour than the front cockpit. It often happened that the planes landed carrying an injured or even a dead gunner. That's why the few single-seat aircraft left in the regiment were in great demand. It was better if you were killed yourself, than if you brought back a dead friend.

Lenya Bukreev was one of the first pilots who began to master flights with a gunner. His first two gunners, Misha Bubakin and Leonid Boldin, were killed, but with Vasiliev he had already made forty-five sorties.

Once the air gunners came to the canteen for a dinner and brought a stray dog with them. The dog was skinny; its red hair was covered with burrs. Though the dog was obviously famished, it did not beg for food. Somebody threw up a piece of bread and cried, 'Catch it!', but the red guest only looked reproachfully at the joker. It lay under the table near Sergeant Nikolai Naumov, who had caressed it, and did not want to attract attention.

Naumov was about thirty. In his free time he liked to walk near the airfield gathering camomile. When I watched him I could not help thinking 'Why was he sent to the war, where men are killed?' Naumov sat down and began to feed the dog. To our amazement it did not snap the food from his hands, but waited patiently until a bone or a helping of porridge was put on a piece of plywood which Naumov had brought to the canteen.

Kostya Averianov began to say what a smart dog a mongrel could be. At that moment the stout sergeant who was in charge of the canteen entered the room. His sleeves were rolled up to his elbows showing his hairy arms. It looked like he had been busy cutting pork, and suddenly had some urgent business. We wondered what the reason was for his coming to the canteen at that time. Nobody was complaining about the food, or asking for an extra portion. The flies which he was fond of hunting were sitting peacefully on the ceiling.

He walked through the room, stopped near the gunners, and looked around. Then he looked under the table and said: 'Take this filth out!'

It became very quiet in the canteen. Naumov bent over his plate. Sasha Chuprina looked at him reproachfully and shook her head. Gunner Vasiliev gave a start and eyed the master sergeant from head to foot. Sergeant Vasiliev had a big bald spot on his head and a scar on his face. The gunners called him *batya*.★

'What filth?' he asked severely.

★ *Batya* means 'father' in Ukrainian; in Russian it carries a rather warm and respectful connotation.

The sergeant kept silent, as if he did not hear.

Vasiliev was not a person to be trifled with. He was a very harsh man. He had been a gunner in the infantry, and was even sent to a penal battalion, but not for showing cowardice to the enemy. He had not shown enough deference towards his commander once. He returned to his unit with a scar across his cheek and a medal on his breast. He was the first to volunteer when the courses for air gunners were organised.

'If the Motherland tells us to fly, it's time to stop crawling on the ground!'

Now Vasiliev was our most experienced and sharp-sighted gunner. He had already shot down two Messerschmitts.

'What filth, I ask you?' he repeated severely.

'The one that is hiding under your table...'

The dog stopped gnawing the bone, as if it knew what the talk was about. Vasiliev's eyes darkened and his scar turned purple. 'Since when are you calling a dog 'filth'?'

'But it's shedding hair... If it gets on your plate, you'll be the first to complain.'

'You'd better watch your own hair!' Vasiliev cast a glance at the sergeant's arms. Dead silence followed his words. We all knew that after his hundred grams Vasiliev was unlikely to be satisfied with a peaceful agreement. After a moment of confusion Junior Lieutenant Kostya Averianov jumped up from his seat.

'All the men in the regiment are ready to take responsibility for this dog,' he said. 'We'll feed it, and it won't shed hair any more. We won't ask you for extra food, and we won't complain about hair on the plate. Is it a deal, master sergeant?'

'If anything happens...'

'Nothing will happen,' Averianov interrupted him and clapped him on the shoulder.

And so our red guest was allowed to stay in the canteen, and after dinner it went to the dormitory with the air gunners.

I had met Averianov two months ago at an airfield near Nevinnomyssk, and actually 'stole' him. I had arrived there to get a new plane and noticed a pilot loitering around the canteen. His face was pale and his cheeks were hollow. He looked an exhausted hawk.

'What unit are you from?' I asked him.

215

'I don't belong to any unit...'

'What do you mean?'

'I ferry aircraft...'

There were by now such pilots, whose only task was to ferry aircraft from rear airfields to the front. Many of them dreamed of joining a military unit, but they were not allowed to do it. Some of them went to the front without permission, and the command searched for them. Such men were considered deserters.

I thought that Averianov could become a good military pilot, and there was no sense putting it off. 'Let's have dinner,' I suggested.

'I don't have a ration card... I've been here for two days already. They don't fuel up my plane, and I can't get to my destination.

'Why don't they give you fuel?'

'They say it's only for the front planes.'

'Come with me to the canteen!'

We shared my portion. I asked him: 'Do you want to join the 7th Guards Regiment?'

'You don't need to ask!'

'Let's fly together. I'll pilot my plane, and you will take yours.'

'Will I not become a deserter?'

'No, you won't. We'll enroll you officially.'

Thus Kostya Averianov joined our regiment and became an excellent pilot.

From that day the gunners and the dog were inseparable. It accompanied them to the dormitory, to the canteen and to the airfield. After some time our mongrel looked really different. Its hair became glossy, its hollow sides fattened out, its ears were now held upright, and its brown eyes were laughing. The red dog relieved our monotonous life, and it was somehow easier now to overcome dangers and the inevitable deaths of friends. The regiment command did not object to the new member, and many men did not find it ridiculous to spend their free time with the dog. It was everybody's pet, but it remained faithful to Naumov. It slept under his bed in the dormitory, and it followed him everywhere at the airfield. Naumov did not pet it really, but we could see that it cheered him up. Every evening he gathered flowers, brought them to the canteen and put them in a glass near Sasha Chuprina. 'Take it, daughter,' he said once.

'Don't act like a father,' answered Sasha.

Reddy quickly learned our rules. She did not go to the landing strip, did not run after the Naumov's plane when he taxied to the take-off and did not approach the rotating propeller. Nevertheless she had her own way of seeing his crew off and meeting them. She followed Naumov and pilot Papov from the command post to the aircraft. As they were putting on the parachutes, Reddy barked encouragingly. After the take-off she kept sitting at the same place waiting patiently for the return of 'her' plane. And when the plane came back and was taxiing along the airfield, the dog rushed around in circles making steep turns, jumped up, and yelped with joy.

Many were surprised to see that: '*We* can distinguish the planes by the numbers, but how does she know 'her' plane?'

'If the plane is close, she can nose it out, and if the plane is far away, she can sense it,' Vasiliev explained.

'How can a dog sense anything?'

'I'm not a vet! But I've experienced it myself once before the war. We were sleeping and our dog was howling. I could not understand what was going on with it. But soon our house quaked! Our bed began shaking like mad, and plaster was falling off the ceiling. It was an earthquake... The dog had sensed it!'

Soon nobody had any doubts that the dog was able to distinguish Naumov's plane from the rest at a distance. Reddy was delighted to meet her master. She stood on her hind legs setting her front legs against Naumov's breast, and tried to lick him in the cheek. Only in those moments did the gunner pat her slightly on the head.

Days, weeks and months passed one by one. It was already autumn. In the morning the ground was hidden with a thick mist, and our boots shone from the dew. The year of 1943 was coming to the end. It was the year of our great victories near Stalingrad and Kursk. The troops of the North Caucasian Front advanced for 500 kilometres from Ordzhonikidze, but already in spring the offensive slowed down considerably. Three of our armies moved up to the German Blue Line, which blocked the way to the Straits of Kerch and the Crimea. The hundred-kilometre line extended from the Sea of Azov to Novorossiysk. Our repeated attempts to break the defence line failed, and the offensive was delayed on the Taman peninsular.

Good news came from the Kuban. For the first time during the war our Air Force won an aerial combat and gained air superiority.

For two months our fighters fought with the enemy aircraft at every altitude from dawn until night. Even the elite squadrons of the German fighters suffered losses in that area. The fascists failed to beat our aces! Brothers Dmitry and Boris Glinki, Alexandr Pokryshkin, Vadim Fadeev, Nikolai Naumchik and dozens of other pilots displayed great courage pursuing the enemy aircraft both in the air and at the airfields. Now we had advantage in the air.

On that day we attacked high-speed amphibious tanks in the Straits of Kerch. Papov did a very good job, and the tank that he attacked went to the bottom. Many Fritzes were floundering about in the water far from the coast. Sasha Chuprina managed to set on fire her first Messerschmitt, and opened her personal score. She stood near the plane in her flying suit like a bear cub, shaking hands with gunners and pilots.

We were to fly again soon, and dinner was brought to the airfield. We ate watching Reddy feed her babies. (She had given birth to two puppies, which we named Boltik (a small screw-bolt) and Dutik (a small wheel under a plane's tail).) Suddenly Reddy jumped up, pricked up her ears to the west and barked alarmingly. Her hair stood on end. The puppies also started yelping. We looked to the west, but did not see anything which could disturb the dog.

In few seconds though, we heard the distant roar of an engine. Then we noticed a fighter approaching the airfield. It was flying low with landing gear released.

'Guys, a Fritz has got lost!' somebody laughed.

'I hope he won't notice the Shturmoviks...'

'What a fun it will be, if he lands here by mistake!'

At that moment our anti-aircraft guns and machine-guns started firing from the other end of the airfield. Bullets were whizzing above our heads.

'Lie down!' somebody ordered, and we dropped on the spot.

The guns kept shooting, but the Messerschmitt kept descending. In my heart I was angry with the gunners. They were driving the pilot away! The fighter had already levelled out just above the ground, when a sheaf of tracer bullets raced past the cockpit. The pilot's reaction was swift: he throttled up, and the fighter climbed steeply. The landing gear disappeared inside the wings, the plane turned and headed to the west.

'You've scared him off, fools!' Vasiliev cried, but at that moment the Messerschmitt began to descend again and disappeared behind the dispersal area. Dust rose up there.

'It's landed! It's landed!'

Everybody forgot about dinner and rushed to the place where the plane had landed. We all wanted to come first, but nobody could overtake our SMERSH★ officer Captain Tarasov. He was rather stout, but he ran so fast that even skinny Kostya Averianov could not catch up with him. Tarasov took out his pistol, and we followed his example – we were going to capture a fascist.

The Messerschmitt lay on its belly. A blond guy in a blue shirt was standing on the wing with his hands up. In one hand he held a pistol by the barrel, and in the other he held a map-case and his helmet. Tarasov snatched the pistol from the fascist pilot, ran his hands over the pilot's body, and took away some documents. Meanwhile the blond guy was smiling and kept repeating some word that sounded strange, but a bit like a Russian one.

Sergeant Vasiliev stared at his sworn enemy. The enemy looked handsome and kept smiling. 'Wish I could have seen your face when you were aiming at one of our planes.' Vasiliev thought. 'What kind of expression was on your face then? You must have shot down more than one plane, and now you are acting a sheep.'

'What is he mumbling?' Vasiliev asked Naumov, who was standing nearby.

'*Sudrugi*... It means 'friends' in Czech.'

'I would have trampled all of such 'friends' down...'

'He used to be our enemy, but perhaps he has changed his attitude now.'

The regiment commander came up to the pilot and told him to drop his hands. The pilot presented him with his helmet and goggles. The goggles had a light filter that allowed the pilot to fly against the sun without being blinded. 'These bastards seem to have thought of everything,' Vasiliev thought. The pilot was already introducing himself to our commander: 'Sasha Gerich, Sasha Gerich.' For some reason he was pointing at the fuselage. He opened the hatch and

---

★ SMERSH (an abbreviation for the Russian 'death to spies') was a department that dealt with enemy spies and saboteurs.

helped a skinny man in a dark suit to get out. The man was shivering as if he had fever.

'If this one could have seen our anti-aircraft gunners 'saluting' to them, he would have yielded up the ghost,' Vasiliev evaluated the second guest.

Meanwhile Sasha Gerich was walking round the plane apologising for not being able to present an undamaged aircraft to the commander. He had had to land on the fuselage, and the propeller was bent.

We went to the command post to continue our dinner. Gerich and his radio operator friend were offered borsch as well. They shovelled the soup down. Vasiliev watched them and felt his anger vanish, as if he swallowed it with his soup.

Our SMERSH officer went to inform his command, and we showered Gerich with questions. He answered eagerly, and we could understand each other without an interpreter.

'When did you decide to fly to the other side?'

'It's been a long time, but I did not have a chance. The Germans do not allow Czechs to fly alone. One of them accompanies you.'

'And how did you manage to hide Jan in the fuselage?'

'He hid there yesterday. Today I accompanied a reconnaissance aircraft to Novorossiysk. We flew really high, and I was afraid that Jan would freeze.'

'And did a German follow you?'

'He did! But I made a smart dive,' Gerich made a vertical dive with his hand.

'We see, we see!' we nodded our heads and laughed. The skinny Jan could not hear anything after the unexpected diving, because his ears were stuffed up. Still he laughed with the rest.

Vasiliev wanted to ask Gerich how many Soviet planes he had brought down, but he did not have time. Tarasov drove up in a captured Horch,* and asked the 'guests' inside.

Following Gerich's example two more Czech pilots flew to our side on Messerschmitts. All of them later fought in the Czech corps led by General Svoboda.

In the evening of the same day two U-2s landed at our airfield. It

---

* A German automobile.

was our dear friends from the fighters' regiment, Hero of the Soviet Union Vasily Fedorenko, Vladimir Istrashkin and their commissar, Alexander Matveevich Zhuravlev. We were very glad to see them.

'Will you spend the night here? Will you have supper with us?'

'We have an urgent business.'

'Organising co-operation?'

'Is it still not enough? We can already recognise each other in the air by the voice and "by the step",' Zhuravlev was laughing. 'Show us the Messer, we want to touch it.'

'You are welcome,' the commander invited them. The pilots went to have a look, but came back quickly.

'We thought it was undamaged. We wanted to pilot it,' Zhuravlev said keeping his eyes on Dutik and Boltik who were playing nearby. And suddenly he confessed: 'Guys, our regiment asks you to present us one of the puppies! To be honest, that's the reason we came...'

We felt astonished. Naumov answered on behalf of everybody: 'Take Dutik, the one with white paws. Let him be a fighter.'

'Our greatest thanks!' The fighters took the puppy to their plane and flew off.

We followed them with our eyes for a long time. Kostya Averianov was the first to break the silence. 'Well, and Boltik will be a real Shturmovik pilot. You'll see!'

Since that day Averianov often took Boltik to the dispersal area and sat in the cockpit of his Shturmovik number 13 for a long time. The crew believed that he was practising blind training, learning to find all the switches and levers with his eyes closed. But a few of us knew that Boltik was always with Averianov inside the cockpit. The pilot trained the dog to lie in the same place on the left of his seat. Boltik was getting used to the unfamiliar smells of paint and fuel, and to the roar of the engine.

Six Ils, including Boris Papov's aircraft, flew to attack a base station at Gorno-Vesely. As usual Reddy saw her crew off, and was sitting beside the empty caponier. Fifty minutes passed and we could distinguish distant spots on the horizon. But we could only count five of them. Meanwhile Reddy behaved in an unusual way. She tossed about, sniffed at the grass and whined.

'She must have smelled a mole...' Vasiliev was trying not to get nervous.

When the five Shturmoviks were landing we saw the sixth one. It flew slowly wobbling from one wing to the other. The aircraft was obviously damaged. It was Papov's plane. The barrel of the machine gun was sticking out, and we could not see Naumov's head.

The aircraft was taxiing to the dispersal area, when Reddy began to press herself to the ground and whine loudly.

The engine stopped. The pilot did not jump, but crawled down from the wing. The nurses pulled Naumov's body out of the gunner's cockpit, put the stretcher in an ambulance car and drove to the hospital. Reddy ran after the car sniffing at the tracks.

We buried Nikolai Naumov on the day when the alert was called off. Pilots, mechanics, and air gunners walked after the coffin. Reddy dragged along with the rest. Some people made short speeches. Sergeant Vasiliev said: 'We swear to you, we'll annihilate the fascist filth in its den!'

Rifles fired three times. A new mound with a little red pyramid and a tin star appeared at the cemetery.

It was quiet at dinner. The seat near Sasha Chuprina was empty. A piece of plywood was still under the table, but there was no sign of Reddy. Only Boltik hung around playing with a black cat. The sergeant in charge of the canteen walked along the windows, saw a fly, lashed against the glass with a napkin, and muttered angrily: 'Filth...'

Reddy did not appear in the dormitory that night. For several days we looked for her but in vain. Two weeks passed and we had to move further to the west. Vasiliev and Sasha Chuprina went to the cemetery. On Naumov's grave they found Reddy's dead body.

The engines started and the Shturmovik took off. Boltik was flying in number 13 plane together with Averianov. It lay at its place listening to the engine roar. Boltik had flown with Averianov for the first time when he attacked the enemy near the Mitridat peak. Since then Boltik accompanied Averianov many times. We often saw the black dog with white pads jumping down from the wing, when number 13 returned from the mission. The dog used to rush to the nearest bush, stand there for a few seconds and run back to its master.

Many people considered it a whim, but Averianov assured us that Boltik sensed the danger before the pilot noticed it.

'If it starts nuzzling my leg with its head, I know I have to manoeuvre. It can be anti-aircraft guns, which I did not notice, or a Messer sneaking from behind.'

Correspondents would not leave Averianov alone: 'Isn't it a superstition that you fly with a dog?'

'People can say anything, but I don't care a damn!..'

The Hero of the Soviet Union Konstantin Averianov served outside our country after the war. Boltik followed him everywhere. During an exercise Averianov, with pilot Bykov, was once imitating an aerial combat with a fighter. Averianov was killed in an accident on that occasion. The brave pilot was buried in Bunzlau in the same cemetery as the heart of Kutuzov.* Boltik walked with the funeral procession, just as its mother had walked after Naumov's coffin. Later the dog had another master.

I remember how sergeant Vasiliev was demobilised.

'Now I'll again breath the piny air of Karelia!'

During the special dinner he told us: 'Do you remember our oath at Naumov's grave? We have annihilated the Fascist filth in its den!.. Let Kolya Naumov, Borya Papov, Sasha Chuprina and all who were killed rest in peace...' Vasiliev wanted to add something, but instead began singing our song about the air gunner. Tears rolled down his cheeks across the scar, and he could not finish the song.

---

* A famous Russian field marshal, who led the Russian troops during the wars with Napoleon.

23

THE WAY TO TAMAN

Our troops kept trying to break the Blue Line. Each time the attack by the infantry and tanks was preceded with an hour or more bombardment from the ground artillery and attacks from the air. Each group of planes had its own strictly determined time for the attack. If we flew a bit early, somebody was still 'working' with the target, and if we came a bit late, the next group was close on our heels. The air was rather crowded during the preparatory bombardment. In order to let more planes attack the target we flew in big groups.

Before a new assault we were to attack the village of Gorno-Vesely, which was a German fortified base station. There was not a single house left in the village, but the Germans hid in basements, buried themselves deep under the ground, and thoroughly hid and camouflaged weapon emplacements. Even after a prolonged batter the Germans encountered our infantry with heavy fire.

I led my regiment to the Blue Line. Two more regiments from our division were following us in a single fifteen-kilometre column. I assembled them flying above other airfields. Not far from Krasnodar I could see the starting point of our route – a sharp bend in the Kuban river. I knew I must not cross that reference point earlier than the estimated time. If I were a bit late I could make up for it speeding up on the route, but if I were early that would be real trouble. Then I would have to slow down, the rear groups would come too close to the front ones, the formation would be deranged, and the flight would actually fail. I kept watching the approaching reference point and the indicator of my watch. Finally I crossed the bend strictly on time, and relaxed.

I flew quietly above the railway. The wooded foothills of the

Caucasus ridge glided slowly to my left, and I could already see bare hills ahead. That was the front line of the defence. The ruins of Gorno-Vesely were already coming into view. I looked at my watch and made sure that we were coming on time. Suddenly I heard an alarming beep in my headphones. It was from my gunner Eugene Tereshenko. I felt annoyed: I was expecting a command from the ground radio station any second, and now I had to switch to the internal communication.

'What's up?'

'Bombers are flying above us...'

I looked up and saw three nine-ship squadrons of our bombers right above my head. According to the schedule they must have bombed Gorno-Vesely before us. It was ridiculous to launch the attack with them dropping bombs above our heads, so I had no choice... I turned left and ordered the rest: 'Follow me! Don't approach the target!'

We flew in a circle above our troops and then started the attack. By that time the bombers had already done their part of the job. We dropped bombs, and dived firing at the target. I heard the command from the ground: 'One more attempt!' The division commander wanted us to press the enemy as long as we could. Colonel Getman, as he had become, now spent almost all his time at the front line directing the Shturmoviks from the ground.

We kept circling in a giant merry-go-round raking the base station with fire. It looked as though there was nothing alive left there. Meanwhile our tanks were crawling out of the shelter followed by groups of soldiers. They had to capture the smoking ruins on the hill.

Next morning the chief of staff Gudimenko informed us that the front line had moved. The pilots had managed to break the enemy defences in Gorno-Vesely.

On July 22, 1943, the Shturmoviks launched a new massive attack on the Blue Line. The group of about a hundred planes was led by one of the best pilots in the Air Force, the commander of the 210th Ground-Attack Regiment of our division, Lieutenant Colonel Nikolai Antonovich Zub. Before Zub headed the 210th Regiment, it had suffered heavy losses in the Donets Basin, and became unfit for action in a month. Reformed and trained by the new commander, the regiment fought successfully in the Northern Caucasus and the

Taman peninsular, and had an excellent reputation in the division. Zub was also the author of practical instructions on the operation of the Shturmovik, and the originator of many tactical developments, including operating in a rank of pairs instead of three-plane squads.

The column of planes was approaching an enemy base station near Kievskaya right on time. The Shturmoviks were flying at a height of 600 metres under the lower edge of the shroud of clouds. The infantrymen were throwing up their field caps welcoming us. The aim was close, but the enemy anti-aircraft guns kept quiet. Zub knew very well that the German gunners had zeroed in on the lower edge of the clouds in advance. He began to turn, smoothly changing course. The manoeuvre was made very carefully. Zub must have been afraid to derange the formation before the attack. He was leading many inexperienced pilots and was taking care of them. The enemy guns were silent. Nothing was worse than ignorance. I wished I had seen the first bursts and knew which way to turn.

The leading five-plane squad was already starting to dive when several batteries fired at once. The leading aircraft and the one to its right jerked. Their noses lowered and the planes went down followed by smoking trails. And so on to the ground.

That was a black day for our 230th Kuban Ground-Attack Division. The 210th Regiment lost its commander, the famous pilot of the 4th Air Army, Nikolai Antonovich Zub.

The door of the building swept open, and a stocky figure appeared in the doorway.

'Hello, Guardsmen!' Those were the first words of Galushenko. I rushed to meet him, and Nikolai hugged me.

He had already two big stars at his shoulder straps – meaning he had been promoted to lieutenant colonel, and I had four small stars – I was a captain.

'You owe us,' I told him.

'I'm all for it... We'll also celebrate my departure.'

'What departure?'

'I've been appointed the commander of the 210th Regiment! You will be confirmed the regiment navigator instead of me,' he said. 'You see, you also owe us!'

Galushenko was absent for almost half a year. I saw him only once, in a hospital in Yessentuki. The hospital did not have enough food, and the injured pilots recovered slowly. I brought them a sack of Kuban lard, and a box of eggs.

'I'm dying to fly,' Galushenko said on the next day. 'Do you have any vacant aircraft?'

'We have one. It's being examined. The pilot said that something was wrong with the engine, but the mechanics can't find any malfunction.'

'I'll ask the commander to let me try it.'

The Shturmovik took off. Galushenko circled the airfield several times, dived steeply, and went up. He began such a show, that not only our pilots but also the neighbouring fighters ran out to watch the masterly flight.

'Is it a new model of Il?' they asked.

'No, it's only a pilot...'

'Who?'

'Sergeant Galushenko,' somebody joked. The fighters took the joke seriously and began to reproach us: 'Then why don't you whirl in the air like this sergeant instead of making pasty cakes when you are attacked by a Messer?'

After that we called Nikolai Kirillovich 'sergeant' as a joke.

He landed and got out on the wing. A mechanic asked him: 'Comrade Lieutenant Colonel, what can you say about the work of the engine?'

Galushenko did not say anything. He embraced the cockpit with his arms and kissed the glass three times.

Our troops failed to break the Blue Line with frontal attacks. On 9 September 800 of our guns opened fierce fire on the port in Novorossiysk. At the same time our torpedo boats burst into Cemess Bay from the sea. Squadrons of landing ships approached the shore after a series of deafening explosions at the pier. Units of the 18th Army led by General Leselidze were advancing from inland. After a seven-day assault, on 16 September we listened to the salute in Moscow in honour of the liberation of Novorossiysk. In the following days the 56th Army led by General Grechko delivered a heavy blow in the centre of the Blue Line, and the 9th Army advanced along the Sea of Azov coast. The Blue Line had collapsed!

The red arcs on our maps crawled into the heart of the Taman peninsular. On 27 September one of them rounded Temryuk, where

Misha Talykov was killed half a year ago. On 9 October Moscow again saluted the forces of the North Caucasian Front. The Taman peninsular was freed from the Germans. Now ahead of us lay the Crimea and the Straits of Kerch about 20 kilometres wide.

The division commander summoned me. 'The Front commander Lieutenant General Petrov wants to check the work of the PTAB* on the range. The trophy tanks are already gathered there. Go to Galushenko's regiment. He's been ordered to give you a plane. There's a good range just near the airfield. You can practise before the show'

The idea was to check the efficiency of anti-tank aircraft bombs with cumulative action that had been added to our armoury not long ago. The bombs were small and had to be dropped in vast amounts from low altitude. You could only burn through tank armour with cumulative shot if you hit the tank directly. We had a rather vague idea of what the chances were of hitting a tank.

By evening I was already in Ahtanizovskaya with Galushenko. It was raining. 'Where shall we have dinner?' he asked. 'In the canteen or at home?'

'I'm tired of splashing through the mud. It's better at home.'

Galushenko's adjutant, who was also his air gunner, brought two pots. On that nasty night we sat at the table a really long time. We talked and listened to the sounds outside. The girls from the regiment led by Evdokia Bershanskaya usually flew at that time to attack Kerch, but we did not hear the engines roar.

'Our 'owls' must be forbidden to fly in such weather,' said Nikolai.

The adjutant drove to the girls' regiment and brought two pilots, one of whom was Galushenko's girlfriend. We had a really good time that night, but were awake early in the morning. The rain stopped. Our heads ached, but we were able to fly. We drank some tea quickly. I asked Galushenko: 'Kolya, have you chosen an aircraft for me?'

'I have... You'll take mine. We loaded the bombs yesterday. Everything's ready.'

A lorry was already waiting for us. The regiment commander got in the cabin, and his adjutant and I got in the back of the lorry.

'Let's go!'

The mist rose for about 300 metres and hung in a continuous thin

---

* Anti-tank aircraft bombs.

layer. It would rise higher when the sun warmed up, but we did not need much height to drop the PTAB.

We drove up to the Shturmovik. A mechanic reported on the status of the plane. There were more than 400 bombs in the bomb bay.

'Take the cover off quickly! I'll fly,' Galushenko ordered.

'Is this plane for me?' I asked.

'Yes, it is...' he waved off. 'But first I'll fly.'

'And will I have to wait for two hours until they load the bombs again then?'

'So you'll wait... There's no to hurry... Put on the parachute, what are you waiting for?' he said to his adjutant.

I could not object, since Galushenko was the regiment commander. He took off and flew to the other end of the airfield, where the bodies of the captured cars were gathered. The aircraft began to dive. Galushenko released the bombs from all four bays at once. I heard a deafening blow and saw that all the bombs overshot the target. Galushenko turned steeply and launched a second attack. I could see he was angry. He dropped the second series of anti-tank bombs, but missed again. He fired from the guns, but the bursts scattered along a line instead of hitting the same place. Galushenko zoomed and the plane disappeared in the clouds. I could imagine him tumbling in the sunshine. The engine roar was changing from the highest notes to almost silence, and I guessed that Nikolai Kirillovich was pouring out his heart through forbidden aerobatics. Nobody could see the aircraft now.

Galushenko flew above the clouds for a long time. At some point the roar stopped and all I could hear was the rear flaps, as if the plane was gliding. Suddenly I saw it breaking the shroud of clouds. The Shturmovik was spinning, its wide wings finishing the turn. It stopped rotating and began to reduce the angle flying along a curved glide path. 'Is it a new trick?' A thought flashed through my head, but immediately I realised that the plane was too low to level out. The angle of dive was decreasing fast, but there were just few metres left, and the nose of the aircraft was still aiming at the ground. In a second the plane crashed and the fragments rolled around. I was the first to run up and saw a part of Galushenko's leg. His adjutant was thrown out of the cockpit and his abdomen was ripped open.

We carried the coffins to the officer cemetery in Temryuk, where

Mikhail Talykov had been killed.

An old woman stood near me by the grave. She crossed herself many times. I talked to her. 'Granny, have you been in Temryuk all the time?'

'Yes, son, all the time...'

'Did many of our planes crash down in your town?'

'There was only one plane.'

'Can you remember, when it was?'

'Of course I remember. It was the day of martyr Evdokia...'

'What was the date?'

The old woman counted in a whisper.

'14 March.'

'Where did it fall?'

'Behind my house. It flew very low and swayed like an injured bird. I thought it would hit my chimney. But it flew further on to the yard of the town hall. The fascist commandant's office was there...'

It was an old stone building beside a park. There used to be an emplacement for a gun in the yard, but it had collapsed. There was also a tree without a top, its trunk split as if by a lightning.

The natives gathered around me interrupting each other: 'He fell flat right here... The Fritzes dragged him out. He was dead, but looked alive. A young guy with brown hair...'

'They took off his insignia, his boots and jacket.'

'And then they started to kick him with their boots...'

'At night they buried him somewhere, but nobody knows the place.'

'They dragged the plane to the gully. And we put it to use. We made pans from the metal and soled our boots with the rubber...'

The lorry was driving without lights. Clods of mud plopped down on the back of the lorry. Two dots of light glided in the air above Ahtanizovskaya. A red and a green one. Those were our 'owls' flying across the Straits of Kerch to trouble the Fritzes at night.

The 210th Regiment lost its commander again. The division's flying technique inspector, Major Kondratkov, was appointed there, and I was promoted to his position. I got my first penalty for not having dissuaded Galushenko from the unplanned flight, and my eighteenth citation for a show flight with PTABs.

230

24

INSPECTOR'S WORK

After that I served as a flying technique inspector and was subordinate to the command of our aircraft division. My job was to control the pilots' manoeuvres above the target and to correct mistakes. I held debriefings, pointed out obvious tactical errors and successful solutions. It was common knowledge that the post of inspector was taken up by the best ace among the division pilots. The inspector must show the best flying technique, and must have performed the largest number of 'effective' sorties that had resulted in heavy casualties for the enemy. The inspector also had to carry authority over the pilots. He had to help them survive and at the same time cause much damage to the enemy. It often happened that a pilot was appointed a leader after his fifth operational flight. That was a great responsibility: if you hit your own forces by mistake, you'd pay the price for it in a tribunal. I had experienced all kinds of situations during operational flights, and I had also worked for seven years as an instructor in an aeroclub. Besides I was ten years older than the majority of pilots, and age was also important.

I accompanied squadrons on missions and usually flew behind or at the side of the group. I tried to correct mistakes immediately, when I saw them: 'Where are you going? The target is to the right!' The pilots were a bit afraid of me. They thought that a flying technique inspector noticed everything.

During the attempts to break the Blue Line our division suffered heavy losses. My regiment alone lost twenty pilots and air gunners. The division was reinforced with new men and took part in covering the Crimea landing force in Kerch and in Eltigen. I remembered those days for a long time. The Shturmoviks often had to fly without bombs. Instead they carried containers with cargo parachutes, and dropped ammunition, food and medicine.

On a spring day in April 1944 the wind was drifting low clouds from the sea. It had rained in showers for two days and operational flights from Taman to the Crimea were cancelled. I allowed myself to sleep as long as I wished, and then came to the empty canteen.

'Is there anything left?' I asked the waitress.

'There is, comrade captain,' she was excited for some reason. 'I have something special for you.' she said mysteriously and disappeared in the kitchen.

In the night a German plane had dropped several bombs from behind the clouds. It aimed at our airfield, of course, but the bombs fell in the Ahtanozovsky lake. To be honest, I thought that the waitress was going to serve me a fried carp. I had seen many of them in the morning drifting along the surface with their bellies up.

'Do we have fish for breakfast today?' I asked.

'Fish? And what will you do if I make you a better surprise?'

'Well, I'll try to get some sauce...' I tried to laugh it off and thought: 'What kind of surprise can be better than a fried carp?'

'Take it...' she offered me an issue of *Izvestiya*. I looked at the front page and read: 'Decree of the Presidium of the Supreme Soviet dated 13 April 1944: to confer the Hero of the Soviet Union to the Officer Personnel of the Air Force'. I found my name in the list and it looked strangely unfamiliar...

I looked through the list, and my heart began to pound. Two lines below my name I read: 'Guards Lieutenant Colonel Nikolai Antonovich Zub'. On 22 July 1943 the commander of the 210th Attack Regiment of our division, Lieutenant Colonel Zub, had been killed in my presence.

'You owe us,' said Nikolai Sednenkov. He was one of few pilots who had joined the regiment in Donbass and were still alive.

It was impossible to get what I 'owed' in Taman. The division commander allowed me to fly to Krasnodar on such occasion. I asked Nikolai: 'What would you like?'

'Won't you regret it?' he scratched his head and pointed at my *kubanka*. It was the kind of hat some pilots got in Krasnodar, when our attack division was called the Kuban division. I gave it to him. Nikolai was an ordinary guy, but our mechanics respected him greatly.

'Our Sednenkov can fly a log,' they said.

For some time Sednenkov flew a plane which nobody else wanted to pilot. Its engine emitted smoke, though it worked all right. Nikolai joked: 'It's even better on a smoking plane. The anti-aircraft guns leave me in piece, and Messers also don't pay much attention. They must be thinking that I'm finished already, and I keep flying...'

Sednenkov was shot down half a year later, when our troops were fighting for Narev at the end of October. The regiment fought with maximum effort and suffered enormous losses. Sednenkov, Karabut, Yurkov, all were killed. On 24 October the Shturmoviks were ordered to suppress the enemy artillery near Chernostuv. Averianov led the first group, and Victor Goryachev followed them with his four-plane squad. The correspondents from the *Frontovaya Pravda* arrived at the airfield, when the planes were off. They came 'to congratulate and make photographs'.

'To congratulate with what?'

'With new Heroes!'

They told us that the decree which had long been waited for was finally coming out. Seven pilots were made Heroes of the Soviet Union: Konstantin Averianov, Vladimir Demidov, Petr Kriven, Boris Levin, Ivan Maltsev, Victor Goryachev and Nikolai Sednenkov.

The correspondents shook hands with those who were present, clicked their Leikas all the time, and were going to take an unusual picture of Averianov and Goryachev together with Boltik.

The Shturmoviks landed one by one, but Victor Goryachev was not among them... We were told that two Messerschmitts had attacked his plane from below. The aircraft zoomed, then dived and blew up hitting the ground. But one of the pilots noticed a parachute canopy that opened just above the ground. We did not know who had managed to bale out: Goryachev or his air gunner Malyshev. There was not much chance that he would stay alive after landing in the enemy position, but things happened. We had already witnessed such a miracle once in our regiment!..

On 5 November 1942, I led a nine-plane squad from Point 3 to Ordzhonikidze. There were no fighters to cover us, though Messerschmitts hung above the battlefield in flocks. During that flight two of our Shturmoviks, piloted by Vladimir Zangiev and Nikolai Pismichenko, played the role of fighters. They flew behind the group performing the 'scissors' manoeuvre.

Our target was the German tanks near Khataldon. Volodya Zangiev knew those places very well. He had spent his childhood and youth there. The first flight of four Messers dived at us aiming at the leader's plane. Zangiev managed to fire a defensive burst, and it was so successful that one of the fighters went down followed by a smoking trail. It was Zangiev's first victory, and it averted the inevitable death of the leader. I could not help following the German plane with my eyes until it hit the ground. But soon I saw a burning Shturmovik coming down. I saw a burning lump falling out of the cockpit. The white canopy opened up just above the ground, but fire was running along it as well... I was not the only one who saw the death of Volodya Zangiev near his native village. But two years passed and at the end of 1944 he came back and began to fly again!

Vladimir was badly burnt and broke his leg. He was taken prisoner and tortured by the fascists but did not say anything. In May 1943 he managed to escape from the concentration camp and get to a partisan group, where he fought successfully. He was wounded during a military operation, and the command decided to send him to the rear. After some time Zangiev returned to the 7th Guards Regiment with an unusual medal for a pilot: 'The Patriotic War Partisan' of the first grade. And Volodya's 'third' life began at the end of 1944, when his Shturmovik hit pine-trees during a snowstorm. He survived again...

The same 'miracle' happened to Malyshev, the air gunner of Victor Goryachev. He returned to the regiment...

25

THE ACADEMY

I got into the Academy quite unexpectedly. After the Germans were smashed in the Crimea, the 4th Air Army, including our 230th Kuban Division, fought as a part of the 2nd Belarussian Front. The pilots did their best, paving the way for our armies and marking their way with crushed columns and burnt enemy tanks. At that time many experienced pilots were sent to study.

Ivan Ostapenko, who was already a squadron leader, was sent to the Air Force Academy. His plane had been brought down during an attack on a railway station in Belorussia, and he survived only thanks to his air gunner Volodya Pimenov. Pimenov was a record-holder among the air gunners, and by the end of the war he had made 137 operational flights. He was a former student of Chelyabinsk Air School, had served in the infantry as a scout, had taken part in the landing operation in Novorossiysk, and became an air gunner only in the autumn of 1943. He came on foot to the regiment base, carrying our Ivan on his back.

At the farewell party Ostapenko wept.

'Don't snivel, Ivan,' said Vladimir Demidov to him. 'When you return to the regiment, we'll have at least one clever head! They say, they teach to fight by formulas...'

Doctors prohibited Senior Lieutenant Vladimir Demidov from flying after a very serious head injury, but he still did so. During an air combat above Kerch he had managed to bring down a Junker 87, but his damaged Shturmovik was intercepted by ten Messerschmitts. Misha Fedorov, his air gunner, shot one fighter down, but the mutilated Il hit the ground. Vladimir survived by a miracle, and Misha was buried at the bridgehead...

Nikolai Smurygov was sent to some advanced training courses. The

235

same with Petr Demakov, the squadron leader's deputy. But Petr came back soon.

'Have they sent you down?' the pilots asked him.

'Nobody sent me down. I ran away!'

'Are you crazy? Go back before it's too late!' his friends tried to convince him.

'I won't go!' Demakov persisted. 'The war is almost over, and sines and cosines can wait.' Demakov led a group but did not come back. He did not see the end of the war. The regiment lost one more leader.

The division commander summoned me. 'Fly to Moscow at the disposal of the head of the Main Personnel Administration, Lieutenant General Nikitin's A.V. A plane is going there.' said Colonel Getman to me. It appeared that he had received the request to send me to Moscow four times already, but had ignored them.

The capital did not welcome me. As I was trying to get to the Air Force Headquarters from the central airfield, I had to show my documents many times. The reason was my clothes. Except for a dark-blue cap nothing proved that I was an aviator. I was wearing a worn American pilot jacket without any insignia, and breeches that our armourer Klava Kalmykova had sewn for me from a captured coat. My boots, which mechanic Shevchenko had made from a parachute case, were covered with oil spots...

I got a pass in the Air Force Headquarters and was told to go to a member of the Military Council of the Air Force, Lieutenant General Shimanov.

Rather excited I opened an enormous black door and entered a large room. A long table covered with a green cloth reminded me of a runway at the Krasnodar airfield. The General came to meet me from the other end of the room. 'How are you?' I was surprised to hear that simple question.

'I'm fine...'

'How does the fighting go?'

'Excellent...'

The General asked me why I came so late. 'They wouldn't let me go,' I answered.

'Did you write this yourself?' he asked me pointing at a file of Stalin's *sokol* magazines. He leafed through the papers, and I recognised my seven articles, titled 'The Components of Airmanship'.

'Yes, I did,' I answered, thinking nervously to myself that I had neither praised nor criticised anyone in the articles, and trying to guess what lapses the General had found there. All I did was share my battle experience.

'Didn't you exaggerate a bit in this place?' he showed me a paragraph marked with red pencil. The 'suspicious' paragraph described my personal achievements in accuracy in shooting and bombing, which I had demonstrated many times during show flights at the front. Among other data there was a table of the range of deviations of the bombs from the target. General Shimanov asked me about one of the numbers in the table which surprised him: 6 metres.

'I wrote as it is,' I answered him.

'To be honest, General Nikitin and I doubted if that it's true. Nobody has yet shown such results in training units and regiments. Can you demonstrate it to the pilots?'

'I can!'

'That's why we summoned you. Make a tour through our training units, share your battle experience, demonstrate... And after that we'll have a special talk.'

I was used to the fact that high command was always keeping something back, so I forgot about the 'special talk' as soon as I received the travel allowance. All I was thinking of was how to show the best performance.

The General told me about a training regiment that was based in the outskirts of Moscow. It was preparing pilots and sending them to fighting units. That was where I had to make a 'show'.

During my trip I tried to do everything just as it was at the front, so I refused to have a look at the targets in advance: 'At the front you see your target only on the map, there are no preliminary flights.' I told the commanders of the units. 'And give me real aircraft bombs and full ammunition.'

They complied with my conditions.

I also made a secret 'deal' with the person in charge of the training ground. The problem was that the target for bombing was a cross, made of white birch trunks, and the target for gun-shelling was a column of trophy lorries. A person would usually go and mark the new holes after each session. I knew that the cars were already punched all over. So I asked the head of the ground to put some straw inside the lorries and pour fuel over it before my flight.

Representatives of the Air Forces, including General Shimanov, came to watch my first show. Together with other pilots they stood near a loudspeaker and listened to my explanations during the flight.

I took off and had no difficulties in finding the training ground in the forest.

'Speed 300, height 800, the target is to the left,' I transmitted to the ground, watching the cross of white trunks approaching the cursor.

'I begin the dive at one o'clock and... release!'

When I levelled out and turned back I saw the logs scattered around. The bombs hit it right! Good!

I reduced height and hedgehopped behind the forest. I wanted to show my 'partisan technique', which I used to attack trains and cars unexpectedly. The speed was rather high, but the height was minimal. I made two turns behind the forest, so that the audience could not see me, found the railway track, and flew along it until I saw the 'column'. I zoomed banking, and then began to lower the nose of the aircraft and take aim at the target. I hadn't yet lifted out when the first lorry caught fire, hit by a sheaf of tracer bullets. Again I disappeared behind the forest getting ready for the second attack. I had always enjoyed shooting at the enemy columns from the guns, and I was really good at it.

My flight had a stunning effect. They had never seen anything like that before. The direct hit of the target with bombs, low and sudden attacks –'That's how you must do it, comrade officers!' said General Shimanov. He told me to give such demonstrations at several training grounds in the outskirts of Moscow and also near Kuybyshev. I told him I knew that place, because I had got planes for my regiment from there. 'So show them what it must look like. They don't know anything!'

After my tour through the training units was over, I came to General Shimanov for the 'special talk'. That time I was wearing full uniform, including gold shoulder straps. I had received all that from central stores thanks to a message from a member of the Military Council.

'Well done,' said General Shimanov. 'Now, there is something I want to ask you. The Monino Air Force Academy has returned from evacuation and is enrolling students. Would you like to study there?'

I was stunned. Having regained control of myself I said: 'May I think it over behind the door for some time?'

'You may think it over until tomorrow,' the General said to my relief. 'Bring me the report.'

I spent the evening dithering. Most of all I worried about the entrance examinations on general subjects. I did not want to enter a preparatory course, because I did not want to waste a year, so I had to pass the exams somehow. There were plenty of advisers around me, but they all had different opinions. Some said I would be a damned fool if I quit fighting now, when the war was so easy. They thought I had a good chance of getting a second Star.* Others said there was no sense risking my life any longer. But the majority advised me to study: 'It's not enough to have a Star, you must also have something inside your head. And don't be afraid of the exams. If you have Shimanov's behind you, they'll take you in automatically.'

My report was lying on Shimanov's table. He looked through it and wrote in a bold hand: 'Enrol in the Academy'. He put a full stop after the phrase and I felt I was going to fly. 'Enrol means I won't have to pass the exams,' I thought. But for some reason the General did not withdrew the pen from the paper. He thought for some time, and then suddenly attached a long tail to the full stop and wrote another line: 'if he passes the entrance examinations.'

My foreboding did not deceive me. At the very end of the examinations, when I had already passed maths, physics and other subjects, I had to face a young blonde girl. She began to cross-examine me on the map of America. For some reason she was especially interested in sheep-breeding. My only geographical knowledge had been picked up from a book by Ilf and Petrov.† The duet of writers just about saved me from complete failure.

Thus I entered the basic course and later graduated from the Academy with the golden medal. As for Hero of the Soviet Union Ivan Ostapenko, he entered the preparatory course and had to learn general subjects. He did not like it very much, to be honest, and

---

* The Golden Star of the Soviet Union.

† This is a reference to the popular book *One-Storied America* by the Soviet writers Ilya Ilf and Evgeny Petrov, who describe a journey they made through the USA in 1935–6.

dreamed of returning to the regiment. There were so many front officers in the Academy that for some time Ostapenko and I had to share one old bed in the dormitory. We couldn't help remembering our wooden beds in barracks!

I was in the Academy on Victory Day. I still remember everything in detail: everyone around me was firing pistols and shouting: 'Victory!!!' At first I could not understand what was going on, and when I did, I took a local train and went to Moscow. The train was crowded, and we felt drunk from happiness!!! I remember a woman of about fifty, who could not restrain tears. She smiled apologetically, tears running down her cheeks. I wished I could hug her!

Moscow was celebrating the triumph. People were shouting 'Hurray!' and lifted up each officer they saw. There was an American embassy on Gorky Street in the centre of Moscow, and I remember American soldiers sitting on the window-sills, shouting and throwing something to us. We were all friends on that day. Everyone was mad from joy! That was happiness!!!

EPILOGUE

In 1932 I heard a slogan, 'Komsomolets – to aircraft!', quit studying at the composition department of the Moscow Conservatoire, and entered a flying school. From that time my whole life was connected with aircraft. I was an instructor in an aeroclub, a military pilot, a flying technique instructor in the Frunze Military Academy...

The years of my flying work have passed long ago, and now I can say that the strongest impressions from that period I gained during the war. They are engraved in my memory, and left scars in my heart. They still stir up my feelings and don't leave me in peace... I will be ninety-four soon, and sometimes Faust's thoughts come into my mind. I imagine a wizard coming to me and saying: 'I can make you young again, but your life will repeat just the same as it was. Again you'll be shot down three times at the war, and again you will survive. You'll go through it for the second time, but you will be young again.' And in my mind I answer: 'NO, I DON'T WANT IT A SECOND TIME', because what I have experienced is too much! It's psychologically impossible! There is a limit. We waited for death every day... We could only calm down in the evening, when we went to sleep. After the 300 grams of vodka and the food I could relax and went to sleep feeling that I have a guarantee that I will live until the morning. And in the morning it began again: you woke up, sipped a cup of tea and ran to get a mission. And all the horror came back. Imagine a sportsman before a start. Nothing serious can happen to him, he won't be killed for sure, but still he feels nervous. And I was thinking that I had been lucky the previous day, but I did not know what to expect from today. I was trying to suppress that kind of thought, and I succeeded. That's why everything was all right. I survived, and I was fighting rather well, I suppose. In that fierce cruel struggle we managed to crush the enemy that brought war to our land, and there is my part of strain, blood, and sweat in it. But the victory over the strong and experienced army of Germany and its allies cost us thousands of people's lives. During the four years of fighting five regiments of my 230th Kuban Ground–Attack Aircraft Division lost 717 men. Two hundred and two of those men served in our 7th Guards Regiment. Few of those who entered the war in 1941 survived it. Few people lived through the war without deep scars on their bodies and in their hearts.

On 9 May 1968 veterans of the division met in Kerch at the uncovering of an obelisk commemorating our lost friends. The obelisk was built with our own money. The curtain fell down to expose five white wings rising up to the sky, their tips closing up in firm handshake. Five wings - five fraternal regiments.

Before leaving the town we gathered near the obelisk late at night. It was illuminated with red light. The town was already sleeping. We stood in silence passing a glass of red wine along the circle. Before taking a sip each of us pronounced the names of his friends, with whom he had flown wing to wing during the war. I heard Fedya Artemov and Misha Talykov mentioned... Our former armourers, whom we still called 'our girls', remembered them.

My friends said to me then: 'Those who were killed must live in a book. People must know about them. And write the truth only!'

That sounded like a military mission, when nobody asks you whether you are capable of doing it.

I have done my best.

TABLE OF PERSONNEL

Name	Aircraft	Role	Date of Birth	Date of Event
Gricevich, Nikolai	Il-2-1	pilot	1919	27.06.1941

KIA. Shot by anti-aircraft fire destroying crossing over Berezina river. Bobruysk region.

Komakha, Roman	—	maint.*	1917	28.06.1941

Killed in attack on an airfield, Gomel region.

Krysin, Aleksandr	—	pilot	1908	28.06.1941

Killed in attack on an airfield, Gomel region.

Mescheriakov, Aleksandr	—	pilot	1918	28.06.1941

Killed in attack on an airfield, Gomel region.

Zakharkin, Ilia	—	pilot	1911	28.06.1941

Killed in attack on an airfield, Gomel region.

Barenov, Vasili	Il-2-1	pilot	1919	29.06.1941

KIA. Destroying crossing over Berezina river. Bobruysk region.

Filipov, Viktor	Il-2-1	pilot	1909	29.06.1941

Returned from captivity 19.8.41.

Gottelf, Solomon	Il-2-1	pilot	1908	29.06.1941

MIA. Bobruysk region.

Kuzmin, Aleksandr	Il-2-1	pilot	1906	29.06.1941

KIA. Shot by anti-aircraft fire destroying crossing over Berezina river. Bobruysk region.

* Maintenance personnel.

Table of Personnel

Name	Aircraft	Role	Date of Birth	Date of Event

Pushin, Abram — Il-2-1 pilot, 1919, 29.06.1941
Shot by anti-aircraft fire when destroying the crossing over the Berezina river. Bobruysk region.

Sosnin, Evstafi — Il-2-1 pilot, 1916, 29.06.1941
KIA. Shot by anti-aircraft fire destroying crossing over Berezina river. Bobruysk region.

Golubev, Nikolai — Il-2-1 pilot, 1906, 30.06.1941
KIA. Shot by anti-aircraft fire destroying crossing over Berezina river. Bobruysk region.

Lapshov, Aleksandr — Il-2-1 pilot, 1918, 30.06.1941
MIA. Destroying crossing over Berezina river. Bobruysk region.

Podlobnyi, Valentin — Il-2-1 pilot, 1908, 30.06.1941
KIA. Shot by anti-aircraft fire destroying crossing over Berezina river. Bobruysk region.

Shulgin, Vasili — Il-2-1 pilot, 1916, 30.06.1941
KIA. Shot by anti-aircraft fire. Returned to regiment 19.8.41.

Sigida, Fedor — Il-2-1 pilot, 1912, 30.06.1941
KIA. Shot by anti-aircraft fire destroying crossing over Berezina river. Bobruysk region.

Sleptsov, Semen — Il-2-1 pilot, 1908, 30.06.1941
MIA. Bobruysk region. Did not want to take part in missions. Afraid of flying even in pre-war times.

Bulanov, Aleksandr — Il-2-1 pilot, 1910, 01.07.1941
Accident, forced landing in bad weather. Sescha region.

Valkovich, Aleksandr — Il-2-1 pilot, 1912, 01.07.1941
MIA. Bobruysk region.

Shiroki, Vasili — Il-2-1 pilot, 1906, 02.07.1941
KIA. Bobruysk region. Crashed in column of tanks. Witnessed by Denisyuk.

Volkov, Petr — Il-2-1 pilot, 1916, 02.07.1941
MIA. Bobruysk region.

244

Table of Personnel

Name	Aircraft	Role	Date of Birth	Date of Event
Alekseikin, Aleksandr MIA. Bobruysk region.	Il-2-1	pilot	1919	03.07.1941
Dryukov, Serafim KIA. Bobruysk region.	Il-2-1	pilot	1907	03.07.1941
Koshelev, Vasili MIA. Bobruysk region.	Il-2-1	pilot	1911	03.07.1941
Krivich, Anatoli MIA. Rogachev region.	Il-2-1	pilot	1914	03.07.1941
Vasilenko, Vladimir Shot down during attack on Bobruysk airfield. Taken prisoner and later released by soldiers who broke the encirclement. As a result of the torture he was put into a mental hospital.	Il-2-1	pilot	1905	03.07.1941
Sorokin, Vasili MIA. Bobruysk region.	Il-2-1	pilot	1916	08.07.1941
Tkachenko, Nikolai MIA. Bobruysk region.	Il-2-1	pilot	1918	08.07.1941
Kuzmichev, Aleksandr MIA. Bobruysk region.	Il-2-1	pilot	19	09.07.1941
Stalkin, Nikolai KIA. Shot by anti-aircraft fire destroying crossing over Berezina river. Bobruysk region.	Il-2-1	pilot	1904	09.07.1941
Shakirdzhanov Accident in bad weather. Mogilev–Mukhamedzhan region.	Il-2-1	pilot	1917	11.07.1941
Soldatenko, Ivan KIA. Mogilev region.	Il-2-1	pilot	1921	11.07.1941
Alekseev, Andrei MIA. Plane on fire. Mogilev region.	Il-2-1		1915	13.07.1941
Osipov, Konstantin Natural death. Bryansk region.	—	maint.	1915	15.07.1941

Table of Personnel

Name	Aircraft	Role	Date of Birth	Date of Event
Denisov, Feofan MIA. Mogilev region.	Il-2-1	pilot	1912	17.07.1941
Ivanov, Vladimir MIA. Kirichev region.	Il-2-1	pilot	1916	20.07.1941
Lesnikov, Vladimir MIA. Mogilev region.	Il-2-1	pilot	1903	20.07.1941
Konov, Nikolai KIA. Mogilev region.	Il-2-1	pilot	1912	25.07.1941
Stoletnii, Grigori MIA. Mogilev region.	Il-2-1	pilot	1914	25.07.1941
Riazanov, Vasili MIA. Mogilev region.	Il-2-1	pilot	1919	26.07.1941
Pleshakov, Sergei MIA. Mogilev region. Forced landing on. Afraid of flying.	Il-2-1	pilot	1910	29.07.1941
Zaitsev, Vladimir MIA. Mogilev region.	Il-2-1	pilot	1913	29.07.1941
Karpenko, Konstantin Accident, blew up on his own bombs. Smolensk region.	Il-2-1	pilot	1915	03.08.1941
Sorokov, Semen Taken prisoner. Returned by 18.8.41. Smolensk region.	Il-2-1	pilot	1909	03.08.1941
Ivanov, Ivan MIA.	Il-2-1	pilot	1917	07.08.1941
Koshelev, Pavel Died from the wounds sustained repulsing machine-gun attack by German soldiers. Pisarevka airfield, Orel region.	—	maint.	1918	12.08.1941
Zhulev, Pavel KIA. Shot by anti-aircraft fire. Turned upside down and caught fire. Donetsk region.	Il-2-1	pilot	1912	28.09.1941
Varfolomeev, Mikhail MIA. Shot down by a tank gun. Donetsk region.	Il-2-1	pilot	1916	01.10.1941

Table of Personnel

Name	Aircraft	Role	Date of Birth	Date of Event
Morozov, Vasili	Il-2-1	pilot	—	09.10.1941

MIA. Zaporozhje region.

Ivanov, Ivan	Il-2-1	pilot	1917	15.10.1941

Disappeared in strange circumstances. Perhaps deserted. 'On October 15 he got lost after the mission and made a forced landing near Zhelannaya village. His aircraft was blown up on October 21. Ivanov still hasn't returned to the unit.'

Sinyakov, Nikolai	Il-2-1	pilot	1918	30.10.1941

KIA on his birthday. Donbass region.

Krasnobaev, Viktor	Il-2-1	pilot	1913	01.11.1941

MIA. Donbass region.

Maslennikov, Petr	Il-2-1	pilot	1919	08.11.1941

KIA. Rostov region.

Getman, Nikolai	Il-2-1	pilot	1918	15.11.1941

MIA. Donbass region.

Vypritski, Nikolai	Il-2-1	pilot	1915	08.01.1942

Accident, lost in fog after take-off, lost, spun and crashed. Voroshilovgrad region.

Shahov, Victor	Il-2-1	pilot	—	19.01.1942

Shot down trying to reach friendly units, frostbite in both legs. Tried to resume flying after amputation, but not allowed.

Egorov, Mikhail	Il-2-1	pilot	1915	19.02.1942

Kharkov region. Did not return from mission. Taken prisoner and returned from the occupied territory (Kvantun).

Chernikov, Daniil	Il-2-1	pilot	1908	21.03.1942

MIA. Donetsk region. Shot by anti-aircraft fire. Landed near Slavyansk.

Shemyakin, Vasily	Il-2-1	pilot	1907	28.03.1942

KIA. Shot by anti-aircraft fire, Donetsk region.

Sergeev, Petr	Il-2-1	pilot	1918	13.05.1942

MIA. Donetsk region.

Table of Personnel

Name	Aircraft	Role	Date of Birth	Date of Event
Smurnov KIA.	Il-2-1	pilot	—	21.05.1942
Ryzhikov, Vladimir MIA. Donetsk region.	Il-2-1	pilot	1918	31.05.1942
Zubov, Nikolai MIA. Donetsk region.	Il-2-1	pilot	1916	31.05.1942
Eliseev, Tikhon MIA in attack on enemy airfield, Kharkov region.	Il-2-1	pilot	1908	09.06.1942
Alimov Student on probation at front. Fate unknown. Donbass.	—	maint.		07.42
Bodikov Student on probation at front. Fate unknown. Donbass.	—	maint.		07.42
Danilychev Student on probation at front. Fate unknown. Donbass.	—	maint.		07.42
Efimov Student on probation at front. Fate unknown. Donbass.	—	maint.		07.42
Karabanov Student on probation at front. Fate unknown. Donbass. Seen in captivity by Elagin in 1943.	—	maint.		07.42
Korneev Student on probation at front. Fate unknown. Donbass.	—	maint.		07.42
Latyshev Student on probation at front. Fate unknown. Donbass.	—	maint.		07.42
Limanski, Andrei Donbass. Escaped on second day at front. Later returned and served in regiment.	—	maint.		07.42
Markov Student on probation at front. Fate unknown. Donbass.	—	maint.		07.42
Nikolaev Student on probation at front. Fate unknown. Donbass.	—	maint.		07.42

Table of Personnel

Name	Aircraft	Role	Date of Birth	Date of Event

Romanov — maint. 07.42
Student on probation at front. Fate unknown. Donbass.

Tantsyura, Aleksei — maint. 07.42
Student on probation at front. Fate unknown. Donbass.

Boiko, Ivan Il-2-1 pilot 1916 16.07.1942
KIA. Donbass. Shot by enemy fighters. 'Around 11 a.m. he was shot down by three Me-109s near Erimeevka village.'

Kudinov, Petr Il-2-1 pilot 1916 17.07.1942
MIA. Rostov region, Kamensk.

Kladko, Anatoly Il-2-1 pilot — 23.07.1942
KIA. Shot down by Me-109 approaching crossing over the Don.

Nikolayev, Nikolai Il-2-1 pilot 1910 23.07.1942
KIA Shot down by Me-109 approaching crossing over the Don.

Bessarabenko, Vasili maint. 1915 24.07.1942
Killed by shrapnel, enemy attack on Kagalnitskaya airfield, Rostov region.

Starcev, Pavel Il-2-1 pilot — 24.07.1942
MIA. Rostov region.

Kniazhev, Grigori Il-2-1 pilot — 25.07.1942
KIA. Shot by Bf-109, Rostov region.

Mospanov, Ilya Il-2 pilot 1913 25.07.1942
KIA. 'Shot down by Me-109, when he was taking off from the Kagalnitskaya airfield. The aircraft set on fire.' Rostov region.

Bobrov, Ivan Il-2-1 pilot 1912 29.07.1942
Died in plane crash landing at the Voroshilovsk airfield. 'Had been previously convicted of breaking machinery.'

Artemov, Fedor Il-2-1 pilot 1918 05.11.1942
KIA. Shot by anti-aircraft fire, North Ossetia.

Kuznetsov, Lev Il-2-1 pilot 1918 05.11.1942
KIA. Shot down by enemy fighters, enemy territory. North Caucasus.

Table of Personnel

Name	Aircraft	Role	Date of Birth	Date of Event
Zangiev, Vladimir	Il-2-1	pilot	—	05.11.1942

Shot down. Taken prisoner, escaped May 1943, fought as a partisan. Injured and evacuated to the rear. Returned to regiment autumn 1944.

Pismichenko, Nikolai	Il-2-1	pilot	1921	08.11.1942

KIA. North Caucasus.

Seleznev, Andrei	Il-2-1	pilot	1909	08.11.1942

MIA. North Caucasus.

Shamshurin, Vasily	Il-2-1	pilot	1920	18.11.1942

KIA. Shot by anti-aircraft fire. North Ossetia.

Bobikov, Ivan	Il-2-1	pilot	—	27.11.1942

KIA. North Caucasus.

Gevorkian, Vartan	Il-2-1	pilot	1923	27.11.1942

KIA. North Caucasus, Aruba region.

Mikhailov, Ilya	Il-2-1	pilot	1921	27.11.1942

KIA. North Caucasus.

Agarev, Ivan	Il-2-1	pilot	1917	05.12.1942

Shot himself. North Caucasus.

Snopko, Grigory	Il-2-1	pilot	1918	08.12.1942

KIA. North Caucasus.

Lebedev, Petr	Il-2-1	pilot	—	10.12.1942

MIA. Shot by enemy fighters, taken prisoner.

Rudenko, Petr	Il-2-1	pilot	1919	10.12.1942

KIA. Shot by enemy fighters. Krasnodar region.

Musienko, Ivan	—	pilot	—	1943

'Shot down, put into a concentration camp in 1943. Escaped in 1944, retrained to pilot an Il-10. Not allowed to take part in the Victory Parade. Settled in Odessa, drank.'

Tsyganov, Petr	—	pilot	—	09.01.1943

Accident during a military operation.

Table of Personnel

Name	Aircraft	Role	Date of Birth	Date of Event
Volkov, Aleksei	Il-2-1	pilot	—	21.01.1943

'Did not return from "hunting" in Armavir region. His wingman Panov did not see him come down.' Krasnodar region.

Shuvalov, Petr	Il-2	pilot	1918	26.01.1943

'He was shot down and made a forced landing near Gulkovskaya. The gunner survived. He shot himself when the Germans tried to take him prisoner.' Krasnodar region.

Dolginski, Sergei	Il-2-1	maint.	1913	31.01.1943

Il-2 collided with Me-109 in bad weather; it was carrying two mechanics.

Dorogavtsev, Nikolai	Il-2-1	pilot	—	31.01.1943

Il-2 collided with Me-109 in bad weather. 'He was killed by Me-109 above the Getmanovskaya airfield. Two mechanics from Stavropol were killed as well.'

Platonov, Aleksandr	Il-2	maint.	1919	31.01.1943

Il-2 collided with Me-109 in bad weather; it was carrying two mechanics.

Zhukov, Ivan		pilot	1917	07.02.1943

Shot by anti-aircraft fire. Krasnodar region.

Slepov, Sergei	Il-2-1	pilot	1921	09.02.1943

Shot by enemy fighters. Killed by policemen. Krasnodar region.

Smirnov, Sergei	Il-2-1	pilot	1913	13.02.1943

Shot by anti-aircraft fire. Krasnodar region. Taken prisoner in Czechia. Escaped and fought as a partisan.

Maximchuk, Boris	Il-2	gunner	1922	23.02.1943

MIA. Crew pilot Proletaev, gunner Maximchuk. Krasnodar region.

Olenin, Victor	Il-2-1	pilot	1918	23.02.1943

KIA. Krasnodar region.

Protalev, Nikolai	Il-2	pilot	1914	23.02.1943

MIA. Krasnodar region. Crew pilot Proletaev, gunner Maximchuk.

Table of Personnel

Name	Aircraft	Role	Date of Birth	Date of Event
Abramov, Mikhail	Il-2-1	pilot	1915	25.02.1943
MIA. Krasnodar region.				
Zakharov, Aleksandr	Il-2-1	pilot	1919	25.02.1943
KIA. Krasnodar region.				
Bubakin, Mikhail	Il-2	gunner	1918	26.02.1943
Gunner in Bukreev's crew. 'On February 23, 1943 he was injured in an aerial engagement, and died in a hospital.' Krasnodar region.				
Bobkov, Sergei	Il-2-1	pilot	1913	01.03.1943
MIA. Krasnodar region.				
Vozgaev, Petr	Il-2-1	pilot	1922	04.03.1943
MIA. Krasnodar region.				
Timofeev, Petr	Il-2	gunner	1921	10.03.1943
KIA. Shot by enemy fighters. Krasnodar region.				
Gladkov, Pavel		maint.	1912	11.03.1943
A joiner. Killed by shrapnel in enemy attack on airfield. Krasnodar region.				
Chelpanov, Valeri	Il-2-1	pilot	1914	13.03.1943
KIA. Shot by anti-aircraft fire. Krasnodar region.				
Boldin, Leonid	Il-2	gunner	1921	14.03.1943
KIA. Krasnodar region. Gunner in Bukreev's crew.				
Talykov, Mikhail	Il-2-1	pilot	1921	14.03.1943
KIA. shot by anti-aircraft fire. Krasnodar region.				
Kuznetsov, Nikolai	Il-2-1	pilot	1903	15.03.1943
MIA. Krasnodar region.				
Romantsov, German	Il-2-1	pilot	1922	15.03.1943
MIA. Krasnodar region.				
Kolesnikov, Petr	Il-2-1	pilot	1923	24.03.1943
Accident after successful military operation. Collided with Zlobin's aircraft. Krasnodar region.				

Table of Personnel

Name	Aircraft	Role	Date of Birth	Date of Event

Muhin, Nikolai — Il-2, gunner, 1922, 24.03.1943
Accident after successful military operation. Kolesnikov's aircraft collided with Zlobin's aircraft. Zlobin and gunner Muhin were killed. Krasnodar region, Baranikovskaya village.

Zlobin, Ivan — Il-2, pilot, 1920, 24.03.1943
Accident after successful military operation. Kolesnikov's aircraft collided with Zlobin's aircraft. Zlobin and gunner Muhin were killed. Krasnodar region.

Iakovlev, Pavel — Il-2, pilot, 1921, 30.03.1943
—

Antonov, Boris — Il-2-1, pilot, —, 04.43
Injured during mission. Kept fighting then sent to the rear. Had plastic surgery fifty times on his face. Discharged from hospital June 1945.

Drobilin, Mikhail — Il-2-1, gunner, 11.05.1943
Accident. Crew pilot Petrov, gunner Drobilin. Skin on wing torn off. Krasnodar region.

Petrov, Vladimir — Il-2-1, pilot, 1920, 11.05.1943
Accident. Crew pilot Petrov, gunner Drobilin. Skin on wing torn off. Krasnodar region.

Aleshin, Nikolai — Il-2, gunner, 1919, 23.07.1943
KIA. Shot by enemy fighters. Krasnodar region. Crew pilot Shevchenko, gunner Aleshin.

Shevchenko, Andrei — Il-2, pilot, 1920, 23.07.1943
KIA. Shot by enemy fighters. Krasnodar region. Crew pilot Shevchenko, gunner Aleshin.

Gurkov, Aleksandr — Il-2, gunner, 1920, 26.07.1943
KIA. Shot by enemy fighters. Krasnodar region. Crew pilot Novak, gunner Gurkov.

Novak, Leonid — Il-2, pilot, 1921, 26.07.1943
KIA. Shot by enemy fighters. Krasnodar region. Crew pilot Novak, gunner Gurkov.

Table of Personnel

Name	Aircraft	Role	Date of Birth	Date of Event

Naumov, Nikolai Il-2 gunner 1910 06.08.1943
Gunner of Panov's crew. Injured in aerial combat with enemy fighters. Died in hospital, Crimea.

Rudometov, Evgenii Il-2 gunner 1919 08.08.1943
Injured in aerial combat with enemy fighters. Died same day in hospital. Krasnodar region.

Fedorichev, Ivan Il-2 pilot 1924 09.08.1943
MIA. Crew pilot Luchko, gunner Fedorichev. Krasnodar region.

Luchko, Grigori Il-2 pilot 1922 09.08.1943
MIA. Krasnodar region. Crew pilot Luchko, gunner Fedorichev. Krasnodar region.

Popkov, Petr Il-2 gunner 1920 09.08.1943
MIA. Krasnodar region. Crew pilot Scherbakov, gunner Popkov. Krasnodar region.

Scherbakov, Semen Il-2 pilot 1922 09.08.1943
MIA. Krasnodar region. Crew pilot Scherbakov, gunner Popkov. Krasnodar region.

Fominyh, Anatoly Il-2 pilot 1922 18.08.1943
MIA. Crew pilot Fominyh, gunner Godilov. Shot by anti-aircraft fire. The burning aircraft crashed near Spirtstroy. One person bailed out. Krasnodar region.

Godilov, Georgi Il-2 gunner 1919 18.08.1943
MIA. Crew pilot Fominyh, gunner Godilov. Shot by anti-aircraft fire. The burning aircraft crashed near Spirtstroy. One person bailed out. Krasnodar region.

Chulimkov, Anatoli Il-2 gunner 1923 11.09.1943
KIA. Shot by anti-aircraft fire. Crew pilot Volkov, gunner Chulimkov. Krasnodar region.

Volkov, Stepan Il-2 pilot 1917 11.09.1943
KIA. Shot by anti-aircraft fire. Crew pilot Volkov, gunner Chulimkov. Krasnodar region.

Table of Personnel

Name	Aircraft	Role	Date of Birth	Date of Event
Gopkin, Ivan	Il-2	gunner	1922	14.09.1943

KIA. Shot by two Me-109s. Crew pilot Lotak, gunner Gopkin. Krasnodar region.

| **Lotak, Mikhail** | Il-2 | pilot | 1922 | 14.09.1943 |

KIA. Shot by two Me-109s. Crew pilot Lotak, gunner Gopkin. Krasnodar region.

| **Verdlis, Ivan** | Il-2 | gunner | 1915 | 14.09.1943 |

KIA. Krasnodar region. The aircraft was attacked by two Me-109s and set on fire. The pilot survived.

| **Baikulov, Ivan** | Il-2 | pilot | 1920 | 19.09.1943 |

KIA. Crew pilot Mamota, gunner Baikulov. Krasnodar region.

| **Mamota, Nikolai** | Il-2 | pilot | 1922 | 19.09.1943 |

KIA. Crew pilot Mamota, gunner Baikulov. Krasnodar region.

| **Bondarenko, Georgy** | Il-2 | pilot | 1921 | 23.09.1943 |

KIA. Shot by anti-aircraft fire. Crew pilot Bondarenko, gunner Glebov. Krasnodar region.

| **Glebov, Aleksei** | Il-2 | gunner | 1922 | 23.09.1943 |

KIA. Shot by anti-aircraft fire. Crew pilot Bondarenko, gunner Glebov. Krasnodar region.

| **Sokolov, Anatoli** | Il-2 | gunner | 1922 | 04.10.1943 |

MIA. Shot by anti-aircraft fire. Baled out and landed in the enemy territory. Krasnodar region.

| **Larskikh, Vasili** | Il-2 | pilot | 1922 | 07.10.1943 |

Accident during take-off. Crew pilot Larskikh, gunner Miroshkin. Krasnodar region.

| **Miroshkin, Petr** | Il-2 | gunner | 1923 | 07.10.1943 |

Accident during take-off. Crew pilot Larskikh, gunner Miroshkin. Krasnodar region.

| **Avdeev, Aleksandr** | | pilot | 1923 | 11.10.1943 |

MIA.

Name	Aircraft	Role	Date of Birth	Date of Event

Belykh, Nikolai — Il-2 — gunner — 1918 — 30.10.1943
KIA. Shot by anti-aircraft fire. Crew pilot Sergienko, gunner Belykh. Crimea.

Sergienko, Aleksei — Il-2 — pilot — 1923 — 30.10.1943
KIA. Shot by anti-aircraft fire. Crew pilot Sergienko, gunner Belykh. Crimea.

Kaverin, Aleksandr — Il-2 — pilot — 1923 — 11.43
Died from wounds.

Chuprina, Aleksandra — Il-2 — gunner — 1920 — 03.11.1943
Accident. Crew pilot Mosolov, gunner Chuprina – sole female gunner in regiment. Aircraft came down in Black Sea in fog.

Mosolov, Nikolai — Il-2 — pilot — 1918 — 03.11.1943
Accident. Crew pilot Mosolov, gunner Chuprina. Aircraft came down in Black Sea in fog.

Ivantsov, Ivan — Il-2 — pilot — 1920 — 07.11.1943
KIA. Shot by anti-aircraft fire. Crew pilot Ivantsov, gunner Kravchenko. Crimea.

Kravchenko, Pavel — Il-2 — pilot — 1923 — 07.11.1943
KIA. Shot by anti-aircraft fire. Crew pilot Ivantsov, gunner Kravchenko. Crimea.

Murodian, Sergei — Il-2 — gunner — 1921 — 14.11.1943
KIA. Shot by enemy fighters. Landed near Kotremez. Injured, but crawled to front line. Shot crossing line. Crimea.

Churochkin, Andrei — Il-2 — pilot — 1921 — 02.12.1943
KIA. Shot by anti-aircraft fire near height 110.8. Crimea.

Gumanov, Igor — Il-2 — gunner — 1923 — 04.12.1943
MIA. Crew pilot Morgachev, gunner Gumanov. 'Made a forced landing during the attack on Eltigen. Was injured trying to escape the encirclement, and remained in the southern part of Kerch.'

Korotkevich, Pavel — Il-2 — gunner — 1922 — 04.12.1943
KIA. Shot down. Crew pilot Panov, gunner Korotkevich. Crimea.

Table of Personnel

Name	Aircraft	Role	Date of Birth	Date of Event
Morgachev, Ivan	Il-2	pilot	1922	04.12.1943

KIA. Crew pilot Morgachev, gunner Gumanov. Shot down. Morgachev and gunner Tereshenko fought on ground, killed.

Panov, Boris	Il-2	pilot	1922	04.12.1943

KIA. Shot by anti-aircraft fire. Crew pilot Panov, gunner Korotkevich. Crimea.

Sklizkov, Sergei	Il-2	gunner	1913	06.12.1943

KIA. Shot by two Bf-109. Crew pilot Skvortsov, gunner Sklizkov. Crimea.

Skvortsov, Nikolai	Il-2	pilot	1917	06.12.1943

KIA. Shot by two Bf-109. Crew pilot Skvortsov, gunner Sklizkov. Crimea.

Chapaikin, Ilia	Il-2	pilot	1920	28.12.1943

KIA. Shot by enemy fighters. Crew pilot Chapaikin, gunner Kulikov. Crimea.

Chumakov, Igor	—		1923	28.12.1943

MIA.

Kulikov, Aleksei	Il-2	gunner	1923	28.12.1943

KIA. Shot by enemy fighters. Crew pilot Chapaikin, gunner Kulikov. Crimea.

Titov, Ivan	Il-2-1	pilot	1920	28.12.1943

KIA. Shot by anti-aircraft fire near Katergez. Landed on water and drowned. Crimea.

Leonov, Vasili	Il-2	gunner	1925	31.12.1943

KIA. Shot by enemy fighters. Crew pilot Stepanov, gunner Leonov. Crimea.

Stepanov, Boris	Il-2	pilot	1921	31.12.1943

KIA. Shot by enemy fighters. Crew pilot Stepanov, gunner Leonov. Crimea. 'He was killed on Yukov's aircraft during the last evening flight. Yukov was furious about losing his aircraft, not the man.'

Table of Personnel

Name	Aircraft	Role	Date of Birth	Date of Event

Kovalkin, Aleksandr Il-2 pilot 1919 04.01.1944
KIA. Shot by enemy fighters in attack on Bagerovsky airfield. Crew pilot Kovalkin, gunner Urmin. Crimea.

Urmin, Fedor Il-2 gunner 1923 04.01.1944
KIA. Shot by enemy fighters in attack on Bagerovsky airfield. Crew pilot Kovalkin, gunner Urmin. Crimea.

Alekseev, Vasili Il-2 pilot 1922 12.01.1944
KIA. Shot by enemy fighters. Crew pilot Alekseev, gunner Degtiarev. Crimea.

Degtiarev, Vladimir Il-2 gunner 1917 12.01.1944
KIA. Shot by enemy fighters. Crew pilot Alekseev, gunner Degtiarev. Crimea.

Tereshenko, Eugene Il-2 gunner 1919 25.01.1944
KIA. Shot by anti-aircraft fire in attack on northern slopes of Mitridat. Crimea.

Fedorov, Mikhail Il-2 gunner 1921 26.01.1944
KIA in forced landing. Pilot Demidov survived. Crimea.

Paukov, Sergei Il-2 pilot 1922 26.01.1944
KIA. Shot by anti-aircraft fire during attack of rear units in western part of Kerch. Aircraft burnt, pilot died. Crimea.

Krivoshein, Vasily Il-2 gunner 1917 16.03.1944
Accident. Two aircraft collided.

Poplavski, Vasili Il-2 gunner 1914 16.03.1944
KIA. Shot by enemy fighters approaching target near Kotergez. Crimea.

Zhdanov, Aleksandr Il-2 pilot 1922 16.03.1944
Accident. Two aircraft collided.

Makarov, Pavel — 1924 15.04.1944
KIA.

Kalashnikov, Aleksandr Il-2 gunner 1922 07.05.1944
KIA. Killed by anti-aircraft fire. Crimea.

Table of Personnel

Name	Aircraft	Role	Date of Birth	Date of Event
Makshanov, Vasili	Il-2	gunner	1922	08.05.1944

KIA. Shot by enemy fighters. Crew pilot Panyukhno, gunner Makashanov. Crimea.

Mediantsev, Aleksandr	Il-2	pilot	1912	08.05.1944

KIA. Shot by enemy fighters. Crimea. 'Crashed above the target near Bezymyannaya height.'

Panyukhno, Aleksei	Il-2	pilot	1922	08.05.1944

KIA. Shot by enemy fighters. Crew pilot Panyukhno, gunner Makashanov. Crimea.

Garanina, Praskovia		maint.	1921	26.05.1944

'Shot herself at 2 a.m.' Crimea.

Beletski	Il-2	gunner		06.44

Flew with Rudenko. Badly injured in crash-landing in forest. Mogilev region.

Rudenko, Aleksandr	Il-2	pilot	—	06.44

KIA. Mogilev region.

Chetverikov, Vladimir	Il-2	gunner	1923	24.06.1944

Accident. Crew pilot Lyashenko, gunner Chetverikov. Shot by anti-aircraft fire, made wrong manoeuvre, collided with another aircraft carrying Prosianik and Morozov. Nobody survived. Mogilev region.

Lyashenko, Georgi	Il-2	pilot	1924	24.06.1944

Accident. Crew pilot Lyashenko, gunner Chetverikov. Shot by anti-aircraft fire, made wrong manoeuvre, collided with another aircraft carrying Prosianik and Morozov. Nobody survived. Mogilev region.

Morozov, Vasili	Il-2	pilot	1915	24.06.1944

Accident. Crew pilot Prosianik, gunner Morozov. Collided with Lyashenko's aircraft, which was shot by anti-aircraft fire. Mogilev region.

Prosianik, Ivan	Il-2	pilot	1923	24.06.1944

Accident. Crew pilot Prosianik, gunner Morozov. Collided with Lyashenko's aircraft, which was shot by anti-aircraft fire. Mogilev region.

Table of Personnel

Name	Aircraft	Role	Date of Birth	Date of Event
Petrichenko, Viktor	Il-2	gunner	1924	26.06.1944

MIA. Crew pilot Pronin, gunner Petrichenko. 'Lost the formation during the attack by eight Me-109s.' Mogilev region.

| **Pronin, Aleksandr** | Il-2 | pilot | 1922 | 26.06.1944 |

MIA. Crew pilot Pronin, gunner Petrichenko. 'Lost the formation during the attack by eight Me-109s.' Mogilev region.

| **Tsukrov, Evsei** | Il-2-1 | pilot | 1917 | 27.06.1944 |

KIA. Shot by anti-aircraft fire during attack on column. Mogilev-Ilyincha. Aircraft crashed in forest.

| **Popov, Dmitri** | Il-2 | gunner | 1924 | 24.07.1944 |

KIA. Shot by anti-aircraft fire. Crew pilot Scherbina, gunner Popov. Poland.

| **Scherbina, Pavel** | Il-2 | pilot | 1924 | 24.07.1944 |

KIA. Shot by anti-aircraft fire. Crew pilot Scherbina, gunner Popov. Poland.

| **Popkov, Nikolai** | Il-2 | pilot | 1921 | 26.07.1944 |

KIA. Shot by anti-aircraft fire. Crew pilot Popkov, gunner Zaigraev. Poland.

| **Zaigraev, Vladimir** | Il-2 | gunner | 1922 | 26.07.1944 |

KIA. Shot by anti-aircraft fire. Crew pilot Popkov, gunner Zaigraev. Poland.

| **Afanasev, Aleksei** | Il-2 | maint. | 1918 | 29.07.1944 |

KIA. Shot by anti-aircraft fire. Poland.

| **Ivanov, Leonid** | Il-2 | pilot | 1924 | 02.08.1944 |

KIA. Shot by enemy fighters. Crew pilot Ivanov, gunner Novikov. Poland.

| **Novikov, Mikhail** | Il-2 | gunner | 1925 | 02.08.1944 |

KIA. Shot by enemy fighters. Crew pilot Ivanov, gunner Novikov. Poland.

| **Demakov, Petr** | Il-2 | pilot | 1921 | 07.08.1944 |

Name	*Aircraft*	*Role*	*Date of Birth*	*Date of Event*

KIA. Shot by anti-aircraft fire. Crew pilot Demakov, gunner Rakaev. Poland.

Rakaev, Nurgali Il-2 gunner 1919 07.08.1944
KIA. Shot by anti-aircraft fire. Crew pilot Demakov, gunner Rakaev. Poland.

Bystrov, Aleksandr Il-2 pilot 1923 15.08.1944
KIA. Shot by anti-aircraft fire. Crew pilot Bystrov, gunner Kuparev. Poland.

Kuparev, Mikhail Il-2 gunner 1924 15.08.1944
KIA. Shot by anti-aircraft fire. Crew pilot Bystrov, gunner Kuparev. Poland.

Yurkov, Aleksandr Il-2 pilot 1911 17.08.1944
KIA. Poland. Crew pilot Yurkov, gunner Zabrodin. 'Exploded after dropping 2,100 kilos of bombs. He was a friend of Karabut. He never said goodbye and never flew in a parade uniform. Before the flight he came to Karabut in a new uniform, and bade him good-bye.'

Zabrodin, Nikolai Il-2 gunner 1917 17.08.1944
KIA. Poland. Crew pilot Yurkov, gunner Zabrodin. Exploded after dropping 2,100 kilos of bombs.

Nogotkov, Anatoli Il-2 pilot 1913 22.08.1944
KIA. Shot by anti-aircraft fire. Poland. 'The aircraft exploded in the air and fell burning to the west from Zambrov. The pilot and the gunner baled out. The pilot was badly wounded and considered dead.'

Selivanov, Sergei Il-2 gunner 1925 27.08.1944
Accident. Pilot took wrong course and hit a roof. Gunner was badly wounded and died same day.

Burov, Ilia Il-2 gunner 1923 03.09.1944
MIA. Crew pilot Karabut, gunner Burov. Poland. 'Shot by anti-aircraft fire when leaving target (10 km to the east of Ostrolenok). Made a forced landing. The fate of the crew and the plane is unknown. The pilots from Sednenkov's group flew to the same area in 10–15 minutes and saw an Il on the ground.'

Table of Personnel

Name	Aircraft	Role	Date of Birth	Date of Event
Karabut, Ivan	Il-2	pilot	1914	03.09.1944

MIA. Crew pilot Karabut, gunner Burov. Poland. 'Shot by anti-aircraft fire when leaving target (10 km to the east of Ostrolenok). Made a forced landing. The fate of the crew and the plane is unknown.'

| **Sednenkov, Nikolai** | Il-2 | pilot | 1919 | 03.09.1944 |

KIA. Poland. Shot by anti-aircraft fire. Crew pilot Sednenkov, gunner Zaitsev. 'It was his day off. He said that he would fly anyway, because he wanted to get the 100 grams. On that day he was awarded the Hero of the Soviet Union, but we did not have a chance to congratulate him.'

| **Zaytsev, Nikolai** | Il-2 | gunner | 1923 | 03.09.1944 |

KIA. Shot by anti-aircraft fire. Crew pilot Sednenkov, gunner Zaytsev.

| **Gladkikh, Vasili** | Il-2 | gunner | 1925 | 22.09.1944 |

Shot by anti-aircraft fire. Poland. Crew pilot Misan, gunner Gladkikh. Taken prisoner and released in 1945.

| **Misan, Ivan** | Il-2 | pilot | 1921 | 22.09.1944 |

MIA. Poland. Shot by anti-aircraft fire. Crew pilot Misan, gunner Gladkikh. Taken prisoner.

| **Pyshnyi, Petr** | Il-2 | gunner | 1923 | 01.10.1944 |

KIA. Shot by anti-aircraft fire. Poland.

| **Goryachev, Victor** | Il-2 | pilot | 1918 | 24.10.1944 |

Shot by 2 Bf-109. Crew pilot Goryachev, gunner Malyshev. Malyshev baled out. Poland.

| **Lev, Georgii** | Il-2 | gunner | 1921 | 24.10.1944 |

MIA. Crew pilot Stepanenko, gunner Lev. 'A burning aircraft was seen falling in the forest 10 km to the south from Makuv. Presumably that was Stepanenko's plane.'

| **Malyshev, Firs** | Il-2 | gunner | 1922 | 24.10.1944 |

MIA. Crew pilot Goryachev, gunner Malyshev. Shot by two Bf-109s. Taken prisoner and returned to the unit on March 13, 1945.

| **Stepanenko, Nikolai** | Il-2 | pilot | 1921 | 24.10.1944 |

MIA. Crew pilot Stepanenko, gunner Lev. 'A burning aircraft was seen

Name	Aircraft	Role	Date of Birth	Date of Event

falling in the forest 10 km to the south from Makuv. Presumably that was Stepanenko's plane.'

Semenov, Sergei Il-2 pilot 1922 27.10.1944

'Died in hospital from burns. On October 24 a bomb fell out of the bomb compartment and exploded during take-off. The pilot got out burning. The plane was burnt.'

Kriven, Petr Il-2 pilot 1922 20.01.1945

KIA. Crew pilot Kriven, gunner Stepanovski. Prussia.

Stepanovski, Nikolai Il-2 gunner 1922 20.01.1945

KIA. Crew pilot Kriven, gunner Stepanovski. Prussia.

Tsaplin, Petr Il-2 pilot 1923 31.01.1945

MIA. Eastern Prussia. 'Fell behind the group near Dotheinberg. Was shot down and taken prisoner. Later returned.'

Goncharenko, Ivan Il-2 gunner 1920 15.02.1945

'On February 13, 1945 the aircraft was attacked and shot down by two Me-109s. The gunner baled out. He was injured from four FB-190s.'

INDEX

Entries in italics refer to illustrations. Ranks are given as most commonly used in the text.

265

Index

Index

Index

Index

Index